Georges Feydeau
Three Farces

Fitting for Ladies
Tailleur pour Dames

A Close Shave
Champignol Malgré Lui

Sauce for the Goose
Le Dindon

Translated by Peter Meyer

Published by the British Broadcasting Corporation,
35 Marylebone High Street, London W1M 4AA
ISBN 0 563 12417 2
First published 1974
English translation © Peter Meyer 1974

Printed in England by Tonbridge Printers Ltd

Introduction

Georges Feydeau was born in Paris on 8 December 1862.
His father, Ernest Feydeau, was originally a stockbroker and
later became a prolific, if not particularly successful, author. His
works ranged from novels to a study of funerary customs in
ancient Egypt, but the only one of his books to be widely
read was a novel, *Fanny*, which had the good fortune to be
denounced as indecent by the Archbishop of Paris from the
pulpit. Ernest Feydeau was a friend of Flaubert and Gautier and,
so he thought, of the Goncourts, but their references in their
diary to both him and his books are scathing.

Georges decided to become a dramatist when he was first taken
to the theatre at the age of six or seven. He was encouraged in
this by his father and wrote steadily during his schooldays, finding
it a convenient excuse to escape from his lessons. When he left
school in 1879, he and his friends formed a group of actors
and, although he showed considerable talent in this field and
at one time contemplated taking it up professionally, he was more
successful as a mimic and also as the author of monologues,
which he continued to write throughout his career. At that time
leading actors and actresses frequently performed in salons and
at charity concerts and the monologue was greatly in demand.

Feydeau then turned to the one-act play and between 1882
and 1886 wrote four, all of which were performed with some
success. Although they are comparatively slight, they already
show his gift for dialogue and are remarkable among curtain-
raisers of the period for having survived at all.

In November 1883 Feydeau was called up for a year's military
service and while in the army wrote his first full-length play,
Tailleur Pour Dames. It was not produced until 1887, when it
achieved a great success with both critics and public. This is not
surprising: it is an amusing play and although it has not the

complexity of his later works, it is acutely observed and beautifully constructed.

In the next few years Feydeau wrote, alone or in collaboration, four full-length plays, one short play and a musical comedy, all of which failed completely. In 1889 he married Marianne Carolus Duran, the daughter of a fashionable painter, and their first child was born the following year. He thus particularly needed a success when at the end of 1891 he submitted two new plays to the management of the Palais Royal Theatre. They agreed to stage one of these, *Monsieur Chasse*, in the spring of 1892, but refused the other, *Champignol Malgré Lui*, saying it was worthless.

On his way home from receiving this news at the Palais Royal, Feydeau met an old friend, Micheau, the owner of the Nouveautés Theatre, who was then facing bankruptcy after a succession of failures. Micheau insisted on seeing the rejected script in spite of Feydeau's protests that it was unplayable and, as soon as he had read it, rushed to see his mother, who had already gone into a decline at the prospect of bankruptcy, to announce that she could leave her bed, as they were saved. He was right. *Monsieur Chasse* was a success, but *Champignol* was a triumph. It was even enjoyed by Feydeau's former company commander, whose speech to his recruits had been reproduced verbatim.

In the next few years Feydeau had an almost unbroken run of successes, including *Un Fil à la Patte* (1894), *L'Hôtel du Libre Echange* (1894), *Le Dindon* (1896), *La Dame de Chez Maxim* (1899), *La Duchesse des Folies Bergères* (1902) and *La Main Passe* (1904). *Le Dindon* is one of his best plays, as was shown by the 1951 production by the Comédie Française with Robert Hirsch as Rédillon and Jacques Charon as Pontagnac. The title means dupe, not turkey, and refers to Pontagnac, who realises in the last line of the play that this is all he has been.

Feydeau was now a rich man and assembled a remarkable collection of pictures by Corot, Courbet, Boudin, Monet, Renoir and Cézanne. But he also acquired a taste for gambling on the

Stock Exchange and after some initial success lost heavily. This led him to overcome his innate laziness and write some of his greatest plays such as *La Puce à L'Oreille* (1907) and *Occupe toi d'Amélie* (1908), but he was forced to write others which showed a marked lack of inspiration and eventually had to sell his pictures and dispose of part of his wife's dowry.

His wife must have had a difficult time. She was a beautiful woman, who bore him four children, but at any rate in later years (his friends' recollections are vague about dates) he led an independent life, leaving her at home alone, so it is not surprising that she was grossly extravagant. Feydeau usually rose late and from six to eight in the evening would be at a café with a circle of literary and theatrical friends. He would end the night at Maxim's, where he stayed until it closed, never drinking anything but mineral water, which was served to him in a champagne bottle.

Although Marianne Feydeau had a difficult life, she too cannot have been an easy person to live with, to judge from the portrait which Feydeau drew of her in his four great one-act plays of 1908 to 1911, a character (it is the same one in each play, though the names are different) which Marcel Achard has described as an untamed shrew. In 1909, after a particularly violent quarrel, Feydeau left home and took a room in the Hotel Terminus at the Gare Saint Lazare, where he intended to stay only temporarily, but remained, apart from unsuccessful attempts at reconciliation, for ten years. In 1914 Marianne sued for divorce and obtained it eighteen months later.

After leaving his wife, Feydeau wrote, in 1910 and 1911, three of the four one-act plays already referred to, but was by then finding it increasingly difficult to work. In 1911 the first two acts of a play were put into rehearsal, but he was unable to finish it, and two years later a similar thing happened, though on this occasion only one act was rehearsed. In 1914 he had a great success with a play, which he had helped a friend to rewrite, and in 1916 wrote his last play, a slight piece in one act, which was also very successful, though today it is chiefly of interest for the fact that the cast included Raimu.

By now Feydeau was suffering from venereal disease and in 1919 his sons had to put him in a home. His condition deteriorated rapidly and at times he was insane, thinking he was Napoleon III and sending out invitations to his coronation. On 5 June 1921 he died.

In all Feydeau completed two musical comedies, twenty full-length and fifteen one-act plays and twenty-two monologues, of which one musical comedy, one short play and nine long plays were written in collaboration. He called his works, variously, plays, comedies or vaudevilles, but he is generally referred to as a writer of vaudevilles and this is how he described himself.

The vaudeville originated in the fifteenth century as a satirical song, but by the beginning of the nineteenth century it had become a play in verse, set to music, a form which first tempted Alfred de Musset to write for the theatre. By the second half of the century the verse and musical components had developed into operetta, notably the works of Offenbach, while the vaudeville itself remained akin to what we would call slapstick farce, where movement was more important than character. In France it was nevertheless to be distinguished from farce itself, which André Roussin has defined as containing an element of tragedy.

Feydeau once told his son, Michel, that to make people laugh you have to place your cast in a dramatic situation and then observe them from a comic angle, but they must never be allowed to say or do anything which is not strictly demanded, first by their character and secondly by the plot. On another occasion he told one of his collaborators to cut a line because it was witty and wit must never be used unless required by the play or it would interrupt the action.

These are precepts which he always followed and they were the foundation of his success. In most of his plays he confined the vaudeville elements to the second act and, after introducing a set of ingeniously created characters in the first act, used his

comic gifts and boundless invention to weave a plot of almost
mathematical ingenuity, which proceeded inevitably from one
situation to another. He was a perfectionist, not only in writing
his plays, but also in their performance, providing detailed stage
directions and, when he was his own producer, which was usually
the case, insisting on three months for rehearsals.

After Feydeau's death his plays continued to be performed in
France during the twenties and to a lesser extent in the thirties.
In 1941 *Feu la Mère de Madame*, one of his late one-act plays,
entered the repertory of the Comédie Française with Madeleine
Renaud in the lead and it was no doubt her success in this which
led the Renaud-Barrault company to stage *Occupe toi d'Amélie*
in 1948. A critic on this occasion, who could recall the slapstick
vaudevilles of the twenties, noted that Barrault, in using a
classical company, had imposed upon the play a new style, which
justified including it in repertory with Marivaux and Shakespeare.
This is the style to which we have become further accustomed
by the productions of the Comédie Française and the National
Theatre, and which has resulted in Feydeau being accepted as
the greatest French comic dramatist since Molière.

Peter Meyer

Fitting for Ladies
Tailleur pour Dames

Translator's Note

This translation was commissioned by the BBC for broadcasting, but I have here ignored my radio adaptation and reverted to the original text. Feydeau's stage directions frequently include the relative positions of the characters, which are numbered from left to right, so that, for example, 1 is always left of 2 but may be anywhere on the stage.

This translation was first broadcast on 30 October 1968 with the following cast:

Moulineaux	*Leslie Phillips*
Etienne	*Andrew Sachs*
Yvonne	*Jan Edwards*
Bassinet	*Wilfred Carter*
Mme Aigreville	*Gladys Spencer*
Suzanne	*Betty Huntley-Wright*
Aubin	*Ralph Truman*
Pomponette	*Marjorie Westbury*
Mme d'Herblay	*Kathleen Helme*
Rosa	*Jenny Lee*

Produced by Archie Campbell

Characters

In Order of Appearance

ETIENNE	*Moulineaux's butler*
YVONNE	*Moulineaux's wife*
MOULINEAUX	*A doctor*
BASSINET	*A friend of Moulineaux*
MME AIGREVILLE	*Moulineaux's mother-in-law*
SUZANNE	*A patient of Moulineaux*
AUBIN	*Suzanne's husband*
POMPONETTE	
MME D'HERBLAY	
ROSA	*Aubin's mistress*

ACT I   Moulineaux's flat

ACT II   The first-floor flat at 70 Boulevard
Amsterdam. A few minutes later

ACT III   The same as Act I. The next morning

Paris in the Nineties

Act I

(Moulineaux's living-room.
In the back wall, a door leads into the hall. Downstage
left, the door of Yvonne's bedroom. Upstage left,
another door. Downstage right, the door of Moulineaux's
bedroom. Upstage right, another door.
There is a desk on the right, with a large armchair
left of it. A doctor's papers and equipment. On the
left are two chairs side by side. Other furniture as
desired.
When the curtain rises, the stage is empty. It is only
just daylight.
Etienne enters upstage right. He is about to start
the housework and carries a broom, a feather duster,
an ordinary duster, etc. He puts it all down and opens
the door into the hall to let in some air)

Etienne *(Yawning)* I'm still sleepy . . . How ridiculous! . . .
It's a scientific fact that you need sleep most, when
it's time to get up. So that's when you ought to
go to bed . . . I'm yawning enough to make my
jaw drop off. Perhaps it's my stomach. I'll ask the
doctor. It's wonderful being in service with a doctor.
He can be a lot of service to you. Especially if
you're always ill like me. A hypochondriac
condition the doctor calls it . . . I'm very comfortable
here. It was even better six months ago. Before
he got married. But I mustn't complain, his wife's
charming . . . If he had to have a wife, she's the
right one for us: the doctor and me. Ah well, it's
time to wake him. It's very peculiar . . . He sleeps
in his room, she sleeps in that one. You can't
help wondering why they got married . . . Ah well,
apparently that's the fashion in Society. *(He knocks*

on the door of Moulineaux's room) Sir! . . . Sir! . . .
(*Aside*) Fast asleep! (*Aloud*) No one there! The bed's
not been slept in! He hasn't been home all night!
. . . He's out on the loose! . . . And his poor little
wife sleeping there so innocently! It's not right!
    (*Yvonne enters*)
Oh! . . . Good morning. (*He goes to 2*)

Yvonne   (*Downstage left*) Is the doctor up yet?

Etienne   (*Stammering*) Eh? No, no . . . Yes, yes . . .

Yvonne   What? No! Yes! . . . You seem worried.

Etienne   Me, worried! Certainly not. Look at me. Worried?

Yvonne   Yes. (*She goes towards the door of Moulineaux's room*)

Etienne   (*Quickly*) Don't go in.

Yvonne   (*Surprised*) What do you mean? Why not?

Etienne   (*Very embarrassed*) Because . . . because the doctor's ill.

Yvonne   Ill, well in that case . . . it's my duty . . .

Etienne   (*Recovering*) No, ill, I'm exaggerating. No, the window's open . . . I'm doing the room, it's full of dust.

Yvonne   When my husband's ill! What are you talking about? (*She goes into Moulineaux's bedroom*)

Etienne   No, look . . . (*To the audience*) Caught, he's caught. Ah well, too bad, I did all I could . . .

Yvonne   (*As she re-enters*) The bed's not been slept in! My husband hasn't been home all night! I congratulate you, Etienne. You must be well paid for all you do.

Etienne   I wanted to avoid . . .

Yvonne   (*Moving across*) You're too kind! Thank you very much . . . After being married only six months! How terrible!
    (*Yvonne goes into her own room*)

Etienne   Poor girl! But serve her right! For that sort of thing I'm unbribable.
    (*Knocking at front door of flat*)

	What is it?
Moulineaux	(*Off*) Open the door. It's me.
Etienne	(*At 1*) Ah, the doctor!

(*He goes and opens the door, then returns, followed by Moulineaux, looking terrible, in evening dress with his tie undone*)

	You've been out all night, sir?
Moulineaux	(*At 2*) Yes, sh! . . . No . . . I mean, yes . . . My wife doesn't know?
Etienne	Well . . . she's just gone back to her room . . . From the way she looked . . .
Moulineaux	(*Anxiously*) Yes? . . . Oh, damn! (*He moves to 1*)
Etienne	Oh, sir, it's all wrong, sir, what you're doing, sir. If you'll believe a friend . . .
Moulineaux	What friend?
Etienne	Me, sir.
Moulineaux	Really! . . . (*He moves to 2*) What a night! . . . I slept on the landing . . . I must have caught rheumatism in twenty different places . . . No one will ever get me to the Opera Ball again.
Etienne	You went to the Opera Ball?
Moulineaux	Yes . . . I mean, no! Mind your own business.
Etienne	All right. I must say, you look marvellous! I don't have to be your worst enemy to see you've been celebrating all night.
Moulineaux	(*Ironically*) Thank you. Etienne, go back to your pantry.
Etienne	All right, I'm going.
	(*Etienne goes out*)
Moulineaux	Ohhh! Nobody will ever get me to the Opera Ball again . . . I didn't want to go . . . Ah well . . . yes, that enchanting little Madame Aubin can make me do anything. If ever you meet an attractive married woman, don't be her doctor. It's too dangerous. The Opera was her idea. 'Two a.m. under

the clock!' Meaning 'Wait for me'. I did wait . . .
till three, like a fool. So when I saw her . . . when I
saw her . . . intention was to make a fool of me, I
left in a fury. Exhausted . . . I come home, consoling
myself with the thought of a good night's sleep.
I get to the door, disaster, no key! I'd left it in my
other suit. If I rang, I'd wake my wife. I'd nothing
to pick the lock with. So I had to spend the night
on the landing. (*He sits down right*) If you've never
spent a night on a landing, you've no idea what it's
like. I'm aching all over and frozen stiff. (*Suddenly*)
I know, I'll write myself a prescription. Yes, but
if I look after myself the way I look after my
patients, I'll be ill for weeks. . . . I might send for
a faith-healer . . .

(*Yvonne enters from her bedroom*)

Yvonne   So here you are at last.

Moulineaux   (*Jumping up, as if moved by a spring*) Yes, here I am.
. . . Hm! You've . . . you've slept well? You're
up early.

Yvonne   (*Bitterly*) What about you . . .?

Moulineaux   (*Embarrassed*) Me? . . . Yes, well, I had a job to do.

Yvonne   (*Hammering each syllable*) Where did you spend the
night?

Moulineaux   (*As before*) What?

Yvonne   (*As before*) Where did you spend the night?

Moulineaux   Yes, I heard . . . Where did I spend the . . . Didn't
I tell you? . . . Yesterday, when I went out,
didn't I tell you I was going to see Bassinet? Poor
Bassinet, he's very ill.

Yvonne   (*Incredulous*) You spent the night there?

Moulineaux   (*With assurance*) Exactly . . . You don't know how
ill he is!

Yvonne   (*Ironically*) Really?

Moulineaux   So I had to sit with him.

Yvonne (*As before*) In evening dress?

Moulineaux (*Floundering*) In evening dress, yes . . . I mean, no.
Let me explain. Bassinet . . . Hm . . . Bassinet is so
ill, you see . . . the slightest excitement would kill
him. So to keep it from him . . . we arranged a
little party there . . . lots of doctors. We had a
consultation, then we danced . . . just to keep it
from . . . We danced you see . . . as if there was
nothing the matter. (*He dances and sings to the tune
of the Blue Danube*)

He's going to die, to die, to die.

It won't be tomorrow, today, today.

We had a marvellous time . . . When people are ill,
you have to use all sorts of tricks.

Yvonne Very ingenious. Then there's no hope?

Moulineaux (*Firmly*) Hope? He'll never get out of bed again.
(*Etienne enters*)

Etienne (*Announcing*) Monsieur Bassinet!
(*Bassinet enters*)

Bassinet (*At 2*) Good morning, doctor.

Moulineaux Damn the man! (*He runs to Bassinet and whispers
quickly*) Sh! Shut up, you're ill.

Bassinet (*Bewildered*) Who? Me? Never felt better. (*He
moves to 3*)

Yvonne (*Slyly*) You're quite well, Monsieur Bassinet?

Bassinet (*Good-natured*) As you see.

Moulineaux (*Quickly*) Yes, as you see, terribly ill, he's terribly
ill . . . (*Aside*) Will you shut up, I tell you you're
ill.

Yvonne Why do you insist that he's ill, he's just said . . .

Moulineaux How does he know? . . . He's not a doctor. I tell
you he's dying.

Bassinet I'm dying? Me?

Moulineaux Yes, you! . . . Only we wanted to keep it from you.
(*Aside*) Let him die, if he wants to. (*He goes upstage*)

Bassinet   Good heavens, what did he say?

Yvonne   (*Deliberately*) Poor Monsieur Bassinet! That's why my husband spent the night with you.

Moulineaux   (*Aside*) Here we go. Crash! Ohhh!

Bassinet   *He* spent the night with me?

Moulineaux   Of course, didn't you notice? (*To Yvonne*) Leave him alone, he's delirious. (*Aside to Bassinet, descending on him*) Shut up. Can't you see you're putting your foot in it? (*He goes upstage to 1*)

Bassinet   (*Aside*) If anyone's ill, it's the doctor.

Yvonne   (*Moving to 2. To Bassinet*) Take good care of yourself. But I must say you look remarkably well for a man who's dying . . . Especially as you're taking so long about it.

Moulineaux   (*At 1*) Yes . . . it's a lingering disease.

Yvonne   They're not usually fatal. (*Aside*) It's obvious. He's unfaithful . . . I'll tell my mother the whole story.

    (*Yvonne goes out into her bedroom*)

Moulineaux   (*At 1, Bassinet at 2*) Can't you see you've been dropping brick after brick for the last half-hour? You'll never take a hint!

Bassinet   (*Frightened*) What about?

Moulineaux   The situation!

Bassinet   What situation?

Moulineaux   If I put you at death's door, I've good reason to. You might have the decency to stay there.

Bassinet   I beg your pardon?

Moulineaux   Why do you have to come blundering in here?

Bassinet   What?

Moulineaux   Couldn't you have the tact to stay away?

Bassinet   How do you expect me to guess?

Moulineaux   (*Getting angry*) The day after the Opera Ball people don't go calling on friends who've used them as an excuse.

Bassinet   If you'd told me . . .

Moulineaux	(*As before*) I always have to dot every i for you.
Bassinet	It's only natural.
Moulineaux	(*Sharply*) Anyway, what is it you want?
Bassinet	What I want is this. (*Jovial*) You know I only call on friends when a helping hand is wanted.
Moulineaux	(*Calming down*) Well, that . . . that's different . . . A helping hand . . .
Bassinet	(*As before*) Is what I need, exactly.
Moulineaux	(*Moving to 2*) You need . . . (*Aside*) The other way round would have surprised me. (*Aloud*) I'm sorry, I'm rather tired. I spent the night on the landing. (*He sits down at 2*)
Bassinet	That's all right. (*He sits down at 1*)
Moulineaux	Thank you. I'm expecting my mother-in-law, she's arriving in Paris today. So you understand . . .
Bassinet	Yes . . . these things happen.
Moulineaux	(*Aside*) You're a bore, go away. (*Aloud*) Excuse me. (*He rings the bell. Etienne enters*)
Etienne	(*Upstage*) You rang, sir?
Moulineaux	(*Aside*) Yes, for heaven's sake get rid of him. In five minutes' time, ring the front door bell and bring me a visiting card, anybody's . . . Say someone's asking for me. That will make him go.
Etienne	I understand. The cure for bores! (*Etienne goes out*)
Bassinet	You know, a year ago, when I got my legacy . . .
Moulineaux	Legacy?
Bassinet	Yes, from my uncle . . . I bought a house here in Paris, 70 Boulevard Amsterdam . . . It's divided into flats and I can't let them . . . (*He gets up*) That's why I'm here . . . You see a lot of patients . . . so I want you to get them to take my flats. (*He gives him cards*)
Moulineaux	(*Furious, moving to 1*) You've hunted me down for that?
Bassinet	(*Moving to 2*) Now wait . . . don't get angry. You've

nothing to lose . . . The drains are terrible . . .
You'll get a lot more business.

Moulineaux (*Erupting*) Do you think I'm going to recommend
your filthy flats . . . ? (*He moves across*)

Bassinet (*Quickly*) One of them's all right . . . A little
furnished flat on the first floor. A bargain! A
dressmaker had it. She vanished without paying the
rent. Actually it's a very funny story . . . You see,
this dressmaker . . .

Moulineaux I don't give a damn for your story, your flat or
your dressmaker. What am I expected to do with
a dressmaker?

Bassinet No, it's not the dressmaker . . .

Moulineaux All right, but you might have chosen a better
moment. When I think that all this time my wife,
my poor wife . . . (*He moves upstage left*)

Bassinet (*Bitterly*) It's true. *You're* married, you are. But
me! (*He sighs*) I've lost my wife.

Moulineaux (*Absent-minded*) Splendid, splendid! (*He is almost in
front of the door of Yvonne's room*)

Bassinet What do you mean, splendid?

Moulineaux (*Recovering*) I mean, dreadful, dreadful! (*He comes
back downstage right*)

Bassinet (*Bitterly*) You'll never believe it . . . She was taken
from me. In two minutes.

Moulineaux (*Bored*) A heart attack?

Bassinet No, a soldier. I left her sitting in the Tuileries
Gardens. I said: 'I shan't be long, I'm going to the
tobacconist to buy a cigar'. I never saw her again.
  (*The door-bell rings*)
There's someone at the door.

Moulineaux (*Aside*) That will be Etienne. (*He goes upstage*)
  (*Etienne enters*)

Etienne Sir, a gentleman would like to see you. Here's his
card.

Moulineaux (*Exchanging a smile of understanding with Etienne*) Let me see . . . Ah, of course . . . (*To Bassinet*) My dear fellow, I'm sorry, this man's an awful bore, but I must see him.

Bassinet A bore! I know all about bores, show him in. (*He sits down, right*) I'll stay here, that will make him go.

Moulineaux (*Aside*) He's going to sit there! What cheek! (*Aloud*) You see, he wants to speak to me privately . . .

Bassinet That's different. Who is this awful bore? (*Taking the card out of Moulineaux's hand*) Chevassus! . . . It's Chevassus! I've known him for years. I'd love to see him . . . I'll go later.

Moulineaux (*Taken aback*) What? . . . No, you can't! . . . It isn't him, it's . . . his father.

Bassinet He never had one.

Moulineaux Then it's his uncle, and he doesn't want to see anybody. Go away. Go away. (*He makes him get up*)

Bassinet All right. (*He goes towards the door into the hall, but when he gets there, swerves and makes for the door midstage left*) I'll wait in the next room.
    (*Bassinet goes out*)

Moulineaux He'll never go. Too bad, I'll drug him unconscious for a week.
    (*Bassinet appears at the door*)

Bassinet I say! I've an idea. If this bore of yours really is a bore, I know how to get rid of him. I'll ring the bell and send in my card, you can say a bore's arrived and you have to see him . . .

Moulineaux Yes, yes, all right, go away, go away. If you're tired, there's a sofa, have a good sleep.
    (*Bassinet goes out*)
    (*At 2*) Whew! . . . I must say, life's complicated! (*He collapses into an armchair*)

Etienne (*At 1*) Sir, you're a doctor. It's easy for you to get rid of a nuisance like that.

Moulineaux I thought he'd never go.

Etienne If I were you, sir, I'd drug him unconscious.

Moulineaux There've been too many excitements this morning, I'm exhausted. I'll try to get an hour's sleep. (*He lies down on a sofa*) See I'm not disturbed.

Etienne (*Going upstage*) Very good, sir.

Moulineaux (*Closing his eyes*) That's better . . . I can feel it won't be long . . .

Etienne (*At the door*) Shall I wake you, sir?

Moulineaux (*Eyes closed*) Yes, tomorrow . . . or the day after . . . Not if I'm asleep.

Etienne Very good, sir. I'll see you in a few days' time, sir. Goodnight, sir.

(*Etienne goes out. A pause. Moulineaux goes to sleep. After a moment, the door-bell rings. Noise offstage*)

Mme A. (*Off*) My daughter! My son! Where are they?
(*Etienne enters like a bomb*)

Etienne Sir, it's your mother-in-law . . . (*He reaches the door of Yvonne's room*) Madame, your Mother's here.
(*Mme Aigreville erupts through the door from the hall, carrying a travelling bag, which she puts down as soon as she enters*)

Mme A. (*Centre stage*) Children! Children!
(*Yvonne enters midstage left*)

Yvonne Mother! Mother!

Moulineaux (*Startled out of his sleep; at 3*) What is it? . . . A hurricane? (*Taken aback*) My mother-in-law!

Mme A. (*At 2*) In person!

Moulineaux What a silly way to wake people up!

Mme A. (*Embracing Yvonne*) My daughter! My son! . . . Well, aren't you going to kiss me?

Moulineaux What? . . . That's what I was going to say. But, you know, the surprise, the confusion . . .you go to sleep without a mother-in-law and wake up to find one. It takes a moment or two . . . Kiss me, mother.

(*Mme Aigreville puts her arms round his neck*)
Oh! Don't shake me too hard . . . When
you've just been asleep . . .

Mme A. You've just been asleep?

Moulineaux Just.

Mme A. Of course . . . You look as though you've had too
much sleep.

Moulineaux Well now . . . isn't that clever of you!

Mme A. (*Bursting into tears*) Children! . . . Children! I'm so
happy to see you again!

Moulineaux Now, now, what's the matter? (*Aside*) My
rheumatism warned me to expect rain.

Yvonne Don't cry, mother.

Mme A. (*Sobbing*) I'm not crying.

Moulineaux (*Aside*) No, it's more like a cloudburst!

Mme A. I'm so happy to see you both again . . . Dear
Moulineaux! How thin you've got, how thin!
(*To Yvonne*) But I must say, you . . . (*To Moulineaux*)
Marriage has its good points, hasn't it? . . . Why
are you dressed like that, are you going to a funeral?

Moulineaux (*Quickly*) Yes. It's . . . it's for you.

Mme A. What!

Moulineaux (*Recovering*) For you to admire.

Yvonne He's been up all night, looking after one of his
patients – who's dying.

Moulineaux (*Recovering*) Exactly.

Mme A. You're on night duty?

Moulineaux No . . . When you've been to a Ball . . . (*Recovering*)
abballing batients you have to mind all night . . .

Mme A. You've got a cold!

Moulineaux A little one, yes.

Mme A. (*To Yvonne*) Aren't you taking care of your husband?

Yvonne (*Sarcastically*) My husband can take care of himself
the same way as his patients . . .with full
choreography!

Mme A. You sound so bitter. (*She pronounces it bittah*)

Moulineaux (*Sharply*) Yes, she's bittah! Horribly bittah!

Mme A. Have we had a little quarrel?

Moulineaux No, but some people get out of bed the wrong side.

Yvonne And other people don't get out of bed at all.

Moulineaux (*To the audience*) That's for me. Straight to the jaw.

Mme A. Now, now, relax, both of you. There's nothing like a mother-in-law for preventing discord between husband and wife.

Moulineaux (*Aside*) That's because it's inherited.

(*Etienne enters midstage right*)

Etienne Sir, the gentleman who was here just now asked me to give you this card.

Moulineaux Excuse me. (*Looking at the card*) Bassinet! This is the limit! (*Aloud*) Tell him I'm not free for a month. (*Aside*) If only he'd be ill, I'd take good care of him!

Mme A. What is it?

Moulineaux Nothing. A man to meet the readers – read the meters. Etienne, go into my room and put out my dressing-gown.

Etienne Thank you very much, sir. That's very kind of you.

(*Etienne goes out downstage right*)

Moulineaux I don't see what's so kind about asking for my dressing-gown.

(*Bassinet enters midstage right*)

Bassinet I say, have you forgotten I'm still here?

Moulineaux (*Pushing him back into the other room*) No, no! Get back there, get back.

Mme A. (*Surprised*) Who is that?

Moulineaux No one. A patient.

Yvonne (*Mockingly*) Really?

Mme A. Why did you chase him away?

Moulineaux (*With assurance*) He has a contagious disease.

Mme A. Has he?

Moulineaux Terribly contagious. Like leprosy.

Yvonne (*Ironically*) But he's a very obliging patient.

Moulineaux Aimed at me again!

Mme A. (*Aside*) Something's going on, that's definite. I must question Yvonne. (*Aloud*) My dear boy . . . leave me alone with my daughter. I want to have a word with her.

Moulineaux With pleasure . . . When my wife's in this sort of mood . . .

> (*Moulineaux goes out downstage right*)

Mme A. (*Pulling her towards a chair, left*) Now then! Why are you treating your husband like this?

> (*They sit down*)

Yvonne (*Bursting into tears*) Mother, mother! I'm so unhappy.

Mme A. Good heavens, what's the matter?

Yvonne He stayed out all night!

Mme A. Really, when was that?

Yvone Last night. Last night. (*Rising*) Perhaps a lot of other nights too, without my knowing.

Mme A. What do you mean, without your knowing? . . . I'd have thought it was obvious . . . at night.

Yvonne How do you mean?

Mme A. Where do you sleep?

Yvonne Who, me?

Mme A. You, him, the pair of you!

Yvonne (*Moving to 2*) Me, there . . . And my husband, there.

Mme A. What! You, there . . . and your husband . . . after six months!

Yvonne It's been like that for a long time.

Mme A. (*Sharply*) That's outrageous, outrageous! A double bedroom is the safeguard of marital fidelity.

Yvonne Is it?

Mme A. Marriage may be the union of free spirits, but

sharing a bedroom stops them being too free. My dear child, that's elementary.

(*Bassinet enters*)

Bassinet (*Coming to 2*) I say . . .

Mme A. (*Taking refuge behind the chairs on the left*) Oh, the leper! Go back in that room.

Bassinet (*To Yvonne*) I wanted to talk to your husband.

Yvonne To make up some other story, no doubt. A pretty game you're playing!

Bassinet (*Dumbfounded*) Me? But I . . .

(*He takes a step towards Mme Aigreville*)

Mme A. (*Fleeing from him, terrified*) Yes . . . Yes . . . Go away . . . Go away . . . Go to bed.

Bassinet (*Advancing on her*) You want me to go to bed?

Mme A. (*Twisting around behind the chairs, to escape*) Yes. If people are ill, they go to bed. So go on, go to bed.

Bassinet (*To the audience*) There's something the matter with everyone in this house. (*Trying to approach Mme Aigreville*) Will you tell the doctor . . .

Mme A. (*Terrified, waving to him to keep his distance*) Yes . . . All right . . . I will . . . I will . . .

Bassinet Thank you. May I kiss your hand?

Mme A. No . . . No . . . (*Aside*) How dare he? (*Aloud*) Go away. Goodbye.

Bassinet Goodbye.

(*Bassinet goes out midstage right*)

Mme A. (*Coming downstage*) How tiresome the doctor is! Why can't he keep his patients in their own homes? . . . You were saying your husband didn't come home all night?

Yvonne No, he didn't . . . Oh, mother, I'm so miserable.

Mme A. Don't cry. Tell me more. Your husband's sleeping in someone else's bed. Whose?

Yvonne Whose?

Mme A. Of course. If a husband's not sleeping in his own bed, he hasn't gone for a cross-country run. Have you discovered anything?

Yvonne (*Pulling a woman's glove from her corsage*) I don't know. Yesterday I found this glove in his pocket.

Mme A. A woman's glove! . . . The first clue! What about his letters?

Yvonne (*Artlessly*) I haven't looked.

Mme A. Not looked? It's the only way to find out what's going on. All women do that.
(*Moulineaux enters from his bedroom*)
Your husband! . . . Leave this to me.
(*Yvonne goes out*)

Moulineaux (*Aside*) I hope everything's all right now. Her mother will have made her see reason.

Mme A. Moulineaux!

Moulineaux (*Very sweetly*) Mother dear!

Mme A. I shan't beat about the bush. Do you recognise this glove?

Moulineaux Do I . . . Splendid, I've searched everywhere for it. (*He tries to take it*)

Mme A. (*Striking him on the hand with the glove*) Hands off. Who does this glove belong to?

Moulineaux Eh? . . . I . . . Who? (*With assurance*) Me.

Mme A. You! This size?

Moulineaux Well . . . It's to make my hand look smaller. You know, if I tuck in my thumb and stretch out my fingers. Like this, look . . .

Mme A. (*Shrugging her shoulders*) Nonsense! It's a woman's glove.

Moulineaux (*With assurance*) It looks like that . . . because it got wet. I left it out in the rain and it's shrunk.

Mme A. (*Displaying the full length of the glove*) An elbow-length glove?

Moulineaux Exactly, it's shrunk, so it's grown longer. Water

	does that. It's gained in length what it lost in width, that's what always happens. So would you, if you got wet . . . (*With his hands, he indicates something very long and narrow*)
Mme A.	Really! Look, the size is marked . . . six and a half.
Moulineaux	(*With assurance*) Nine and a half. The water's turned the figure round.
Mme A.	Do you take me for a fool?
Moulineaux	Oh, no! No!
Mme A.	(*Getting angry*) Do you know what I think? You're behaving like a libertine.
Moulineaux	Me?
Mme A.	Yes, a libertine . . . You stay out all night and I find women's gloves in your pocket.
Moulineaux	It's the damp!
Mme A.	(*Advancing on him*) Remember, if you deceive my daughter, you'll have me to deal with.
Moulineaux	I'm sorry, but . . .
Mme A.	(*As before*) You know you're married.
Moulineaux	(*Between his teeth*) She's getting on my nerves.
Mme A.	So you've sworn to be faithful to us.
Moulineaux	I'm sorry, not to you.
Mme A.	(*As before*) You know that according to the marriage service a wife must obey her husband. So you must obey us.
Moulineaux	Excuse me, the marriage service refers to a wife, not a mother-in-law.
Mme A.	An accidental omission! Unnatural boy, are you trying to separate a daughter from her mother?
Moulineaux	(*Erupting*) Oh, go to hell.
Mme A.	(*Recoiling*) What!
Moulineaux	You've come here . . . to make a nuisance of yourself. After all, I'm master in this house. I don't have to answer to anyone. You're driving me mad.
Mme A.	*I* am! . . . Ohhh!

Moulineaux (*Furious*) Yes, you are. Now clear out.

Mme A. And people say it's always the mother-in-law's fault. You'll make me think I'm not wanted here. (*She goes upstage*)

Moulineaux (*Also going upstage*) If you want to start making trouble between us . . .

Mme A. (*Dramatically*) There, you're turning me out! . . . Turning me out of my daughter's home!

Moulineaux Me?

Mme A. (*As before*) That's all right, you don't have to tell me twice.

Moulineaux (*Raising his arms*) Ohhh! Look, I . . . No . . . I'd rather leave her . . . That woman would exasperate . . . the Pope!
(*Moulineaux goes out downstage right*)

Mme A. (*Calming down*) They're all alike . . . Exactly the same as my poor husband with my dear saintlike mother . . . No . . . I shan't spend the night here. . . . I'd rather seek refuge in the poorhouse.
(*Bassinet enters midstage right*)

Bassinet I've never heard of anyone being kept waiting like this.

Mme A. In the meantime I'll try and find a furnished flat.

Bassinet You're looking for a flat? . . . I've just what you want.

Mme A. (*Terrified*) The leper again! Go away.
(*She moves quickly to the right, to put the table between them*)

Bassinet (*Aside*) She's got another attack. (*Aloud*) I've just what you want: a charming little first-floor flat. Fully furnished. Ready to walk in to.

Mme A. Really?

Bassinet Yes, just round the corner, 70 Boulevard Amsterdam.
(*He offers her a card; she tries to avoid taking it and*

he finally passes it to her on top of his hat)

Mme A. (*Anxiously*) Do *you* live there?

Bassinet No, it was a dressmaker's. Actually it's a very funny story. You see this dressmaker . . .

Mme A. How amusing! Is this flat perfectly all right?

Bassinet That depends . . . Are you actually going to live in it?

Mme A. I beg your pardon?

Bassinet You know, sometimes people take a flat to have a bit of fun in the afternoon.

Mme A. (*Scandalised*) What!

Bassinet (*Recovering*) You don't want it for that . . . It's all right . . . like any other flat. As long as you don't catch anything. (*Aside*) After all I don't know her . . . and she is Moulineaux's mother-in-law. You must always try to help a friend.

Mme A. We shall visit it today.

Bassinet If only I can get rid of it!
         (*Moulineaux enters*)

Moulineaux Dammit, I can't find my dressing-gown.

Mme A. My son-in-law! I yield the floor to him.
         (*Mme Aigreville goes out into Yvonne's room*)

Moulineaux She doesn't seem to have calmed down yet.

Bassinet The old girl's causing a spot of bother, eh?

Moulineaux (*Noticing him*) Ah! I'm glad to see you.

Bassinet (*At 1*) It's the first time I've heard that.

Moulineaux (*At 2*) Yes, I've been thinking about what you were saying.

Bassinet What was that?

Moulineaux I'll take that little flat of yours.

Bassinet Will you? (*Aside*) I should have put it up to auction.

Moulineaux It's just what I need. I can tell you – I know you're discreet – I'm having an affaire. Oh, platonic, still. With a married woman. She's been a patient of mine for ages.

Bassinet   What was the matter with her?

Moulineaux   Nothing. I cured her in the end.

Bassinet   What about her husband, what does he say?

Moulineaux   I've no idea. I don't know him. Never mind.
How much is your flat?

Bassinet   Two hundred and fifty francs.

Moulineaux   A year? That's nothing. I'll take it.

Bassinet   I'm sorry. Two hundred and fifty a month.

Moulineaux   Raising it already? . . . No matter. Done. I'll take it.

Bassinet   When?

Moulineaux   Today of course.

Bassinet   (*Mechanically arranging the lapels of Moulineaux's coat*) Damn . . . You see, it's still upside down. All the dressmaker's things are there, you know, I told you. Actually it's rather a funny story. You see, this dressmaker . . .

Moulineaux   (*At 1*) No, you can tell me tomorrow.

Bassinet   Yes . . . It's in an awful mess.

Moulineaux   That's all right, you can clear it up later.
(*Etienne enters, wearing Moulineaux's dressing-gown*)

Etienne   Sir! Madame Aubin's here.

Moulineaux   Ah! Good. (*To Bassinet*) Now, you go in there. You can start drawing up the lease.
(*Bassinet goes out*)
Phew! (*To Etienne*) Make yourself at home! Why are you wearing my dressing-gown?

Etienne   (*Innocently*) You told me to put it on.

Moulineaux   I said 'Put it out', not 'Put it on'.
(*Suzanne enters quickly*)

Suzanne   Good morning, dear Monsieur Moulineaux.
(*Moulineaux signals to Etienne to go out. Etienne goes out*)

Moulineaux   Here you are, you wicked creature! After keeping me waiting all those hours at the Opera!

Suzanne   I'm terribly sorry. I was hoping my husband would

	go off on his own, so I'd be free. He never left my side the whole evening.
Moulineaux	Yes, I suspected as much.
Suzanne	For days now he's gone everywhere with me. He gets attacks like this. He's downstairs at the moment, waiting in the carriage. He wanted to come up. I told him to stay where he is.
Moulineaux	Quite right. I don't exactly want to meet him. (*Aside*) I might get a conscience. (*Aloud*) Suzanne darling . . . (*He pulls her towards the two chairs*)
Suzanne	It's very wrong of me to listen to you like this . . .
Moulineaux	No, it isn't. You mustn't think that.
Suzanne	Yes . . . yes . . . But it's too late now, isn't it?
Moulineaux	Of course it is.
Suzanne	You know, it's the first time this has ever happened. (*They are now both seated, left*)
Moulineaux	You've said that before. And it makes me wonderfully happy. But it's not going to be very easy to see each other. Visiting your doctor's a good excuse, but it can't go on for ever. Our friends and relations are going to notice how often you come here. They'll start talking and in the end they'll find out the truth. They'll understand it's not a patient and her doctor, but two hearts in love, two noble souls that have taken wing together for the land of eternal romance . . .
Suzanne	(*Very firmly*) Yes, that would let the cat out of the bag.
Moulineaux	Yes . . . If you like, we could meet . . . on neutral ground.
Suzanne	(*With a pout*) Not on *any* ground! I'd rather have a little flat somewhere.
Moulineaux	Exactly . . . I've got one . . . 70 Boulevard Amsterdam. We could meet there . . . today. It's just round the corner.

Suzanne   (*Hesitating*) I'm tempted . . . (*Sharply*) You know, it
          must be completely honourable . . . Spiritual
          love . . .

Moulineaux   Oh, yes! Yes!

Suzanne   Because I'm faithful to my husband.

Moulineaux   Are you faithful to your husband? . . . Who would
          ever dream you weren't?

Suzanne   (*Rising and passing to 2*) Then it's settled, today, in
          an hour's time, 70 Boulevard Amsterdam. Oh, it's
          so wrong! . . . You know, it's the first time this
          has ever happened!

Moulineaux   Yes . . . Yes . . . I know. (*Aside*) She agrees. When
          they really want to, respectable women always
          make the least fuss.
          (*They both go upstage*)

Suzanne   Now, I must rush away.
          (*Etienne enters*)

Etienne   (*Coming downstage left*) Sir, Monsieur Aubin's here.

Suzanne   My husband!

Moulineaux   (*With Suzanne, near the door into the hall*)
          Oh, no! I don't want to see him!
          (*Aubin enters*)

Suzanne   (*Etienne at 1, Aubin 2, Suzanne 3, Moulineaux 4*)
          Darling! . . . I was just going downstairs.

Aubin   (*Very offhand*) Good, go on then. I'll be with you
          in a moment. I want a word with the doctor.
          (*Seeing Moulineaux in evening dress, he throws his
          overcoat into his arms; to Moulineaux*) Be off with you.
          (*Stretching out his hand to Etienne, who is in a dressing-
          gown*) Doctor!

Moulineaux   (*Dumbfounded; aside*) Really . . . !

Suzanne   (*To Aubin*) But, darling . . .

Moulineaux   Sh, let him be, it's better like this.
          (*He quickly shows Suzanne out into the hall, then
          goes out downstage right*)

Aubin (*Going downstage; Etienne at 1, Aubin at 2*) I was downstairs, so I thought I'd come up and see you professionally. You see, for a long time now, my nose keeps bleeding and my circulation just stops.

Etienne (*Surprised*) Eh? . . . Use your dining-room key.

Aubin It must be the dining-room?

Etienne If possible, yes, the dining-room. Take it and put it down your back.

Aubin The dining-room! . . . Good God!

Etienne Then fill a basin with water, plunge your nose and mouth in it and stay there for an hour and a half.

Aubin What! . . . How do I breathe?

Etienne Breathe? . . . Just keep your nose and mouth in the water. That's all. That will stop it . . . completely.

Aubin Well! I'd prefer something else. Now, look at my tongue. What do you think of that? (*He sits, left, at 2*)

Etienne (*Sitting next to him at 1*) Pooh! Mine's longer. (*He puts out his tongue*)

Aubin What!

Etienne Besides, yours is fat, mine's thin. (*He puts his tongue out again*)

Aubin Really, doctor . . .

Etienne I'm not the doctor.

Aubin (*Rising*) Not the doctor!

Etienne (*Also rising*) It comes to the same thing . . . I'm his servant.

Aubin A servant! And you sit here, chatting to me!

Etienne I'm not proud . . . Anyway I've nothing else to do.

Aubin (*Aside*) Who did I give my overcoat to? (*He goes upstage*)

(*Moulineaux enters downstage right, wearing an overcoat. Almost at the same time Bassinet enters midstage right*)

Moulineaux I'm ready.

Bassinet Here's your lease. (*He gives it to him*)

Moulineaux (*Etienne at 1, Aubin 2, Bassinet 3, Moulineaux 4*)
Thanks . . . My dear fellow!

Bassinet By the way, I still haven't told you that story.
You see, this dressmaker . . .

Moulineaux (*Escaping*) Yes, some time later . . . later. Now
I've got to rush away . . . to ecstasy! (*He goes
quickly upstage*)

Aubin (*To Moulineaux, stopping him as he passes*) Excuse me,
doctor . . .

Moulineaux (*Aside*) Oh no, now's the time for his wife! (*Aloud*)
I'm not the doctor.
(*Moulineaux goes out*)

Aubin (*Aside*) Oh, he's a patient . . . I'm sorry . . .
(*Seeing Bassinet and going to him*) Then that's the
doctor. (*Aloud*) I've been waiting to apologise to
you.
(*Bassinet is polishing his hat and doesn't understand.
He turns round to see who Aubin is talking to and
realises it's himself*)

Bassinet Apologise?

Aubin Yes, about the overcoat.

Bassinet (*Not understanding*) The overcoat, yes . . . Not at all.
Look, let me tell you a marvellous story. You see,
there's this dressmaker . . .

Aubin (*Having been unwillingly accompanied upstage by
Bassinet*) Yes, of course . . . Forgive me. I'm
delighted to have met you.
(*Aubin goes out*)

Bassinet (*Taken aback*) He's gone too. (*Noticing Etienne, who
has not moved and is looking at him with a stupid smile*)
Ah, the servant! Let me tell you a marvellous story.

Etienne (*Serious again*) I've something in the pantry . . .

Bassinet (*Not listening and making him sit down next to him left; Etienne at 1, Bassinet 2*) Yes . . . You see the dressmaker had a gentleman friend . . .

(*Taking advantage of a moment when Bassinet, engrossed in his story, is not looking, Etienne steals away into the hall. Bassinet is taken aback to find himself alone. He looks to see where Etienne could have gone, going upstage, then coming down again*)

He's gone! (*To the audience*) Well, it's not a very long story. You see this dressmaker . . . had a friend . . .

(*The orchestra cuts him short. Bassinet tries to dominate it and goes on talking. Finally the curtain comes down in front of his face*)

CURTAIN

Act II

(*The first-floor flat in the Boulevard Amsterdam. A few minutes later.*

In the back wall there is a door, opening on to the landing which is visible to the audience. On each side of this door is a chair. Upstage left, not far from the door, a tailor's dummy with a woman's dress. Doors left and right midstage. Left and right downstage, dressmaker's benches on which are piled bits of material, fashion engravings, scissors, etc. Left, near the bench, a chair. A sofa on the right.

When the curtain rises, the stage is empty. Then

Moulineaux enters from the landing)

Moulineaux So this is the first-floor flat! Very nice! The lock's broken! Marvellous! The door won't shut. I must tell Bassinet to get it mended. (*He turns round sharply and finds himself face to face with the dummy. Instinctively he bows*) A lady! No, it's a tailor's dummy. Of course, a dressmaker used to live here. Bassinet told me. It will be very nice when everything's cleared out . . . I know what I'm doing is wrong . . . when you've a charming wife like me. I do have a conscience. But I shan't take any notice of it.

(*Suzanne enters from the landing*)

Suzanne Here I am.

Moulineaux Suzanne!

Suzanne (*Trying to shut the door*) It won't shut!

Moulineaux (*Who has gone upstage in front of her*) Don't worry. I'll put a chair under the handle. (*He does so*)

Suzanne I can come in? There's no danger?

Moulineaux (*Coming downstage with her*) What danger could there be?

Suzanne I mean if anyone saw us . . . I'd be so much to blame.

Moulineaux (*Aside*) Enchanting creature! (*Aloud*) We're completely alone, Suzanne darling. Come here next to me. (*He sits down on the sofa and takes both her hands*) Don't tremble. (*Moulineaux at 1, Suzanne 2*)

Suzanne It won't last long. My husband was a soldier – in the Service Corps, on the Reserve – he says the bravest men always tremble when they first go into action, but it doesn't last long.

Moulineaux He says . . . Well then, you see! . . . Do take off your hat.

Suzanne Oh no! Impossible. I can only stay a moment. Anatole's downstairs. He might come up.

Moulineaux (*Puzzled*) Anatole?

Suzanne Yes, my husband. He insisted on coming with me again.

Moulineaux You told him . . .

Suzanne Yes.

Moulineaux (*Very angry*) It's ridiculous! People don't do such things!

Suzanne I told him . . . I told him I was going to see my dressmaker. I knew a dressmaker used to live here, so that gave me the idea . . .

Moulineaux Phew! That's a relief.

Suzanne I was furious. But if I'd tried to stop him, he'd have been suspicious . . . and I didn't want to disappoint you. It's nice, isn't it?

Moulineaux Yes, yes it is . . . Dear, darling Suzanne! (*Aside*) I must say the thought of Anatole downstairs freezes me completely . . . (*Aloud, absentmindedly*) Dear, darling Suzanne . . .

Suzanne (*Smiling*) You've said that already.

Moulineaux (*Stammering*) Have I? . . . Perhaps I have. Dear, darling Suzanne . . .

Suzanne (*As before*) That's the fourth time.

Moulineaux The fourth time, exactly. Dear, darling . . . no . . . no.

Suzanne (*Serious again*) Tell me I'm not doing something dreadful.

Moulineaux (*bored*) Oh, no. No.

Suzanne You know this is the first time . . .

Moulineaux Yes, I know . . . (*Aside*) It's incredible how that husband embarrasses me. I feel as if I'm sunning myself on the edge of a precipice.

Suzanne Are you happy?

Moulineaux Me . . . I . . . Well, really! . . . Am I happy! . . . Well, really! (*Singing gently as if completely exhausted*) Well, really! Well, really! Well, really! (*Aside,*

after a moment's thought) I must say this flat's damned
expensive. Two hundred and fifty francs a month!

Suzanne What are you thinking about?

Moulineaux Me? . . . Nothing. Hm. You. I'm thinking about
you.

Suzanne You seem so cold. I'm sure you must despise me.

Moulineaux (*Getting enthusiastic without much feeling*) Suzanne,
how can you say that? . . . I'd like to spend my
whole life at your feet!

Suzanne You say that!

Moulineaux (*Going down on his knees*) Look, let me prove it . . .
(*The chair overturns with a crash. Aubin enters*)

Aubin There I go, ruining everything!

Moulineaux (*Completely dumbfounded; still on his knees*) Her
husband! . . . Don't come in.

Aubin Don't come in?

Moulineaux (*As before*) I mean, do come in. (*He gets to his feet*)
(*Aubin at 1, Moulineaux 2, Suzanne 3*)

Aubin Thank you, I am in. I got bored downstairs, so I
thought I'd come up.

Moulineaux Splendid! (*Aside*) I was thinking he might do this.

Aubin (*Jovial*) Don't let me disturb you. You know, carry
on as if I weren't here.

Moulineaux Oh? . . . It's easy to say that.

Aubin You were taking my wife's measurements. I saw you.

Suzanne (*Seizing the opportunity*) Exactly. He was measuring
my waist.

Moulineaux (*Floundering*) That's it . . . Your waist . . . Your
waist . . . Forty-eight round the waist.

Suzanne (*Sharply*) Forty-eight! . . . Twenty-two, in fact!

Aubin (*Laughing*) Yes, twenty-two!

Moulineaux (*Trying to recover*) Exactly! . . . That's what
fashionable dressmakers always do. Everything's
double.

Aubin Including the bill?

Moulineaux No, the bill's triple . . . Yes, that's what marks
us out from the ordinary trade. Besides, you know,
like this, without a tape-measure . . . by eye . . .
Hm. You . . . wouldn't have a tape-measure on you?

Aubin (*Laughing*) No, I wouldn't. Haven't you?

Moulineaux No . . . I mean, yes . . . Dozens. But they're in
the workroom . . . my workrooms. . . . my
enormous workrooms!

Aubin (*Aside*) Eccentric sort of fellow! (*Aloud*) Tell me,
Monsieur . . . Monsieur . . . ? I don't know your
name.

Suzanne (*Seeking a name*) Monsieur . . . (*She nudges Moulineaux
hard in the ribs*)

Moulineaux (*Taken by surprise*) Oh! . . . er, Monsieur Oh.

Aubin Oh! I don't think I've heard that name before.

Moulineaux It's a very common name. There are lots of Oh's.

Aubin I do seem to know your face. Where can I have
met you?

Moulineaux (*Trying to hide his face and half turning away*) I don't
know (*Aside*) I hope he doesn't recognise me.
(*Aloud*) Probably in the street . . . or in church.
I go to lots of churches.

Aubin No. I know at Moulineaux's, he's my wife's doctor.
I caught a glimpse of you there. Does he take good
care of you?

Moulineaux (*Trying to appear offhand*) He does very little for me.

Aubin I'm not surprised. The man's a charlatan.

Moulineaux (*Taken aback*) Now look here . . .

Aubin (*Surprised*) Why, what's it to do with you?

Moulineaux Well . . . he's my doctor.

Aubin Anyway I don't care. (*He sits down on the chair, left,
which he places facing Moulineaux*) Tell me, what does
my wife want you to do?

Moulineaux (*Quickly*) Nothing . . . You mustn't think . . .

Aubin Nothing?

Moulineaux (*Recovering*) I mean, yes. . . . A . . . dress, yes, a
dress . . . in pink satin . . . with panels of . . . of fur.
Embroidered with pearls . . . on the trousers.

Aubin What trousers?

Moulineaux What trousers? . . . There are trousers underneath.
You can't see them.

Aubin What an extraordinary concoction! Panels of pearls
on the trousers! Don't wear anything too outlandish,
Suzanne. (*To Moulineaux*) You haven't a model of
this dress?

Moulineaux Model? . . . Yes, yes, dozens of models. But you
can't see them. They're in the workshops . . . You
know, competition . . . You only have to whisper . . .

Aubin Then we can't choose?

Moulineaux Yes, you can choose, but you can't see them.
(*Aside*) Won't he ever go?
(*Pomponette enters*)

Pomponette (*Coming to 3*) Afternoon, everyone.

Suzanne (*At 4*) A woman!

Moulineaux (*Dumbfounded*) Who on earth is this?
(*A moment's silence. They all look at each other
inquiringly*)

Pomponette Madame Durand's not here?

Moulineaux Madame Durand? . . . (*A pause. He looks in turn at
Suzanne and Aubin*) . . . No, Madame Durand's not here.

Pomponette Oh! I wanted to see her about my bill.

Moulineaux Bill? . . . What bill?

Pomponette For the dresses she made me.

Moulineaux Of course, Madame Durand! She's the dressmaker!

Aubin Don't you know her?

Moulineaux (*Quickly*) Naturally! . . . Do I know her! Dear
Madame Durand! . . . She's my partner. (*Aside*)
Bassinet might have said she didn't take her
customers with her. A lot of fun it will be if we
have any more of them!

Pomponette   Good. If you're her partner, I can talk to you.
I am Mademoiselle Pomponette.

Moulineaux   (*After a pause*) Why shouldn't you be?

Pomponette   I want you to take something off my bill. You've
charged far too much.

Moulineaux   Why not! Whatever you like! (*Aside*) It won't
cost me anything . . . And it will get rid of her.
(*He takes a pencil out of his pocket*)

Pomponette   (*Showing him the bill*) Look. Three hundred and forty
francs, that's enormous for one tiny little dress.
You know, my scarlet one.

Moulineaux   Of course . . . Your scarlet one. I can see it now
. . . Yes, I can see you're scarlet!

Pomponette   It's far too much.

Moulineaux   Yes, isn't it, far too much. For that dress! It's
indecent. How much do you want me to take off?

Pomponette   I don't know. I think three hundred francs is
enough.

Moulineaux   (*Off-hand*) Agreed. So we'll take off three hundred
francs . . . leaving forty. All right?

Pomponette   What? You've got it wrong.

Moulineaux   No, no. I deal in round figures . . .

Pomponette   Thanks very much. I never dreamt you'd take off
as much as that. (*She goes upstage*)

Aubin   (*Laughing; to the audience*) They must all be robbers
if they can afford that sort of rebate.

Pomponette   Goodbye then. I'll be back soon.

Moulineaux   No, no, I shouldn't bother.
(*Pomponette goes out*)

Aubin   (*Rising*) Good heavens! Half past one! . . . I must
go too. (*Aside*) Rosa's waiting for me, I must hurry.
(*Aloud*) I leave my wife in your hands. Give her
whatever she wants.

Moulineaux   Eh? He's telling me to . . .

Aubin   Goodbye then.

(*Aubin goes out. Moulineaux immediately rushes to the door, puts the chair against it and collapses on the chair, exhausted*)

Moulineaux He's gone. Phew!

Suzanne (*Going upstage*) This is terrible. What are you going to do?

Moulineaux (*Firmly*) What am I going to do? . . . Disappear. I swear nothing like this will ever happen again.

Suzanne You're not serious! You can't!

Moulineaux What do you mean, I can't? Whyever not?

Suzanne Because my husband thinks you're my dressmaker . . . He might come back. If he doesn't find you, he'll guess the truth. I know him, he'll kill you.

Moulineaux (*Rebelling*) He's not entitled to. He's not a doctor. (*Collapsed*) Suzanne, what sort of a mess have we got ourselves into?

(*Bassinet enters, overturning the chair with a crash and sending Moulineaux flying over to the sofa*)

Bassinet (*Bumping into the chair*) Oh! What's happened?

Moulineaux (*Having half-dislocated his thumb*) Ohhh! Look where you're going. What a way to come into a room!

Bassinet (*Hopping down to 2, rubbing his knee*) Why do you sit up against the door?

(*Suzanne at 1, Bassinet 2, Moulineaux 3*)

Moulineaux It's your door and it won't shut. Do you always let flats that are falling to bits?

Bassinet I must say, I did warn you. I only let it to you an hour ago. I've had no time to do anything to it.

Moulineaux You ought to have locks that work. People walk in here, like a shop . . . It's impossible! The first damned fool who arrives . . .

Bassinet Oh, who?

Moulineaux Never mind . . . You! (*He goes upstage and comes back to 2*)

Bassinet	(*Moving to 3*) Me, that's all right. I'll write to the builder. I was going to tell you. After the dressmaker left, I had to force the door; then the builder went off for lunch . . . and never came back. But he will. Apart from that, is everything all right? (*He goes upstage*)
Moulineaux	(*Moving to 2*) Yes, well, you'd better do something about it. (*Pointing to Suzanne who has half-turned away*) Excuse me, I'm not alone.
Bassinet	(*Bowing, at 3*) I am sorry, I didn't see the lady. (*To Suzanne*) Don't you worry, I'm not going to talk about anything private. Don't let me drive you away. (*He sits down on the sofa*)
Moulineaux	(*Aside*) He sticks like a leech. This is the last straw. (*Madame d'Herblay enters*)
Mme d'H.	Excuse me, is Madame Durand here?
Moulineaux	Not again! Ohhh! No, no, no! (*He moves to 3*)
Suzanne	(*At 1*) This is too much!
Mme d'H.	(*At 2*) You see, I've come about my coat.
Moulineaux	(*Moving to the extreme right, then upstage, then coming down again*) Yes. All right. Not today . . . What's your coat got to do with me?
Mme d'H.	(*Offended*) Very well then, I shan't pay, I don't care.
Moulineaux	Nor do I.
Mme d'H.	A charming way to treat a customer! (*Madame d'Herblay goes out*)
Suzanne	(*Aside to Moulineaux*) What about him, won't he go?
Moulineaux	(*At 2*) I'll get rid of him. (*He goes towards Bassinet*)
Bassinet	(*To Moulineaux who tries in vain to interrupt him*) My dear fellow, I've just had a dreadful shock. You'll never believe it, I thought I'd tracked down my wife. Someone pointed out a Madame Bassinet in the street . . .
Moulineaux	Yes. Tell me about it later.
Bassinet	No. It's all right . . . I don't mind this lady

hearing . . . You'll never believe me, it wasn't
her. I said 'I'm sorry, I was looking for a woman'.
She replied: 'Really, what sort of woman do you
want?'

Mme A. (*Off*) The first-floor flat! Very nice!
    (*Bassinet rises with a start*)

Moulineaux My mother-in-law! At this moment!

Suzanne (*Furious*) Another woman! Someone must have had
a bet.
    (*Mme Aigreville enters*)

Mme A. (*Seeing Bassinet*) The leper! (*Aloud*) I've come to see
your flat.

Bassinet (*At 4*) Damn! I was going to tell you . . . It's let.

Mme A. (*At 3*) Let! You told me . . . (*As she turns round,
she sees Moulineaux*) My son-in-law!

Moulineaux (*At 2. Very pleasantly*) In person, mother dear!

Mme A. (*Seeing Suzanne. Very severely*) What is this lady doing
here? I've a right to know.

Moulineaux Well . . .

Mme A. You refuse to speak? . . . Take care, I'm entitled
to draw my own conclusions.

Moulineaux (*Coolly*) What do you mean? This lady's a patient
of mine. It's her flat. She's ill.

Mme A. What!

Moulineaux (*To Suzanne, with a wink*) Isn't that so, you are my
patient?

Mme A. (*Quickly and pleasantly*) I never dreamt you weren't.

Suzanne (*Playing the part of mistress of the house*) I'm afraid
I don't know your name . . .

Mme A. (*Embarrassed*) I do apologise. Let me explain. Little
do you know how fortunate one is to have a
mother . . .

Suzanne (*With a mocking seriousness*) I always support
anything for orphans. Here's five francs.

Mme A. (*Dumbfounded*) She's given me money!

Moulineaux	Aren't you ashamed to go begging in people's houses?
Bassinet	Would you believe it? The old thief!
Mme A.	I didn't ask for anything . . . Take it back, I'm not collecting for charity. I'm looking for a flat.
Suzanne	I am sorry . . .
	(*Mme Aigreville holds out the coin to Moulineaux for him to pass to Suzanne. He absentmindedly puts it in his pocket*)
	(*To Moulineaux*) Hm!
Moulineaux	(*Returning the coin*) Oh, sorry.
Suzanne	(*Coolly*) Now, introduce us.
Moulineaux	(*Dumbfounded*) You want me . . .
	(*Suzanne nods*)
	(*Acidly*) Madame Aigreville, my mother-in-law. (*Yearningly*) Madame Aubin.
Mme A.	My son-in-law's looking after you?
Suzanne	(*Embarrassed*) Yes. Yes. (*Quickly*) My husband too.
Mme A.	(*At 3*) I'm glad to hear it. What is the matter with your husband?
Moulineaux	(*Quickly; at 2*) Eczema . . . combined with impetigo, aggravated by peeling of the epidermis . . . the . . . the aftermath of pregnancy.
Mme A.	Pregnancy? A man?
Moulineaux	(*Recovering*) Not him, his wife!
Suzanne	Me?
Mme A.	You are a mother?
Suzanne	Certainly not!
Moulineaux	(*Floundering*) No, not her, him . . . I mean, no, her husband. You see, her husband imagined he was. . . . So when he learnt he wasn't . . . you know . . . the . . . the . . . the worry, the relief . . . his blood just . . . he had eczema. There! . . . Phew! Now, mother, if you'll leave me with my patient . . .
Mme A.	(*Going upstage*) Of course . . . I must be on my way.

	If my daughter arrives, tell her I've gone.

Moulineaux (*Going with her*) Of course. Goodbye, mother dear.

Mme A. (*In the doorway*) Don't be so charming, I forget nothing. (*With dignity*) But I know how to behave in front of other people.

Moulineaux (*Very pleasantly*) I'll take care I'm never alone in future. This way.

Mme A. (*Bowing to Suzanne*) Goodbye.

Suzanne Goodbye.

Moulineaux (*On the landing, seeing Aubin coming upstairs*) Oh, no! (*To Suzanne*) Your husband's coming back.

Suzanne (*Terrified*) Great heavens!
    (*Suzanne goes out quickly, left*)

Mme A. (*Dumbfounded to Moulineaux who is trying to make her go out left too*) What's the matter?

Moulineaux Nothing. Go in there with her.
    (*He pushes Mme Aigreville, completely dumbfounded, through the door left, and goes out with her. Bassinet follows him to the door*)

Bassinet You'd like me to go too?

Moulineaux (*Pushing his head through the half-open door*) No, you deal with him. He'll ask for me, Monsieur Oh, because he thinks I am Monsieur Oh. Tell him anything you like . . . I'm busy, I'm in conference with . . . with the Queen of Iceland, if you like, I don't care, but don't let me see him. (*He slams the door in Bassinet's face*)

Bassinet All right . . . Another bore, eh? . . . I know 'em. (*At 1*) No doubt about it, he is a bit cracked. Have to make the doctor see a doctor!
    (*Aubin enters*)

Aubin (*At 2*) It's me again. Monsieur Oh's not here? (*He puts his hat on one of the chairs near the door*)

Bassinet (*Facing the audience, his back to Aubin*) No, Monsieur Oh is engaged.

    Aubin (*Recognising him*) The doctor!

  Bassinet (*Turning round*) Exactly, the doctor . . . You know
        then? . . . (*Aside*) Why does he call himself
        Monsieur Oh? (*Aloud*) No, he's engaged.

    Aubin (*Coming downstage*) I didn't expect to meet you here.
        Of course I know Monsieur Oh often sees you. He
        was talking about you just now. You look after him?

  Bassinet (*Not understanding*) I look after him . . . I look after
        him . . . because he looks after me.

    Aubin I see. You mean you do it for nothing.

  Bassinet Yes, I . . . eh? (*Aside*) What the devil's he talking
        about?

    Aubin Tell me, Monsieur Oh is ill then?
        (*Bassinet, as he talks, automatically unbuttons Aubin's
        overcoat. Each time, Aubin does it up again*)

  Bassinet You've noticed it too. I think he must be ever so
        slightly cracked in the head.

    Aubin I must say I wondered . . . What do you prescribe
        for him? A douche perhaps?

  Bassinet (*Unbuttoning Aubin again*) A douche . . .?

    Aubin (*Escaping and doing up his buttons*) Please don't bother.

  Bassinet It's no concern of mine. But frankly a douche
        would do him a lot of good.

    Aubin I'm sure it would. Tell me, as I've found you here,
        I'm very hot-blooded . . .

  Bassinet (*From time to time removing a thread or a speck of
        dust from his coat*) Splendid! Splendid!

    Aubin But there seems to be something wrong with my
        blood. I keep going numb.

  Bassinet Dreadful! Dreadful!

    Aubin I mentioned it to your servant just now.

  Bassinet (*Arranging the lapels of his coat*) Ah, you know my
        servant. Which one, Joseph or Baptiste?

    Aubin (*Breaking away*) I don't know. He prescribed the
        most extraordinary things.

Bassinet My dear fellow, take my word for it, there's nothing like massage.

Aubin I've tried that, it wasn't any use.

Bassinet That's because you go about it the wrong way. You find a masseur, eh? Make him undress and lie on a bed, then massage him as hard as you can for an hour. If your blood doesn't circulate after that, may I be eaten alive by cannibals!

Aubin Really? I've always done it the other way round. Thanks very much, I'll try it. What are we talking about? . . . I can't see Monsieur Oh?

Bassinet (*Mysteriously*) No, no. He's in conference . . . with the Queen . . . the Queen of Iceland.

Aubin (*Dumbfounded*) The Queen of . . . what did you say?

Bassinet The Queen of Iceland.

Aubin (*Admiringly*) Well, well, well, well! The Queen of . . . Phew! . . . He dresses Queens! . . . He must be damned expensive.

Bassinet So would you mind coming back another day.

Aubin I can't. I'm bringing him a new customer, Madame de Saint-Anigreuse, a friend of mine. She wanted me to take her to my wife's dressmaker. So I came on ahead, because I don't want her to meet my wife. I thought I'd make sure she's gone.

Bassinet (*Undoing Aubin's buttons*) That was your wife who was here just now?

Aubin Yes, yes.

Bassinet You let her come here like that, on her own?

Aubin Don't worry, I came with her.

Bassinet (*Mockingly*) Well, then . . .

Aubin I say, tell me, do you think he'll be long?

Mme A. (*Off*) What do you mean, I've an appointment . . . I must be going.

Bassinet (*To the audience*) His mother-in-law! Damn, I mustn't let her get away. I'll wait for her on the stairs and

    try to get her to take the flat above.
     (*Bassinet goes out*)

Aubin (*Not having seen him go*) Tell me, doctor . . .
    (*Turning round*) Where is he? (*Calling*) Doctor! . . .
    He's gone. Extraordinary fellow!
     (*He goes upstage. Mme Aigreville enters*)

Mme A. (*At 1*) I'm going. I don't know why they're keeping
    me.

Aubin (*Upstage, having taken his hat; aside*) The Queen!
    (*Aloud*) Your Majesty! (*He bows*)

Mme A. (*Aside*) What did the man say? (*Aloud, bowing*)
    Good afternoon.

Aubin (*Bowing continually*) Highness!

Mme A. (*Astonished*) What did you say?

Aubin Nothing. I was just overawed by your Majesty.

Mme A. (*Coquettishly*) My majesty! . . . He sees majesty in
    me. I'm afraid I don't know your name . . .

Aubin (*Bowing*) Anatole Aubin.

Mme A. Ah, Madame Aubin's husband . . I met her just
    now, a charming woman. (*Suddenly*) How is your
    eczema?

Aubin (*Dumbfounded*) What?

Mme A. I said, How is your eczema?

Aubin (*He moves to extreme right and carefully inspects his
    hands*) I'm sorry, I haven't got eczema.

Mme A. Forgive me. (*Aside*) I was wrong to mention it, he
    seems embarrassed. (*Aloud*) I see I've been indiscreet.
    I must go now.

Aubin Indiscreet? Certainly not.

Mme A. You're too kind. (*Aside*) I'm not sorry to have seen
    the husband. (*Bowing*) Good afternoon.

Aubin (*Bowing*) Your Majesty.
     (*Madame Aigreville goes out*)
    She seems very nice. Who'd have thought she was
    a queen! . . . She looks like anybody's mother-in-

law. And certainly not proud.
    (*Moulineaux enters*)
There you are! (*He comes downstage*)

Moulineaux Him! . . .Back again!
    (*He sees Suzanne has followed him in, pushes her back
    into the other room and slams the door on her*)
    Go back in there.

Aubin (*Turning round*) What's the matter?

Moulineaux (*Very innocent*) Eh? Nothing.

Aubin Tell me, my wife's gone?

Moulineaux Ages ago. She said, if you came I was to tell you
she's at the Louvre. If you want to join her.

Aubin (*Taking him down to the footlights*) No, I do not . . .
That's splendid, because, you see, a lady . . . a
friend of mine . . . is coming here to collect me.

Moulineaux Here? (*Aside*) He's making dates with his girl
friends in my flat!

Aubin I particularly don't want her to run into my wife.

Moulineaux Of course . . . An affaire, eh?

Aubin (*Laughing*) Just a tiny one. So there's no point in
my wife . . .

Moulineaux (*Deliberately*) Yes, she might retaliate in the same way.

Aubin (*With conviction*) Impossible.

Moulineaux (*Mockingly credulous*) Oh!

Aubin I keep my eyes open . . . I've had affaires with
married women all my life. You can't teach me
anything. I know the lot.

Moulineaux (*As before*) Oh, you . . .

Aubin (*Bluntly*) The lot. I'm not like all those other damn
fool husbands. (*Laughing*) Would you believe it, I
knew one man who went with his wife to all our
rendezvous. She said she was going up to see her
fortune-teller. The fortune-teller was me! . . . Her
husband waited down below! (*He roars with laughter,
clutching his knees*)

Moulineaux (*Also laughing and tapping him on the shoulder*) Nobody could really be as stupid as that.

Aubin Anyway my wife would never dabble with that sort of thing. She knows if I caught her, I wouldn't hesitate for a moment.

Moulineaux (*Anxiously*) A duel, eh?

Aubin No, I can't use a sword.
    (*Moulineaux sighs with relief*)
I'd just shoot him. When I found him, bang, I'd kill him.

Moulineaux (*Aside*) He sends shivers down my spine.

Aubin Anyway I didn't come here to talk about that. (*Changing his tone*) Monsieur Oh!

Moulineaux (*Not with him*) Monsieur . . . ? Ah, yes. (*In the same tone as Aubin*) Monsieur Aubin!

Aubin Monsieur Oh, I've a little surprise for you.

Moulineaux Really I . . . (*Aside*) I'm scared stiff.

Aubin Do you know what?
    (*Moulineaux shakes his head*)
A customer.

Moulineaux A customer? What for?

Aubin Some new clothes.

Moulineaux Again! . . . Oh, a marvellous idea!

Aubin (*Satisfied*) My ideas always are.

Moulineaux (*Forgetting*) Thanks very much! . . . You think I've nothing else to do? What about my patients?
    (*He bites his lip as he realises what he's said*)

Aubin Your patience? Is it exhausted? I've never known a dressmaker complain about too many customers.

Moulineaux Nor have I.

Aubin (*Getting angry*) Just because you make dresses for crowned heads . . .

Moulineaux Dresses for heads?

Aubin Are you a dressmaker or aren't you?

Moulineaux (*Reaching the extreme left*) Of course I'm a dressmaker.

	(*Aside*) If I weren't, he'd kill me.
	(*Madame d'Herblay enters timidly*)
Mme d'H.	It's me again. I've come to see if you're not quite so busy. About my coat.
	(*Aubin sits down on the sofa*)
Moulineaux	(*Seizing the opportunity*) Of course, do come in . . . (*To Aubin*) Am I a dressmaker! Ha!
Mme d'H.	He does seem nice. (*To Aubin*) Excuse me.
	(*Moulineaux at 1, Mme d'Herblay 2, Aubin 3*)
Aubin	Please, please.
Mme d'H.	(*Presenting her back to Moulineaux*) Look, this bodice fits so badly. It's full of creases.
Moulineaux	(*With assurance*) Ah, yes . . . Yes, lots of creases.
Mme d'H.	It's much too big. *You* must have cut it. You'll have to cut it again.
Moulineaux	(*Appalled*) Me?
Mme d'H.	Yes. Right away, I'm in a hurry.
Moulineaux	(*As before*) I've got to cut . . . ?
Aubin	Of course. What's stopping you?
Moulineaux	Me? Nothing . . . You want me to cut . . . Just a moment. (*He gets the scissors and begins to cut the dress*) Heavens, what am I going to do?
Mme d'H.	Heavens, what are you going to do?
Moulineaux	Yes, that's what I . . . You asked me to cut it.
Mme d'H.	No, you know what needs to be done, you can send round for it. (*She goes upstage, then returns*) I don't live where I used to.
Moulineaux	(*Dazed*) Oh! Good.
Mme d'H.	No, I'm on the floor above. Goodbye.
	(*Mme d'Herblay goes out*)
Moulineaux	(*Dazed*) Thanks for telling me. (*He stands there, his eyes fixed, his mind elsewhere, automatically opening and shutting the scissors*)
Aubin	(*Looking at him; aside, laughing*) He looks absolutely flabbergasted. (*Rising, to Moulineaux*) Do you know

what I've been told about you? . . . You ought to
take regular douches.

Moulineaux (*Staring at him dumbfounded*) Who on earth said that?

Aubin Moulineaux.

Moulineaux (*Raising his head and staring at him for a moment to
see if he's gone mad*) Moulineaux?

Aubin Yes, Doctor Moulineaux. I've just left him.

Moulineaux You've just left him. (*Pause*) Are you ill?

Aubin Because I saw the doctor? No, no . . . I happened
to run into him.

Moulineaux (*Coming downstage right*) Ha! I've heard some pretty
big ones in my time, but never anything to beat
that.

(*Rosa enters, with a dog under her arm*)

Rosa Here you are!

Aubin (*Hurrying to meet her*) Good afternoon, my dear.

Moulineaux (*Aside*) Oh, no! His wife's still here!

(*Rosa at 1, Aubin 2, Moulineaux 3*)

Aubin (*Coming downstage*) This is Madame de Saint-
Anigreuse. I told you about her.

Moulineaux (*Turning round*) How do you do. (*Recognising her.
Aside*) Rosa Pichenette!

Rosa (*Aside*) Fancy Pants!

Aubin Madame de Saint-Anigreuse is a member of one
of our most aristocratic families.

Rosa (*Aside*) He recognised me. I've got to talk to him.
(*To Aubin*) Yes, dear, of course, but look, Beautiful's
pricking up his ears. That means he has a little
something he wants to drop on the pavement.
(*Handing him the dog*) So take him for walkies. Come
back when he's finished.

Aubin Oh, no . . . No . . . It's too humiliating.

Rosa (*Frowning*) What did you say?

Aubin (*Humbly*) I said . . . Yes, dear. (*Between his teeth*)
Take the dog for a walk! . . . Rosa has no tact.

(*Aubin goes out*)

Rosa   (*Coming downstage*) Fancy Pants!

Moulineaux   (*Going upstage to meet her*) Rosa Pichenette!
(*They both grip hands. Rosa at 1, Moulineaux 2*)

Rosa   The way you run into people! . . . I haven't seen you since those old Left Bank days.

Moulineaux   Yes, I was a medical student.

Rosa   You became a doctor at last?

Moulineaux   (*Taking a step back, both hands in his pockets*) As you see.

Rosa   But now you're a dressmaker?

Moulineaux   (*After a moment's thought*) What? . . . Ah, yes . . . Yes, to be different. You know, if a doctor practises medicine, it's so ordinary. But for a dressmaker . . . !

Rosa   (*Effusively*) Darling Fancy Pants!

Moulineaux   Sh! Not so loud . . . (*Aside*) Ohhh! Suzanne's in there!

Rosa   (*Surprised*) Why, is somebody ill?

Moulineaux   No. But there's no need to call me Fancy Pants at the top of your voice. I'm not Fancy Pants any more. That was all very well on the Left Bank. Now I've a position in life.

Rosa   It's the only name I've ever known you by. What's your real name?

Moulineaux   My real name? Moul . . . (*Recovering*) Oh . . . My name's Oh.

Rosa   What a ridiculous name!

Moulineaux   There we are . . . I can't help it.

Rosa   (*Passing grandly in front of Moulineaux and reaching 2*) You may not be Fancy Pants any more, but I'm not Rosa Pichinette. I am Madame de Saint-Anigreuse.

Moulineaux   You're married?

Rosa   (*Sitting down on the sofa*) Fixed up, more or less. I started by getting married.

Moulineaux You did?

Rosa Yes. Then once I was a respectable married woman, after a two-day honeymoon, I left my husband for a General.

Moulineaux Phew! A General? . . . There aren't many generals about. Where did you find him?

Rosa In the Tuileries Gardens. My husband had gone to the tobacconist to buy cigarettes.

Moulineaux (*Having looked up during her last words*) I've heard that story before . . . Only it was a cigar.
> (*Noise of broken crockery*)
I'd forgotten Suzanne. She's taking it out on the crockery.

Rosa Who made that noise?

Moulineaux (*Coolly*) Nobody.

Rosa Have you a pet in the flat?

Moulineaux (*Quickly*) Yes, a . . . an ostrich . . . It's just been sent me from Africa. For the feathers.

Rosa (*Rising*) Let me see.

Moulineaux No, you can't . . . It doesn't like people, it's a brute. Talking of brutes did you ever see your husband again?

Rosa No, thank heavens . . . He was useful for launching me in the world, that's all . . . Once I was launched, I took the name of Madame de Saint-Anigreuse.
> (*Noise of crockery again*)
Are you sure that ostrich is all right?

Moulineaux (*Anxious*) Yes, fine. What about you? . . . I mean, wait a moment, I'll go and say something.

Rosa To the ostrich? . . . That won't do much good. Don't go.
> (*Suzanne enters*)

Suzanne (*Coming downstage to 1, furious*) What do you think you're doing? Trying to make a fool of me?

Moulineaux Suzanne . . . This is the last straw!

Suzanne (*Seeing Rosa*) Another woman! . . . This is too much! (*She goes furiously upstage, then comes down again*)

Rosa (*At 3*) Who is this lady?

Moulineaux (*At 2, in a whisper*) Nobody. It's the cashier. She's ill; it's her nerves, don't take any notice. (*To Suzanne who has just come back downstage*) Please, Suzanne, control yourself. Don't make a scandal.

Suzanne (*Very excited*) You might have mentioned you were going to start playing jokes! You might have mentioned you were here with your mistress!

Rosa (*Jumping up*) What do you take me for? I'll have you know I'm a customer. I've come here to order a dress.

(*They have come close to each other, separated only by Moulineaux*)

Suzanne You don't have to tell me that sort of tale!

Rosa What!

Moulineaux I assure you . . .

Suzanne You too! . . . I must say you've a nerve!

Rosa (*Acidly to Moulineaux*) Even if the cashier is your mistress, you should at least prevent her insulting your customers.

Moulineaux (*Exploding*) Splendid! The cashier's my mistress now!

Suzanne (*Quickly*) What cashier? . . . What's she talking about?

Moulineaux (*Appalled*) Nothing. Nothing . . . She's talking to herself.

Rosa (*Quickly*) I'm a respectable woman. This gentleman's my dressmaker.

Suzanne Not again!

Rosa I can prove that's all he is. I came here with my husband.

Suzanne (*Pretending to laugh*) Your husband! I'd like to see him!

Rosa (*Quickly*) You will. He's downstairs taking the dog for a walk.

Moulineaux (*Flabbergasted, at right*) Ohhh! No, no, no, no!

Rosa Listen . . . I can hear him.

(*She goes upstage. Aubin enters, with the dog under his arm; Suzanne at 1, Rosa 2, Aubin 3, Moulineaux 4*)

Come on in. Show yourself . . . This woman won't believe you're my husband!

Aubin (*Turning round*) I . . . Really . . . I . . . (*Recognising Suzanne*) My wife!

Suzanne (*Exploding*) My husband!

Moulineaux Crash!

(*The whole of this last scene must be played with great warmth and without any pauses*)

Suzanne My husband! I won't let him forget this!

(*Suzanne rushes out*)

Aubin (*Wanting to run after his wife*) Suzanne! . . . I . . . Suzanne! . . . (*To Rosa*) Take your damned dog. (*He gives it to her*)

Rosa Anatole!

Aubin (*Pushing her away*) Go to hell.

(*Aubin goes out*)

Rosa (*The dog under her right arm*) What impertinence! Oh, my nerves! Oh, the excitement! (*She faints into Moulineaux's arms*)

Moulineaux (*Catching her in his right arm and taking the dog under his left*) She's ill. Rosa, you're not playing the fool?

(*Yvonne enters*)

Yvonne My mother must still be here.

Moulineaux (*Turning round, finding himself face to face with his wife*) Good God, my wife!

Yvonne My husband! . . . With a woman in his arms! (*Going quickly upstage*) Goodbye! I'll never see you again as long as I live!

Moulineaux Yvonne! . . . Yvonne! . . . Listen . . .

Yvonne No, I won't listen to a word!

(*Yvonne goes out*)

Moulineaux   Wait. Let me explain. Where can I put this woman?
              (*Bassinet enters*)

Bassinet   I say, old man . . .

Moulineaux   (*Passing him Rosa and the dog*) Ah, just in time!
              Hold this woman for me. (*Running out*) Yvonne! . . .
              Yvonne! . . .
              (*Moulineaux goes out*)

Bassinet   What on earth's going on? (*Recognising Rosa*) My
              wife! (*He kisses her*)

Rosa   (*Brought to her senses by the kiss*) My husband! . . .
         Oh!
         (*She slaps his face. Bassinet, amazed, collapses on the
         sofa, as Rosa goes quickly towards the door*)

CURTAIN

Act III

(*Same as Act I. The next morning.*
When the curtain rises, the stage is empty. The door-bell
rings. A moment's silence)

Etienne   (*Off*) That's quite all right, sir.
           (*Moulineaux enters downstage right, very worried*)

Moulineaux   The bell rang. Who is it? (*Calling*) Etienne! . . .
              Well, Etienne?
              (*Etienne enters from the hall*)

Etienne   Sir?

Moulineaux   Who rang?

Etienne   (*Shrugging his shoulders and going towards the door*)
           Nobody.

Moulineaux What do you mean, Nobody?

Etienne Just a patient, wanting an operation. He asked if you were here. I said yes. So he said it didn't hurt any more and went away.

Moulineaux Idiot! If it's no one, come and say someone's there.

Etienne I didn't think there was any point.

Moulineaux (*Annoyed*) All right, go away. (*He moves to 1, deep in thought*)

Etienne (*After watching him for a moment*) You're worried, sir, I understand. I told you the Opera Ball would only cause trouble. If you want to do this sort of thing, you ought to do it properly.

Moulineaux What!

Etienne You should have told me you were going. I'd have slept in your bed.

Moulineaux My bed!

Etienne I'm not particular.
  (*Moulineaux shrugs his shoulders*)
  I'd have changed the sheets.

Moulineaux (*Still pursuing his own thoughts*) Where on earth can my wife be?

Etienne (*Very thoughtfully, like him*) Yes . . . That's what we've been wondering in the kitchen.

Moulineaux (*As before*) It's almost twenty-four hours since she left.

Etienne (*With enthusiasm*) If only you could keep it that way! Do try, sir.

Moulineaux (*Discouraged*) Oh!

Etienne (*Very innocent*) For my sake. Do it for me. I don't like people being miserable . . . I'm so sensitive, sir, it makes me miserable, too. I can't stand it.
  (*Door-bell rings*)

Moulineaux (*Raising his head*) Someone rang.

Etienne (*As before*) Don't worry.

Moulineaux Don't worry!

Etienne   No, they can't come in, if I don't open the door. Well . . . it's agreed? For my sake?

Moulineaux   (*Impatiently*) Yes, all right. Go on.

Etienne   Thank you. (*He stretches out his hand; Moulineaux doesn't take it, so he shakes hands in the air*) Thank you.

Moulineaux   (*Moving to the right*) Remember, except for my wife, I'm at home to nobody.

Etienne   Nobody?

Moulineaux   Not even the Pope. Nobody.

    (*Moulineaux goes out downstage right. Etienne goes out into the hall*)

Etienne   (*Trying to prevent Aubin entering*) No, sir. He's not here.

Aubin   (*At 1*) Nonsense. The concierge told me he is.

Etienne   He just told me himself he isn't. He ought to know better than the concierge.

Aubin   Really? Tell him it's Monsieur Aubin.

Etienne   He said, not even the Pope . . . You aren't the Pope?

Aubin   No. I must see him . . . About my wife.

Etienne   He won't see anyone because of his.

Aubin   Why is that?

Etienne   (*Importantly*) That's his secret . . . and mine. Of course I'm the soul of discretion. If you asked me: 'Etienne, is it true it's been brewing for days, he didn't come home the other night, she didn't come home last night, we're still waiting for her?' . . . I'd say 'No, no, no, I don't know what you mean.'

Aubin   Madame Moulineaux's disappeared?

Etienne   (*Innocently*) How did you know?

Aubin   You've just told me.

Etienne   Me! (*Aside*) He has a nerve!

Aubin   Disappeared. Like my wife. Since that scene yesterday I haven't set eyes on her. It's unbelievable.

Etienne (*Laughing stupidly*) Your wife too? It seems to be catching.

Aubin (*Moving to the right*) It can't go on like this. I've come here, because I know this is when she sometimes sees the doctor.

Etienne The doctor's not seeing anyone today, including your wife . . . till he's got *his* wife back.
(*Door-bell rings*)
There's the bell. Excuse me.
(*Etienne goes out quickly*)

Aubin (*To the audience, moving to the left*) Obviously, I must have it out with my wife. I'll disown Rosa, that's all.
(*Etienne enters quickly*)

Etienne Sir, they're here. You'd better go.

Aubin Who are here?

Etienne Madame Moulineaux and her mother.

Aubin The doctor's wife? Lucky man! *She's* come back!
(*Madame Aigreville and Yvonne enter*)

Mme A. Go and tell Monsieur Moulineaux that Madame Aigreville is here.

Aubin Madame Aigreville! The Queen!

Etienne I will. He'll be so happy.
(*Etienne goes out downstage right*)

Mme A. That is his concern. I should be surprised.

Aubin The Queen . . . Madame Aigreville? I don't understand . . . (*To Mme Aigreville*) Excuse me, you're not . . .

Mme A. Not what?

Aubin The Queen of Iceland?

Mme A. Me? The . . . (*She laughs*) He must have another attack of eczema.

Aubin You're not? No, obviously you couldn't be.

Mme A. What!

Aubin No, I didn't mean that. (*Bowing*) I see you want to

	talk to the doctor. Good morning. (*He bows again*)
Mme A.	Good morning.
Aubin	(*Bowing to Yvonne*) Good morning. (*Aside*) Charming wife the doctor has!
	(*Aubin goes out*)
Mme A.	Remember, Yvonne, don't weaken.
Yvonne	(*At 1, Mme Aigreville 2*) It's all right, mother.
	(*Moulineaux enters and rushes to Yvonne*)
Moulineaux	Yvonne! You don't know how worried I've been! (*At 3*)
Mme A.	(*Barring the way*) Stand back. (*At 2*)
Moulineaux	What!
Mme A.	Let there be no misunderstanding as to why we're here.
Moulineaux	But . . .
Mme A.	You thought I would allow it to blow over. No. I know my duty as a mother.
Moulineaux	Ohhh! . . . If she starts meddling!
Mme A.	My son, for that is what you happen to be, I have brought you back your wife.
Moulineaux	That is nice of you. (*He starts to rush forward*)
Mme A.	(*Stopping him*) Stand back . . . Not in the way you mean. My daughter and I have considered the matter at length. This is what we have decided.
Moulineaux	(*Getting angry*) If your daughter's listened to you, it *will* be charming!
Mme A.	From now on there will be no contact between your wife and you.
Moulineaux	(*With a hollow laugh*) There! . . . What did I say?
Mme A.	At first I thought of taking my daughter home with me. That is why we spent last night at the Grand Hotel . . . Room 423 . . . on the fourth floor . . . at the front. But I do not intend to expose ourselves to vulgar gossip. For appearances' sake, my daughter will live under the same roof as you.

Moulineaux (*Aside*) Will she? Once we're alone, I'll make sure . . .

   Mme A. And I shall stay with her.

Moulineaux (*Startled*) What?

   Mme A. To be her guide and counsellor.

Moulineaux That will be fun.

   Mme A. We shall be two distinct households, each in one half of the flat. (*Pointing to Moulineaux's room*) That side, men. This side, women.

Moulineaux (*With a hollow laugh*) I congratulate you . . . (*Exploding*) It's ridiculous . . . You can't be serious. Anyway, what have I done? Yes, Yvonne, tell me what I've done.

   Yvonne Me?

   Mme A. (*Quickly*) Yvonne, don't answer.

Moulineaux (*Furious*) Let her speak, for God's sake!

   Mme A. Don't lose your temper with me.

   Yvonne (*Moving to 2*) You have the impertinence to ask me what you've done?

   Mme A. Yes, he has.

Moulineaux I'm not talking to you.

   Yvonne Will you please be a little more polite to my mother!

Moulineaux Will you please answer my question?

   Yvonne What! I find you at a dressmaker's, alone with a woman, holding her in your arms!

Moulineaux (*Quickly*) She wasn't mine.

   Yvonne Who?

Moulineaux That woman! She'd just been handed to me. (*He explains in mime*)

   Yvonne Really! So that's why you were clutching her in your arms.

Moulineaux No, if you'd looked . . . I wasn't clutching her!

   Yvonne I tell you, you were clutching her in your arms. And she hated it.

Moulineaux (*Seizing the opportunity*) There, you see! She hated it. That proves she . . .

Yvonne Nonsense! You're having affaires with dressmakers.

Mme A. And you introduce them to me as patients.

Moulineaux (*Glibly, moving to 2*) No, that's different, don't confuse the two. (*To Mme Aigreville*) The woman you saw is Madame Aubin, the wife of Monsieur Aubin. But the other . . .

Mme A. (*At 1, acidly*) Is whose wife?

Moulineaux (*Quickly*) Monsieur Aubin's.

Mme A. (*As before*) Oh? He's a bigamist?

Moulineaux (*As before*) Exactly . . . No, no. There's no way of explaining. (*To Mme Aigreville*) You're muddling everything. It's no business of yours. Why are you poking your nose in?

Mme A. Poking my nose in!

Moulineaux (*Furiously*) You're interfering in our private life. I'm not married to you. The only person I have to explain to is my wife. I don't need you.

Mme A. Don't think I'm going to leave you alone with Yvonne. This poor child exposed to your wiles!

Moulineaux (*Exasperated*) My wiles! My wiles! . . . I tell you I want to talk to my wife alone. I think I'm entitled to.

Mme A. No.

Moulineaux (*Hoarse, stifling a shout of rage*) Ohhh! (*He is clearly about to strangle his mother-in-law but controls himself, strides upstage, then returns downstage extreme left*)

Yvonne Mother, let's do as he asks. Then he'll have no cause for complaint.

Mme A. I know you. You'll let yourself be persuaded.

Yvonne There's nothing to be afraid of.

Mme A. Very well, I shall leave you. Never let it be said that I interfere. Remember, don't yield an inch. (*Aside*) Poor child! If I weren't here, she'd have made it up already. (*Making a face at Moulineaux*) Pah!
(*Mme Aigreville goes out midstage left. A pause.*

*Then Moulineaux goes slowly towards Yvonne, who
is extreme right)*

Moulineaux (*Very calmly*) Listen, Yvonne, forget your mother
for a moment and trust me. These two women are
Monsieur Aubin's secret, not mine. I don't know
them. They're two . . . two patients, there! I was
called in as a doctor . . . A pathological case, most
extraordinary . . . comparative medicine! It's too
difficult to explain, you know . . . science . . . you
need special knowledge. Believe me, it's finished,
completely. You found me making an experiment.
It was not a success. I've abandoned it.

Yvonne It's easy to say that now.

(*Mme Aigreville puts her head round the door*)

Mme A. Will you be long?

Moulineaux No . . . We'll call you when we're ready.

Mme A. Remember. Don't believe a word he says.

(*Mme Aigreville goes out*)

Moulineaux (*Aside, fuming*) Damn the woman, go away. (*Aloud,
gently*) Yvonne, I promise I'm telling the truth.
(*Aside*) As a man of honour, I have to bend it a
little.

Yvonne (*Weakening*) If only I could believe you!

Moulineaux (*Enthusiastically*) You must believe me.

Yvonne It would be wonderful if I could . . . But I can't.
. . . You must be lying.

Moulineaux (*Hotly*) No! What makes you think that?

Yvonne It's mother.

Moulineaux (*Furious. With a bitter laugh*) Your mother! . . .
Your delicious, delightful mother! . . . That's no
reason.

Yvonne (*Longing to give way*) You're prepared to swear . . . ?

Moulineaux But . . .

Yvonne To convince mother. Swear you're telling the truth.

Moulineaux (*Aside with feeling*) Her mother's impossible.

(Raising his hand) I swear it's the truth, the whole truth and nothing but the truth . . . *(Aside)* It's got to be. *(The Aside must follow straight after the oath, without a pause)*

Yvonne Thank you. Then you don't know that woman?

Moulineaux If you ever see us together again, you can think what you like. There! You forgive me?

Yvonne Oh! No . . . No, not like that. Later. When mother's gone.

Moulineaux Kiss me anyway.

(Aubin enters from the hall)

Yvonne That's different.

(Moulineaux kisses her)

Aubin *(Aside. With amazement)* Monsieur Oh's having an affaire with the doctor's wife! *(He remains in the doorway and listens)*

Moulineaux You're an angel.

Yvonne You will be sensible, you won't behave again like you did the other night? Where did you go, instead of sleeping here like a good little boy? We've a lot to talk about.

Aubin *(Scandalised)* Oh!

Moulineaux You'll never have any reason to be angry with me again.

Yvonne I'm not angry with you for being a bad husband, I'm angry with you for not loving your wife.

Moulineaux *You* don't love your husband.

Aubin *(As before)* This is something new. *(Aloud)* Hm! It's me . . . I've just arrived, I didn't hear what you were saying. *(He comes downstage to 1)*

Moulineaux *(Aside)* Oh, no . . . He'll ruin everything. *(Aloud)* Let me introduce Madame Moulineaux.

Aubin Yes, yes, I know . . . I saw you. *(He laughs and bows)* Ah-ha, you rogue, you, congratulations!

Moulineaux *(Surprised)* What's the matter with the man?

Aubin   How's everything else? You've remembered us all right?

Moulineaux   (*Quickly*) Yes, yes, of course. (*Aside*) The bomb's going off any moment now.

Aubin   You've started my wife's dress?

Moulineaux   Yes . . . Let's talk about something else. Have you been up the Eiffel Tower today?

Yvonne   What dress, darling?

Moulineaux   (*Offhand*) Nothing, a nightdress. I mean, no . . . A night-dressing I ordered for his wife.

Yvonne   Night-dressing?

Moulineaux   (*As before*) Yes, a special sort of treatment . . . a dressing charged with electricity, you have to wear at night. Science again. (*Aside*) If only I could bury the man!

Yvonne   It sounds very suspicious to me.

Moulineaux   No, darling, no. You're not going to start getting ideas again?

Aubin   He calls her darling in front of me! Tactless fellow!

Moulineaux   Don't be so suspicious. You must trust me. Just remember you're the only woman I love. And ever will love.

Yvonne   (*Doubtfully*) Oh!
     (*Bassinet enters*)

Aubin   Good heavens! Her husband! (*He pulls out his handkerchief and makes desperate signals to Moulineaux who turns his back on him*)

Moulineaux   I tell you, I love you, I love you, I love you.

Bassinet   (*At 2*) Charming!

Aubin   (*Making signals*) Pst! Monsieur Oh! Monsieur Oh!
     (*He sees Bassinet is looking at him and pretends to be fanning himself with his handkerchief, at the same time bowing to Bassinet. Bassinet, surprised, pulls out his handkerchief and makes the same gestures*)

Moulineaux   (*Tenderly, at 3*) Yvonne! (*He wants to kiss her*)

Yvonne (*At 4*) No, not in front of everybody!

Moulineaux I'm not ashamed.

Aubin This is the limit. And her husband takes no notice.
(*He sees Bassinet move towards Moulineaux*) Yes, he does.

Bassinet (*Advancing with comic gravity and tapping Moulineaux on the shoulder*) I say! I'm here, you know!

Aubin He's going to explode. This will be terrible.

Moulineaux (*Grumpily, not even bothering to turn round*) Eh? What?

Bassinet (*Jovial*) Well . . . Hullo! You're cutting me dead!

Moulineaux Hullo, hullo!

Aubin (*Appalled*) That's all! (*To Moulineaux*) I say, Monsieur Oh!

Yvonne (*Quickly*) Why does he call you Monsieur Oh?

Moulineaux (*Embarrassed*) What? You thought he called me . . . No, he said Monsieur and then he said Oh, two different things . . . (*Aside*) If I don't get Yvonne out of here, he's going to ruin everything. (*Aloud*) I think your mother's calling you.
(*They pass in front of Bassinet who is centre stage*)

Yvonne No, she isn't.

Moulineaux Yes, she is. Hurry up . . . (*To the others*) I shan't be long.
(*He takes Yvonne out midstage left. A pause. Aubin and Bassinet look at each other. Then Bassinet points to the door Moulineaux has gone through and they both burst out laughing*)

Aubin (*Still laughing*) He's absolutely shameless. You don't say a word?

Bassinet What about?

Aubin About . . . nothing. (*Aside*) Is the man deaf?

Bassinet (*Laughing*) I say, I think we disturbed them.

Aubin (*Appalled*) Yes, I . . . (*Aside*) What century are we living in?

Bassinet (*As before*) They're charming.

Aubin (*Laughing out of politeness*) Charming! Charming! . . .

(*Aside*) He has no morals at all. (*Aloud*) My dear
fellow, I'm not prudish, but I don't understand
why you don't keep a closer watch on your wife.

Bassinet (*Bewildered*) My wife? (*Aside*) The man's mad.
(*Aloud*) Give me a little time. I only found her
again yesterday.

Aubin You only found her again . . .

Bassinet Yes. (*Aside*) Why is he talking about my wife?
. . . (*Aloud*) You see, she deserted me.

Aubin For the dressmaker . . .

Bassinet No, a soldier.

Aubin A soldier, too! . . . (*Aside*) What a girl!

Bassinet I'd been searching for her for years. Then yesterday
when I least expected it, I found her in someone
else's arms. Guess whose?

Aubin Monsieur Oh?

Bassinet (*Dumbfounded*) Monsieur Oh . . . Exactly. How do
you know?

Aubin It's not hard to guess. (*Aside*) He's very
philosophical.

Bassinet When she saw me, she was so delighted she slapped
my face . . . I'm so happy!

Aubin She slapped his face and he's happy! I'm not
surprised.

Bassinet (*Aside*) If anyone's surprised, it will be Moulineaux
when I introduce him to my wife.
(*Moulineaux enters*)

Moulineaux There, that's settled . . . I've made her mother see
reason, almost. (*To Bassinet*) Good morning, my
dear fellow, I'm sorry I was a little absent-minded
just now.

Bassinet (*Reaching 2*) That's all right, I understand.

Moulineaux (*To Aubin*) You're still here, are you?

Aubin (*Taking Moulineaux aside, extreme left*) Yes, I want
to have a word with you.

(*Bassinet, very innocently, joins them and listens*)
(*Embarrassed; to Bassinet*) Excuse me.

Bassinet (*Innocently*) Go ahead, don't mind me.

Aubin (*Laughing with embarrassment*) It's a personal matter.

Bassinet Of course. (*He goes to the table, right, sits down and glances through a book during the following scene*)

Aubin (*Quietly*) I wanted to tell you, I'm waiting for my wife. She often has an appointment with you about this time and as I haven't seen her since yesterday . . .

Moulineaux (*At 2*) Oh, hell!

Aubin What did you say?

Moulineaux I said, Oh, hell!

Aubin (*At 1*) That's what I said, Oh, hell! But it doesn't help. I wanted to settle everything, because it's too ridiculous . . . But how can I explain away Rosa?

Moulineaux Yes.

Aubin (*Suddenly*) I've an idea. You won't let me down?

Moulineaux Of course not . . . We men must stick together.

Aubin (*Delighted*) I'll say that Rosa . . . is your mistress.

Moulineaux (*Nodding*) That's it . . . No! What are you saying? Certainly not.

Aubin (*Very naturally*) What difference does it make to you? My wife's the only person who'll know.

Moulineaux Thank you. That's enough.

Aubin (*Begging*) My dear fellow . . .

Moulineaux I tell you it's ridiculous. No, no. I can't do it. What would Madame Moulineaux say?

Aubin (*Appalled, looking at Bassinet*) You think he . . .

Moulineaux Find someone else.

Aubin Who?

Moulineaux I don't know.

(*Bassinet starts humming and attracts Moulineaux's attention*)

Why not him?

Aubin (*Scandalised*) Well . . . !

Moulineaux It's nothing.

Aubin (*Scandalised*) To him? . . . You think Madame
　　　　Moulineaux won't mind?

Moulineaux (*Very innocently*) Why should she?

Aubin (*As before, opening his arms wide*) What morals!
　　　　What morals! Well, it's no business of mine.

Moulineaux (*To Bassinet, who, still humming, has thrown his book
　　　　on the table and risen*) I say, this gentleman wants
　　　　to ask you something. (*He withdraws to the table, right*)

Aubin (*To Bassinet*) Will you do me a great favour?

Bassinet (*Anxious*) Me?

Aubin I need your help very badly.

Bassinet (*Embarrassed*) Well . . . actually . . . I'm rather short
　　　　of money at the moment . . .

Aubin (*Reassuring*) It won't cost you anything.

Bassinet (*Reassured*) Ah! Go on, then.

Aubin I'm having a little trouble with my wife. She caught
　　　　me with my mistress . . .

Bassinet (*Laughing very innocently*) That was silly of you.

Aubin (*Laughing obligingly*) Very silly. (*Seriously*) My wife
　　　　will be here in a moment. You know her. Tell
　　　　her Madame de Saint-Anigreuse is your mistress.

Bassinet (*Joking*) That's an idea.

Aubin Yes.

Bassinet (*Turning round sharply*) A rotten one.

Aubin You're not going to refuse?

Bassinet Precisely.

Moulineaux (*In a whisper to Bassinet; coming downstage to him*) Do
　　　　what he wants. He's chairman of lots of companies
　　　　. . . He might be looking for a flat.

Bassinet Really? . . . I agree.

Aubin Really?

Bassinet It won't mean anything?

Aubin Nothing.

Bassinet Tell me . . . Hm . . . Is she pretty?

Aubin Who? . . . The . . . Very pretty.

Bassinet (*Laughing*) Quite a girl, eh?

Aubin Yes, quite.

Bassinet (*Laughing and nudging him*) A bit of a tart, in fact?

Aubin (*Laughing*) Yes, in the nicest possible way. Here's her photo. (*He takes a photo out of his wallet and gives it to Bassinet*) You can show it to my wife to make it ring true.

    (*Etienne enters*)

Etienne Madame Aubin.

Aubin (*Thrusting the photo into Bassinet's overcoat pocket*) My wife! . . . Sh! Hide it . . .

    (*Etienne goes out*)

Moulineaux (*At 1, Suzanne 2, Aubin 3, Bassinet 4; going towards Suzanne*) Good morning, Madame Aubin.

Aubin (*Timidly*) Good morning, Suzanne.

Suzanne (*Scornfully*) You're here? . . . Very well, I can easily go.

Aubin (*Quickly*) Suzanne! . . . Listen to me . . . I wasn't doing anything.

Suzanne You can explain that to the judge. (*She makes for the door*)

Aubin The judge? . . . Certainly not. Look, let's talk it over. It was all a misunderstanding. You found me with a lady, yes. I don't know her. She belongs to this gentleman. (*To Bassinet*) Doesn't she?

Bassinet (*Without conviction*) Yes, yes . . . Yes, yes, yes.

Aubin You see?

Suzanne Rubbish!

Moulineaux Madame Aubin, don't be so cruel.

Aubin Suzanne, do believe me. I swear you're wrong. (*Aside to Bassinet*) Show her the photograph.

Bassinet (*Searching in his pocket*) Yes. (*He moves to 3*)

    (*Etienne enters*)

Etienne Madame Bassinet.

(*Rosa enters. Etienne goes out*)

Bassinet (*Going quickly upstage*) Come on in.

Suzanne My husband's mistress!

Bassinet (*To Aubin*) Let me introduce . . .

Aubin (*Not having noticed Rosa's entrance and suddenly recognising her*) Rosa! Oh, no!
　　　　(*Aubin escapes through the door downstage right*)

Bassinet What's the matter with him? Moulineaux, my dear fellow, let me introduce my . . .

Moulineaux (*Raising his head*) Rosa! Let's get out of this.
　　　　(*Moulineaux escapes through the door downstage left*)

Bassinet What on earth's the matter with them?

Rosa (*Annoyed*) They're not very polite.

Bassinet Never mind, they're just surprised. (*Going upstage; to Suzanne*) May I have the pleasure of introducing . . .

Suzanne No, you may not.
　　　　(*Suzanne goes out midstage right*)

Rosa What! . . . Again!

Bassinet Yes . . . Phew! Perhaps she didn't understand.
　　　　(*Yvonne enters midstage left*)
Ah! Let me introduce . . .

Yvonne (*Amazed, to Rosa*) You here? . . . (*To Bassinet*) Up to your old tricks again?
　　　　(*Yvonne goes out quickly midstage left*)

Rosa (*Furious*) This is too much!

Bassinet (*Good-natured*) No, it happens all the time.

Rosa Don't you ever say anything?

Bassinet Yes . . . Yes. (*He goes to the door midstage left and knocks on it*) You'll see.
　　　　(*Moulineaux enters downstage left and, thinking Rosa is alone, rushes to her*)

Moulineaux (*Whispering quickly*) How dare you come here! You must be mad.

Rosa What do you mean? I'm with my husband.

Moulineaux   Your husband? Where?

Rosa   There, Bassinet. He found me again yesterday.

Moulineaux   (*Appalled*) Bassinet!

Bassinet   (*Coming between them*) What's the matter?

Moulineaux   Nothing. (*He bursts out laughing*)
　　　　　(*Rosa is now on the right. Aubin enters downstage right*)

Aubin   (*Whispering quickly*) Rosa, for heavens' sake don't make a scene. Go away, my wife's here.

Rosa   (*Going to 1*) You're all of you getting on my nerves.

Bassinet   (*Going towards Aubin*) Why is everybody whispering?
　　　　　(*Mme Aigreville and Yvonne enter left. Suzanne enters right*)

Yvonne   (*To her husband*) This is too much. How dare you bring your dressmakers into our home!

Moulineaux   Who do you mean? What dressmaker?

Yvonne   (*Pointing to Rosa*) That woman!

Rosa   Me?

Mme A.   (*Pointing to Suzanne, who has remained in the doorway midstage right*) No, that one!

Suzanne   Me?
　　　　　(*She comes downstage between Aubin and Moulineaux. Rosa is at 1, Mme Aigreville 2, Yvonne 3, Moulineaux 4, Suzanne 5, Aubin 6, Bassinet 7*)

Moulineaux   Do make up your minds.

Aubin   (*Pointing to Suzanne*) I'm sorry, this lady is my wife.

Bassinet   (*Pointing to Rosa*) And this lady is mine. Please remember that when you talk about her.

All   His wife!

Bassinet   Exactly.

Aubin   (*Making his wife move to the extreme right*) His wife! I gave him her photo! (*To Bassinet*) Give me back that picture.

Bassinet   What? Which . . . ? Ah, of course. (*He takes it out of his pocket and wants to look at it*)

Aubin (*Quickly*) Don't look at it.

Bassinet (*Pushing Aubin away with his left hand and pulling out the photo with his right*) Pah! Why not?

Aubin (*Insisting*) No, please!

Bassinet (*Looking at the photo*) Oh!

Aubin (*Between his teeth*) Crash! Here we go!

Bassinet How funny, she looks like my wife. (*To Aubin*) Doesn't she?

Aubin (*Offhand*) What? She . . . Oh, no. She has a lot too much . . .

Bassinet (*To Moulineaux*) Yes. Look. Don't you think she's like my wife?

Moulineaux Oh . . . she hasn't nearly enough . . .

Bassinet (*To Rosa*) Go on, you look!

Rosa You're very cruel.

Bassinet Am I? Yes, you're right. It's not like you at all.

Suzanne (*To Aubin*) It was all true then?

Aubin I've been telling you so for the last hour.

Suzanne Anatole, darling!

Aubin All right, I forgive you.

Yvonne (*To Moulineaux*) Will you forgive me?

Moulineaux Don't ask me to forgive you, that's too much.

Mme A. Are they going mad? . . . It's lucky I'm here or they'd start all over again tomorrow.

Yvonne My dear husband!

Moulineaux Ohhh!

Aubin Her husband? . . . Then Doctor Moulineaux . . .

Moulineaux (*Embarrassed*) Well, you see . . .

Bassinet (*Pointing to Moulineaux*) He's the doctor.

Moulineaux Bloody fool!

Aubin I thought you were a dressmaker.

Moulineaux You didn't? That's the end! (*To the audience as the curtain starts to fall*) Well, I mean, it is!

(*The curtain falls in front of his face*)

A Close Shave
Champignol Malgré Lui

Translator's Note

This translation was commissioned by the BBC for broadcasting, but I have here ignored my radio adaptation and reverted to the original text. Feydeau's stage directions frequently include the relative positions of the characters, which are numbered from left to right, so that, for example, 1 is always left of 2 but may be anywhere on the stage.

The Italian uncle, Romeo, has been changed from a Swiss, Chamel, to provide jokes about his name and because references to the absence of military service in Switzerland and the prevalence of Swiss porters in Paris would now be unintelligible. I have assumed that he and his family would use the Italian pronunciation of Romeo, but that Saint Florimond in his ignorance would pronounce it in the usual English fashion. In Act II I have made all the recruits Reservists, instead of some of them being Territorials, and for the drill sequences I have adopted the simplifications and clarifications used by Stuart Burge in his production at the Nottingham Playhouse, including the elimination of two additional squads of recruits with their attendant corporals.

This translation was first broadcast on 27 December 1968 with the following cast:

Saint Florimond	*Richard Briers*
Angele	*Gwen Watford*
Joseph	*John Baddeley*
Charlotte	*Rosalind Shanks*
Romeo	*Andre van Gyseghem*
Mauricette	*Pamela Miles*
Dufoulay	*Michael Spice*
Capt Camaret	*Simon Lack*
Adrienne	*Helen Weir*
Celestin	*Graham Armitage*
Police Sergeant	*John Pullen*
Champignol	*John Moffatt*
Lt Ledoux	*Fraser Kerr*
Sgt Belouette	*Frederick Treves*
Lafauchette	*Antony Viccars*
Prince of Valence	*John Humphry*
Major Fourrageot	*Peter Pratt*
Corporal Grosbon	*Victor Lucas*
Barber	*John Baddeley*
Jerome	*David Brierly*

Produced by John Tydeman

The first stage production was at the Nottingham
Playhouse on 10 July 1971 with the following cast:

Saint Florimond	*Jimmy Thompson*
Angele	*Angela Richards*
Joseph	*Geoffrey Drew*
Charlotte	*Susan Littler*
Romeo	*Paul Dawkins*
Mauricette	*Delia Lindsay*
Dufoulay	*Neil Fitzwilliam*
Capt Camaret	*David Dodimead*
Adrienne	*Gail Harrison*
Celestin	*Simon Cadell*
Police Sergeant	*Martin Matthews*
Policeman	*Melvyn Hastings*
Champignol	*Donald Gee*
Lt Ledoux	*Michael Elphick*
Sgt Belouette	*Peter Childs*
Lafauchette	*David Schofield*
Prince of Valence	*Charles Waite*
Lavalanche	*Hywel Davies*
Badin	*Peter Ellis*
Major Fourrageot	*Martin Matthews*
Corporal Grosbon	*Melvyn Hastings*
A Barber	*Geoffrey Drew*
Jerome	*Peter Ellis*
Reservists	*Michael Barnard*
	Michael Barry
	Kevin Cole
	Paul Greenwood
	Timothy Seward
	Harry Stephenson

Directed by Stuart Burge
Settings by Patrick Robertson
Costumes by Rosemary Vercoe

Characters
In Order of Appearance

SAINT FLORIMOND	
ANGELE	*Champignol's wife*
JOSEPH	*Her manservant*
CHARLOTTE	*Her maid*
ROMEO	*Her uncle*
MAURICETTE	*Romeo's daughter*
DUFOULAY	*Her husband*
CAPT. CAMARET	
ADRIENNE	*His daughter*
CELESTIN	*His nephew*
POLICE SERGEANT	
CHAMPIGNOL	
LT LEDOUX	
SGT BELOUETTE	
LAFAUCHETTE	
PRINCE OF VALENCE	*Reservists*
LAVALANCHE	
BADIN	
MAJOR FOURRAGEOT	
CORPORAL GROSBON	
A BARBER	
JEROME	*A manservant*
A POLICEMAN	
SIX RESERVISTS	

Act I   The Champignols' flat in Paris
Act II   The Barracks at Clermont. The next day
Act III Mme Rivolet's House in Clermont. The same
         evening
         The time is about 1890

Act I

(The Champignols' flat in Paris. On the right is the door of Angele's bedroom. On the left, downstage, a door leading to the rest of the flat. Midstage a big window, and in the back wall a door opening into the hall. At the back of the hall is the front door of the flat.

Pictures on easels, sketches on the walls etc. On the right, downstage, is a table, with a chair on each side of it. On the table a cup of chocolate on a tray. On the left a sofa with two upright chairs on its right. Against the back wall on a chair is a canvas with its back to the audience.

When the curtain rises, the stage is empty. A cuckoo clock strikes eight, then a key can be heard in the front door which opens.

Saint Florimond enters)

St Florimond   *(Coming downstage centre)* Phew! I'm here. Oh, it's so silly! My heart's going bang, bang, bang! I can hear it. Oh, if you've anything wrong with your tonsils, don't ever risk a love affaire. *(He goes upstage)* If I were her husband, I'd come in here, calm and collected. But I'm not . . . Ah, well, be brave.

    (He goes behind the right-hand table to the door and knocks on it)

Angele   *(Off)* Is that you, Victoire?

St Florimond   *(Woman's voice)* Yes. . . . *(Aside)* She'll be furious.

Angele   *(Off)* Come in then.

St Florimond   *(As before)* Yes.

    (He opens the door)

Angele   *(Off. Screaming)* Oh! You! . . . Go away.

St Florimond   Oh! She's getting out of the bath.

Angele   *(Off)* Shut the door. Shut the door.

St Florimond   Yes, no . . . Well . . . *(The door slams in his face)* Oh!

7

What did I say? She'd be furious. What did I say?
Women are funny. (*He sits*) If I were her husband . . .
I'd come in here . . . calm and collected . . . I'm her
lover . . . So I'm kicked out. That's life. When I
think I've been cooling my heels for two hours
outside on the pavement! (*He sits at the table, right,
with his back to Angele's door*) Oh, no! My heart! . . .
There are two things that upset me. Excitement.
And hunger. I've had no breakfast this morning.
(*He sees the cup of chocolate and drinks it as he goes on
talking*) . . . And heaven knows when I'll get any.
But, pah! Lovers don't need food. (*He swallows the
rest of the chocolate*)
>   (*Angele enters right and stands facing the audience at the
>   end of the table at which Saint Florimond is sitting*)

Angele	What is the meaning of this behaviour?
St Florimond	Angele, I will only say one word. (*Stuffing a piece of toast in his mouth and talking with his mouth full*) It's love.
Angele	(*Coming downstage*) For heaven's sake! You've been drinking my chocolate!
St Florimond	Your chocolate? It is good!
Angele	*Is* good?
St Florimond	Hm. *Was* good.
Angele	Really, this is outrageous! I forbid you to set foot in this house again and here you are at eight in the morning!
St Florimond	I didn't want to compromise you.
Angele	Pah! . . . Anyway someone must have seen you.

>   (*Saint Florimond rises and goes to the door into the hall to
>   make sure no one's coming, then he comes back downstage
>   next to Angele*)

St Florimond	No, they didn't. I thought . . . this is the moment . . . the moment when the servants go out . . . every day. So I waited till they'd gone. Besides I knew your

	husband had been away for the past month. So I thought: she's alone!
Angele	I told you not to come. I wrote to you, didn't I? 'Everything is finished between us. Send me back my key. The key I so foolishly gave you.'
St Florimond	It's because of the key I'm here. . . . Hm, that's how I got in.
Angele	(*Moving to the extreme left, level with the sofa*) You didn't have to *come*! You could have posted it.
St Florimond	(*Following her*) I thought of that. But apparently you have to write on the parcel what's in it . . . Well, I couldn't put 'Madame Champignol's front-door key'. What would the man in the post office think?
Angele	(*Sitting on the sofa*) You don't have to say everything.
St Florimond	(*Standing next to her*) Besides . . . I did have another reason for coming here. I thought: No, the last word has not been said. That farewell letter can't be final. Or it wouldn't have filled me with hope.
Angele	Hope? What filled you with hope?
St Florimond	'Everything is finished between us.'
Angele	That filled you with hope?
St Florimond	Of course. Everything can't possibly be finished, I thought, because nothing ever started. . . So if she begins with the end, perhaps she'll end with the beginning. (*He sits on the sofa at 2, next to Angele*)
Angele	(*Mockingly*) Oh! Oh!
St Florimond	Angele! (*He tries to seize her by the waist*)
Angele	(*Releasing herself, rising and moving to 2*) No! No more Angele, my dear! Thank you very much. No more little escapades!
St Florimond	(*Rising and following her*) What escapades?
Angele	Well! Like Fontainebleau!
St Florimond	(*At 1*) That was a disaster.
Angele	(*At 2*) It was virtue triumphant.
St Florimond	That wasn't your fault.

Angele (*Sitting on the chair at the left of the right-hand table*)
You think so?

St Florimond (*Passing behind the table, then coming downstage on the other side*) I don't suppose you agreed to spend two days with me at Fontainebleau to look at the palace! (*Sitting on the chair on the other side of the table, facing Angele*) If you hadn't run into those relations of yours from the country . . . your uncle . . . What's his name?

Angele Romeo.

St Florimond A splendid name for an uncle!

Angele He's Italian.

St Florimond If you hadn't run into your Uncle Romeo, his daughter and her husband . . .

Angele (*Rising and moving to the left at 1*) Yes. What about that? It was typical of you.
(*Saint Florimond rises and comes downstage towards her*)
There are hundreds of other towns in France besides Fontainebleau. Dozens of other hotels besides the Golden Lion. But you have to pick the one hotel in the one town that they choose for their honeymoon.

St Florimond How could I know?

Angele You should have found out.

St Florimond (*At 2*) All right! Next time I go to a hotel, I'll ask if they've any Romeos about the place!

Angele (*At 1*) Look what happened! They think you're my husband.

St Florimond You didn't have to tell them.

Angele I didn't tell them. . . . Not knowing my husband and seeing you alone with me at Fontainebleau, of course they thought . . .

St Florimond That I was Champignol. And as your husband's a painter, your uncle kept on pestering me to do a

sketch for him. I did him a 'Mountain Peak',
all on my own. Oh, I won't forget Fontainebleau.

Angele (*Moving to 2*) Nor will I. Thank heavens they never
come to Paris! Anyway, I've decided not to proceed
any further. Give me back my key.

St Florimond (*At 1*) Give me back my key! You really mean you
want it to end like this . . . just fizzle out?

Angele Yes.

St Florimond But that's dishonest. You made me believe you were
in love with me.

Angele I know. You see, you arrived at the psychological
moment. My husband was away, I met you at a party,
you pursued me . . .

St Florimond You fell in love with me.

Angele No, I was bored . . . Perhaps I did believe I was in
love with you. But as Heaven decreed I should
emerge unscathed, I'm now going to be faithful to
my husband. He's charming, intelligent; it's not as
if he were . . .

(*Clock strikes the half-hour: 'Cuckoo'*)
I beg your pardon?

St Florimond (*Midstage at 1*) It wasn't me . . . It was the clock.

Angele (*Extreme right*) I should hope so!

St Florimond (*Going towards her*) You know, you're right. It's
never worth while trying to patch up a love affaire.
This one's a failure, on to the next!

Angele Now you're being sensible. If I were to give you
a word of advice, it would be to give up all these
affaires of yours. And get married.

St Florimond (*Indignant*) Get married! (*Changing*) I'm just going to.

Angele Just going to! . . . You never mentioned it.

St Florimond I was afraid it would annoy you.

Angele (*Going upstage to 2*) How thoughtful! And who are
you thinking of marrying? (*Sitting on a chair to the
left of the table*)

St Florimond (*Standing next to her at 1*) I don't know. A girl I'm
due to meet tomorrow night at a ball her aunt's
giving. A Madame Rivolet; I hardly even know *her*!

Angele Where is this ball?

St Florimond At Clermont, a little town in Brittany.

Angele Oh! That's a long way. Is the girl pretty?

St Florimond Is she pretty! Sixty thousand francs a year!

Angele (*Rising and moving to 1*) Oh! Well, you mustn't
heistate. Go right ahead!

St Florimond That was my intention.

Angele I'd never have believed it. . . After the propositions
you've just made to me!

St Florimond (*At 1*) That! . . . That was for now! . . . But, well,
you're right. If we have to part, let's part.

Angele Exactly. Now you must go. If the servants come
back . . .

    (*They go upstage to the hall door. Voices can be heard*)
Heavens! Here they are!

St Florimond How can I get out? (*He hurries towards the room on
the right, passing behind the table*)

Angele No, not that way! That's my bedroom!

St Florimond Too bad!

    (*Saint Florimond goes out into Angele's room. Joseph
enters from the hall*)

Angele What is it, Joseph?

Joseph (*Upstage, left of the hall door at 1*) I've just done the
shopping.

Angele (*Behind the table, at 2*) I don't care what you've done.
What do you want?

Joseph Didn't you find my message last night?

Angele (*Coming downstage, as does Joseph*) Message?

Joseph Yes. As you were late, I left a message on the table
next to your bed . . . (*Suddenly*) I'll go and get it.
(*He goes towards her bedroom, passing behind the table*)

Angele (*Quickly, passing in front of the table and taking up a*

position in front of the door) No, no! There's no
need to. What was the message?

Joseph I said, very respectfully, that a policeman came last
night for Monsieur Champignol.

Angele (*At 2, passing behind the table and going to Joseph, who
is level with it, midstage*) A policeman? What did he
want?

Joseph It's about Monsieur Champignol's military service.
Apparently he's been called up.

Angele My husband, one of the leading painters in Europe!
Nonsense! He did his military service when he was
twenty, he's never done it since. (*She comes downstage, still at 2*)

Joseph Perhaps that's why they've called him up. The
policeman said he should have been with his
regiment three days ago.

Angele It's too much! Do they think he's nothing better
to do! Run down to the police station and say
I'm very sorry but my husband's away at the
moment. Explain that he's painting a portrait of
Mr Vanderbilt. Remember the name. And he can't
do three dozen things at the same time. He'll do
his military service when he gets back.

Joseph Very good, Madame.

Angele I've never heard of such a thing. Oh, Joseph, my
trunk's packed, take it downstairs. I'm going to
see my nephew in Nice.

Joseph Very good, Madame.

Angele (*Pointing to the cup of chocolate on the table, right*)
Take that away.

> (*Joseph takes the cup and goes out into the hall. Saint
> Florimond appears at the bedroom door*)

St Florimond He's gone?

Angele Yes. Now, take your hat and hurry!

St Florimond (*Going towards the hall door*) Oh, with pleasure!

  Joseph (*Off*) Oh, Madame!

  Angele Oh! Go back in there. (*She pushes him back into the bedroom*)

    (*Saint Florimond goes out. Joseph enters*)

    What is it now?

  Joseph It's the maid you were expecting from the country.

  Angele (*At 2*) All right, later.

  Joseph Oh, here she is.

    (*Charlotte appears at the hall door*)

    Come in, my girl, come in.

  Angele (*Aside, coming downstage*) This man's driving me mad!

    (*Joseph goes out*)

 Charlotte (*Curtsying. Strong country accent*) Madame . . .

  Angele (*Sitting on the chair to the left of the right-hand table*)

    Ah, come here. You've been sent me by the priest at Chatellerault, an old friend of my family's.

 Charlotte (*At 1, centre*) A very good man!

  Angele He recommends you highly.

 Charlotte So he should. I'm in an interesting condition.

  Angele I beg your pardon?

 Charlotte I'm in an interesting condition. My mother put me in it.

  Angele Your mother?

 Charlotte Yes, my mother. She sinned, my mother did.
    You can't know what that is in Paris. It means she was led on by a man . . . well, she sinned.

  Angele Who with?

 Charlotte The Fifth Dragoons. Then she went off after them and left me there, a little baby. Ill I was, too. That's when the priest said I was in an interesting condition.

  Angele Ah! Good! Very good! That's much better.

 Charlotte He brought me up.

  Angele He did?

 Charlotte Yes . . . And my Aunt Pichu. I expect you know her son, he's in Paris. A porter.

Angele No, I've never met him. . . . Well, I don't expect you can do very much?

Charlotte Oh, yes. I can look after cows. Have you any in Paris?

Angele No. Can you sew?

Charlotte Oh, yes. I can sew, I can cook, I can dance.

Angele I'm not interested in your dancing. Have you ever served anyone before?

Charlotte Oh! I'm a virgin!

Angele (*Rising and going towards her*) That is irrelevant. Well, you seem willing, we'll try to make something of you. When my husband gets back, I hope he'll find you're a perfect servant.

Charlotte Oh! You've a man!

Angele As you say. He's away at the moment, but he should be back very soon now.

Charlotte Ah, I look forward to seeing him, bless him!

Angele Very well. I'll take you on. You'll start at forty francs a month.

Charlotte Oh, you're so kind!

Angele And board.

Charlotte Oh, you can't be bored!

Angele Now, run along.

Charlotte Yes, Madame.

> (*Charlotte goes upstage. Angele crosses towards her bedroom door*)
>
> (*Returning*) Madame!

Angele (*Turning round*) Yes.

Charlotte Would you be pleased to accept this basket?

Angele This basket?

Charlotte Yes. I thought you might like some eggs, straight from the country. I chose them myself. They're none of them fresh.

Angele Not fresh?

Charlotte No. I was told you never eat fresh eggs in Paris.

Angele	Charming girl! All right, be off with you . . . What's your name?
Charlotte	Charlotte. (*Aside*) I think I'm going to like it here. (*Charlotte goes out upstage*)
Angele	Phew! Now let's get rid of him. (*Going to her bedroom door and calling*) Come out. (*Saint Florimond appears at the door*)
St Florimond	It's all right now?
Angele	Yes. Hurry up. (*They both go upstage towards the door*)
St Florimond	Well, I'll be off. (*Stopping upstage centre, at 2*) So this is the end of a romance that never happened. Goodbye, Angele, goodbye. (*Pause*) Angele?
Angele	Yes?
St Florimond	We'll never see each other again. Let me give you a farewell kiss.
Angele	What!
St Florimond	Not as a lover. A simple brotherly kiss.
Angele	All right. As it's the last time. But hurry up. (*He kisses her. Charlotte enters upstage*)
Charlotte	Oh!
Angele *St Florimond* }	Oh!
Charlotte	(*Very simple*) Monsieur Champignol!
Angele *St Florimond* }	What!
Charlotte	(*Coming downstage to 3*) Oh, sir, I heard you'd soon be back, but I didn't know it would be as soon as this.
Angele	All right, now go away. I didn't ring.
Charlotte	Don't worry. I'm glad I came. (*To Saint Florimond*) Did you have a good journey, sir? You're not tired?
St Florimond	Yes . . . No . . . Yes . . .
Charlotte	I'm Charlotte, the new maid.
Angele	(*Getting angry*) Oh! Oh! Oh!

Charlotte   Now, sir, you'll be wanting to make yourself comfortable. Give me your coat.

St Florimond   No! No!

Charlotte   Yes! Yes! With all that travelling, it must be full of dust. (*Thumping him on the back*) Look! Filthy!

St Florimond   Ohhh! What a way to behave!

Angele   All right, stop it. Why have you come in here?

Charlotte   I couldn't find my room.

Angele   Well, go and wait in the kitchen.

Charlotte   Oh yes, I will. (*Aside*) What a nice man! I'll go and get his dressing gown.

(*Charlotte goes out upstage*)

Angele   Oh, this is too much. You heard her. She thinks you're my husband too.

St Florimond   It's fate.

Angele   It's my fate. . . Why did you have to kiss me.

St Florimond   How could I know she'd come in?

Angele   'How could I know'! That's all you ever say!

St Florimond   Well, I couldn't.

Angele   You see what happens. Come on. Do please go.

St Florimond   Yes, yes, I'm going. Goodbye, Angele, goodbye. For ever!

Angele   Goodbye, goodbye.

(*Saint Florimond goes out upstage*)

Phew! He's gone at last. (*Coming downstage*) That girl thinks he's my husband. There's only one thing to do. Get rid of her at once.

(*Clock strikes nine*)

Nine o'clock and I'm still in a dressing gown! I've so much to do! . . . I must get dressed!

(*She passes in front of the table and goes out right. Clock finishes striking. Then a noise is heard, off. Saint Florimond bursts in*)

St Florimond   The Romeos! The Romeos are here! On the stairs! Where can I hide? (*He hides behind the sofa, his head still showing above the top*)

> (*Romeo enters, followed by Mauricette and Dufoulay*)

Romeo (*Italian accent*) Champignol, I say, Champignol!

All Three (*Seeing Saint Florimond*) Ah, there he is!

St Florimond (*Aside*) They've caught me. (*Aloud, going towards them*) Oh, what a lovely surprise!

Romeo (*Coming downstage to 3*) Didn't you hear us? We called you.

St Florimond (*Coming downstage to 4*) Was that you? How extraordinary! I thought it came from above. That's why I ran up . . .

Romeo (*Delighted*) It was us! Of course it was!

> (*Mauricette has by now come down to 1 and Dufoulay to 2*)

Mauricette Hullo, Monsieur Champignol!

Dufoulay Hullo, Monsieur Champignol!

St Florimond (*Pretending to be pleased*) Hullo! Ah-ha! What a lovely surprise! (*Aside to audience, crossing to 4*) Well, do you think it's easy to get out of a house?

Romeo (*At 3*) Ah-ha! You didn't expect us, did you?

St Florimond (*At 4*) To be absolutely frank . . . no!

Romeo There, Mauricette, I told you so!

Dufoulay (*At 2*) You see, the Army's called me up for four weeks' training.

Mauricette Delightful when you've just been married!

Romeo Be quiet, darling. It will do you both a lot of good. You've no idea, Champignol, these children are disgusting, the way they carry on!

Dufoulay Well, when you've just been married, no one minds. (*He kisses Mauricette*)

St Florimond Of course not. Anyway it doesn't last long. . . . I say, wouldn't you like to come for a walk?

Romeo No, no, I wouldn't. (*He sits down, left of the right-hand table*)

Dufoulay We'd rather stay here.

(He sits down on the sofa, left, at 2. Mauricette sits next to him, at 1)

St Florimond   *(Aside)* Ohhh! What's Angele going to say when she finds I'm still here? With the family!

Romeo   You understand! We've had such a long journey and now we have to take the ten o'clock train for Clermont. That's where the poor boy has to do his service. So we said to ourselves, we've an hour in Paris, let's go and see the Champignols!

St Florimond   *(At 4)* What a marvellous idea! I was just saying we never see you.

Romeo   *(Rising and going downstage to 3)* Well, here we are! Here we are! *(To Dufoulay and Mauricette who are kissing each other)* Now, now, children, restrain yourselves.

Dufoulay   Don't you bother about us.

Romeo   By the way, what about Angèlà? *(Italian pronunciation)*

St Florimond   Angèlà? *(The same)*

Romeo   Of course, Angèlà. *(The same)* Your wife!

St Florimond   Ah yes, Angèlà *(The same)* My wife!

Romeo   Aren't we going to see her?

St Florimond   Well, no, I don't think so. She's not very well.

Mauricette   *(Rising and coming downstage)* Not very well?

Dufoulay   *(Following her)* What's the matter?

St Florimond   I don't know . . . She hasn't been well for some time . . . feeling sick . . . dizziness . . .

Romeo   *(Nudging him in the ribs and laughing)* I understand. Congratulations!

St Florimond   *(Aside)* What's the matter with him?

Romeo   Yes, yes, I understand.

St Florimond   Do you? Lucky man!

(Angele enters, dressed)

Angele   Who is it? *(Recognising them)* Oh, no!

Romeo   Ah, there she is!

Angele   *(Noticing Saint Florimond)* He's here with them!

Mauricette Good morning.

Angele *(Coming downstage to 3 between Dufoulay and Romeo)*
How delightful to see you! *(Aside)* This is the last
straw!

St Florimond I met your uncle on the stairs. *He* brought me
back.

Dufoulay Angele, good morning!

Romeo By the way! We hear you've some news for us!

Angele What is that?

Romeo Champignol told us. *(To Saint Florimond)* Didn't
you?

St Florimond What? Me! Nonsense!

Romeo He's about to become a father! Congratulations,
Angèlà!

Angele He told you . . .

St Florimond *(At 5)* No, I didn't.

Angele *(Furious, raising her arms to heaven)* You said that?

Romeo *(Making her lower her arms)* Don't raise your arms.
Don't raise your arms.

Angele Stop it, Uncle. It's not true.

Romeo Come now! Why hide it? It's natural for a father
to feel proud.

Angele No, it isn't . . . I mean, you're wrong. *(Crossing
to 5, aside to Saint Florimond)* Are you out of your
mind?

St Florimond Angele, I promise you . . .
(Charlotte enters, carrying a velvet smoking jacket)

Charlotte Here's your smoking jacket.

St Florimond *(Next to Angele, right)* Marvellous! Here's the maid!

Angele What is it now?

Charlotte *(Coming downstage to 4)* Sorry, all! I didn't know
you'd got company. I've brought Monsieur
Champignol's smoking jacket.

St Florimond
Angele }Oh!

Romeo	Well, there's your jacket!
Charlotte	Yes. Come on, sir, give me your coat.
St Florimond	(*Struggling, moving to 4*) No! No!
Charlotte	Yes! Yes! You must be tired after that long journey.
All	Long journey?
Romeo	(*At 3*) You've been away?
St Florimond	Oh, not very far.
Romeo	Never mind us. Put on your smoking jacket.
Mauricette (*At 1*) *Dufoulay* (*At 2*)	} Yes, put it on.
St Florimond	(*Letting Romeo and Charlotte take off his coat*) No! No! Angele, stop them.
Angele	(*Aside*) That man will drive me insane!
Charlotte	(*To Saint Florimond who has put on the jacket, which is much too big for him*) There! Look, that's much better!
Romeo	(*At 3*) Good heavens! You have got thin!
St Florimond	(*At 4*) Thin?
Romeo	(*Bunching up the jacket*) Look how big your jacket is!
St Florimond	I had it made like that. It's more comfortable.
Charlotte	(*At 5, taking his morning coat*) Now I'll go and brush your coat.
St Florimond	No! No!
Charlotte	(*Going upstage*) Yes! Yes! Of course I will! I'll put it next to Madame's bed, ready for when you get up.
	(*Charlotte goes out upstage*)
Angele	(*Whispering*) Look what you've done.
St Florimond	(*At 4, whispering*) How could I know?
Angele	(*At 5, whispering*) Don't keep on saying that.
Romeo	Well, where have you been?
St Florimond	Me? Nowhere. (*Recovering*) Ah, yes, yes, I've been . . . I've been painting a portrait . . . abroad . . . at Tours.
Romeo	(*At 3*) A portrait? That reminds me, I've something

	to tell you. (*He sees Dufoulay and Mauricette, who are sitting on the sofa, kissing*) Oh really! They're kissing again. It's disgusting! Disgusting!
Mauricette	Oh, father!
Romeo	People don't do that in public! Look at Monsieur and Madame Champignol, they love each other, but they're not kissing all the time. They don't behave like a pair of lovers! Dammit all . . . Dufoulay, give me that sketch.
St Florimond	Sketch?
Dufoulay	(*Giving Romeo the sketch, stuck on cardboard, which he had brought in with him and put on the sofa*) Here it is.
Romeo	(*At 3, offering it to Saint Florimond*) Here it is.
St Florimond	(*At 4. Aside*) Damn, my 'Mountain Peak'! (*Laughing*) Ah! My sketch! Yes. . . Isn't it pretty?
Romeo	Well, no . . . apparently it isn't. I showed it to a picture dealer. He said 'That a Champignol . . . rubbish'. I told him you'd painted it and all he said was 'Well if that's a Champignol, you'd better get him to sign it . . . that will make it worth something!' So I've brought it here.
St Florimond	Sign it? (*Aside*) That would be forgery. Oh, no! (*Aloud*) No, no, I never sign sketches.
Romeo	But still . . .
St Florimond	No! Everyone knows that. So if I signed this one, people would say it was forged.
Romeo	Would they? Then I'll put your name on the frame. (*Romeo goes upstage and sits on the sofa, next to Mauricette and Dufoulay. They all examine the sketch*)
St Florimond	Yes, do that. (*Aside*) He'll have something to boast about. (*He laughs*)
Angele	There's nothing to laugh at.
St Florimond	How right you are!
Angele	Why won't they go? (*She passes in front of Saint Florimond and goes towards Romeo*) Uncle, you must

	be in a hurry, I don't want to keep you.
Romeo	(*Sitting on the sofa, looking at the sketch*) What, me?
St Florimond	No, no, don't stand on ceremony. I'll show you out . . .
Romeo	(*At 3, rising and coming downstage with the others*) Not at all, not at all! Who says I'm in a hurry? We have to catch the ten thirty train for Clermont. (*Clock strikes the half-hour*) Half past nine, we've plenty of time.
Angele	But you must have lots of things to do . . . it's years since you were last in Paris. Have you seen the Eiffel Tower?
Romeo	Yes, I've got it on my tiepin. (*Passing in front of Angele and going towards Saint Florimond*) You don't see anything else in the country. I'm fed up with the Eiffel Tower.
St Florimond	(*At 5*) Well, in that case . . .
Romeo	(*At 4*) No, I'll stay here. I said to the children: 'We've an hour in Paris, let's go and see your cousin'. They wanted to go to a hotel . . . because, you know, they . . . but I said: 'Certainly not! People don't go to hotels in the middle of the day'.
Angele	(*At 3*) How nice of you! (*Aside*) They won't go!
Romeo	(*Passing in front of Angele and going to 3*) But could we possibly have a wash . . . the train, you know . . .
Angele	(*At 4*) Of course. (*Aside to Saint Florimond*) This is your chance to get away. (*Aloud*) I'll show you where to go.
Romeo	I wouldn't dream of it. Champignol's here, he'll take us.
St Florimond	(*Moving to 4*) But Angele said . . .
Romeo	Angele's going to stay here. She mustn't tire herself in her condition. (*Mauricette and Dufoulay are still upstage left*)
Angele	Not again! I tell you I'm not . . .

Romeo   No, you must rest. Come along, Champignol.
> (*He takes Saint Florimond by the arm and goes out with him left, following Mauricette and Dufoulay*)

St Florimond   Oh, dear! I am part of the family!
> (*Angele has gone to the door left, and now comes back to the centre of the stage*)

Angele   Oh! What a family! Someone must have had a bet! Everybody's in the plot. What a lesson! Oh, what a lesson!
> (*Joseph enters*)

Joseph   (*At 2*) Oh, Madame . . . I've just been to the police station.

Angele   (*At 1*) All right, all right!

Joseph   No, it's not all right.

Angele   What do you mean? What is it? What did they say?

Joseph   I told them Monsieur Champignol's not here. They said they didn't care. He'd better be.

Angele   (*At 1*) What? They said . . . Oh. I'll deal with them when he gets back . . . Didn't you tell them he's painting a portrait of Mr Vanderbilt?

Joseph   Yes.

Angele   What did they say to that?

Joseph   To hell with it!

Angele   Oh!

Joseph   That's what *they* said. So perhaps you'd better send Monsieur Champignol a telegram . . .

Angele   (*Crossing to 2 in front of the right-hand table*) Where can I send a telegram? He's on Mr Vanderbilt's yacht. His last letter said 'At sea'. I can't address a telegram 'At sea'!

Joseph   (*At 1*) But this is serious.

Angele   All right! But what can they do?

Joseph   I don't know. They just said 'All right, we know what to do'.

Angele	Oh, you should have said so in the first place. They will!
Joseph	Will they?
Angele	Of course! . . . I'd never have believed it! My husband! One of the leading painters in Europe! . . . They will! All right . . . That will be all, Joseph.
Joseph	I'll go and finish the shopping. There's nothing else I can do?
Angele	No.
Joseph	Very good, Madame.

(*Joseph goes out. Saint Florimond enters left*)

St Florimond	I've got rid of them . . . I'll go now.
Angele	(*At 2*) Yes. Hurry up.
St Florimond	My hat!

(*He takes it and goes towards the door into the hall, still wearing his velvet jacket. Romeo enters left, with Mauricette and Dufoulay*)

Romeo	Champignol, what are you doing?
St Florimond	(*Aside*) They're leeches! . . . Caught again! (*Aloud*) I've something to see to. I'm going out.
Romeo	Dressed like that! You are amusing!
St Florimond	(*Coming down to 4, while Angele comes down to 5*) Oh! I forgot! My coat! . . . Where's my coat?

(*Bell rings*)

Oh, no! Who on earth's that?

Angele	A visitor!
St Florimond	Probably a model.
Romeo	A naked woman!

(*Charlotte enters with Camaret, in mufti, and Adrienne*)

Charlotte	Yes, Monsieur Champignol's here . . . That's him!

(*She points to Saint Florimond and goes out*)

Angele	Oh, no! What's she saying?
St Florimond	The idiot!
Camaret	(*To Charlotte*) Thank you very much.

St Florimond	This is the last straw!
Camaret	(*Coming down to 4, while Adrienne comes down to 5; to Saint Florimond*) Monsieur Champignol?
St Florimond	(*Passing in front of Angele and reaching 6*) What! No, no! Hm! Yes, yes!
Camaret	(*At 4*) Delighted to meet you. (*Pointing to Angele*) Your wife, I presume?
St Florimond	(*At 6*) I presume she is!
Camaret	(*Bowing to Angele*) How do you do. (*He greets the company with a circular movement of his head*) Let me introduce you to my daughter.
Adrienne	(*At 5, to Saint Florimond*) I'm so glad to meet you. I adore painters. (*She shakes his hand and goes upstage towards the sofa*)
St Florimond	Ohhh!
Camaret	Well, now we've finished with the introductions . . . (*He sits down on one of the upright chairs by the sofa. Adrienne sits on the other*)
St Florimond	(*Aside*) Now he's finished with the introductions! Who does he think he is!
Angele	(*At 7, aside*) He's making himself at home! (*Aloud*) Excuse me . . .
Camaret	Ah! Of course. (*Rising and introducing himself*) Captain Camaret of the 75th Infantry!
Dufoulay	(*Seated on the sofa with Mauricette and Romeo, leaping up*) Stationed at Clermont?
Camaret	Yes. In fact I must get back there right away. I'm in charge of the reservists.
Dufoulay	Then, Captain, you're *my* captain!
Camaret	Your captain?
Romeo	His captain? You're his captain?
Dufoulay	Yes. I'm joining your regiment.
Adrienne	You're a conscript?
Dufoulay	No, a reservist.
Camaret	Well!

> (*They all sit down in the following order: Mauricette (1), Dufoulay (2), Romeo (3), all on the sofa; Adrienne (4) and Camaret (5), both on upright chairs right of the sofa, with their backs to Angele (6) and Saint Florimond (7) who are downstage near the table*)

St Florimond   (*Aside*) How much longer are they going to go on gossiping? What's this captain here for?

Mauricette   Captain, you must take great care of him, because he's my very own darling husband.

Camaret   Indeed?

Mauricette   Yes, for two whole weeks now!

Adrienne   Really, you've been married for two weeks?

Mauricette   Yes. (*Tapping Dufoulay on the cheek*) You're my very own darling husband, aren't you?

Romeo   Really . . . Mauricette! . . . (*To Camaret*) They're disgusting . . .

St Florimond   (*Who has been standing apart with Angele, approaching timidly*) Excuse me, but . . .

Romeo   Sh! . . . Just a moment. (*To Camaret*) You've been so kind, will you allow me to join my daughter in asking . . . you don't know who I am . . .

Camaret   Monsieur?

Romeo   Romeo.

Camaret   Congratulations.

Romeo   Be good to the boy. Keep an eye on him.

Camaret   Of course. (*To Dufoulay*) Don't you worry.

Dufoulay   Oh, Captain, thank you so much!

Camaret   Not at all.

Mauricette   There's one other thing, Captain. You must make sure he always wears a flannel vest.

Camaret   (*Smiling*) Well . . .

Mauricette   Oh, you must! . . . He never bothers . . . He's such a baby!

Angele   (*Approaching Camaret*) This is all very interesting, but it doesn't explain why we're honoured with your visit.

Camaret Of course . . .

> (*He rises, followed by everyone else. Romeo and Dufoulay go upstage and look at the pictures. Adrienne approaches Mauricette, who is still at 1*)

In a nutshell . . . I'm a great admirer of your husband.

Angele You're too kind.

Camaret I'm not the only one. Everybody thinks he's brilliant.

St Florimond Yes, brilliant! Brilliant!

Angele (*Aside to Saint Florimond*) Be quiet.

Camaret (*Aside*) He's not exactly modest. (*Aloud*) So there we are . . . I suddenly thought I'd ask you to do a portrait of my daughter.

St Florimond What? Me?

Camaret Yes . . . You see, I'll have to lose her some day . . . I must think about finding her a husband.

Mauricette (*At 1, to Adrienne*) You're going to get married?

Adrienne (*At 2*) Yes, I'll have to be put on the market!

Camaret (*At 3*) They've already started looking for a suitor.

Adrienne (*Aside to Mauricette*) Yes, but it's a waste of time. I've an idea of my own.

Mauricette Oh?

Adrienne Yes. Sh!

> (*Charlotte enters, showing in Celestin*)

Charlotte He's in there somewhere.

Celestin (*Coming down to 3*) Ah, Uncle!

Camaret (*At 4, to Angele at 6*) I apologise, but this is my nephew Celestin, my sister's son.

St Florimond (*Aside; at 5*) Why does he think we're interested?

Celestin Do forgive me . . . but I was so longing to see Monsieur Champignol's studio . . .

Camaret That I ventured to invite him.

Angele I'm so glad.

Celestin (*Turning round and going upstage*) Oh, it's marvellous!
　　　　Marvellous! (*He bumps into Mauricette who has gone
　　　　upstage with Adrienne*) Oh! I beg your pardon.

Adrienne (*Introducing him to Mauricette*) Let me introduce my
　　　　cousin Celestin.

Mauricette (*At 1*) How do you do . . .

Adrienne (*At 2. Aside*) Do you think he's handsome?

Mauricette Well . . . Not bad, certainly . . . (*Aside*) So he's
　　　　what she meant by an idea of her own! (*She moves
　　　　across to Dufoulay and Romeo, upstage left*)

Camaret (*Right. To Saint Florimond*) I was just saying that
　　　　when my daughter gets married I'd like something
　　　　to remember her by.

Adrienne (*To Celestin*) You heard! He wants to marry me off!

Celestin Yes, I heard.

Adrienne (*With a melodramatic sigh as she goes upstage with
　　　　Celestin*) Never!
　　　　　(*Camaret is now at 1, Saint Florimond at 2 and
　　　　　Angele at 3, all downstage in front of the right-hand
　　　　　door. The others are all upstage left, talking quietly or
　　　　　looking at the pictures*)

Camaret (*At 1. To Saint Florimond*) Something signed by
　　　　your hand.

St Florimond (*At 2*) Of course . . . I . . . (*Aside*) Ohhh! I can't
　　　　paint a portrait for him!

Angele (*At 3*) Actually my husband has a lot of work at
　　　　the moment.

Camaret A portrait won't take long. Anyway I don't want
　　　　anything very big. (*He goes upstage and, taking the
　　　　canvas which is back to front on the chair, left of the
　　　　door, he returns downstage*) Something like this. (*He turns
　　　　the canvas round. It's a painting of Venus emerging from
　　　　the waves*)

St Florimond (*Laughing*) Like that?

Camaret (*Roaring with laughter*) No, I mean that size.

St Florimond Ah, that's different.

Camaret (*Looking at the canvas*) Very funny! Is it beautiful?

St Florimond Well . . . you can see!

Camaret Oh, I've no idea . . . Pictures don't mean anything to me.

Angele But I thought you admired my husband's work so much.

Camaret I admire it because everyone else does. I mean, you don't buy pictures because you like them, you like them because you've bought them. (*He puts the canvas back on the chair*)

St Florimond Well!

Camaret (*Coming back downstage to 2*) As long as you do a good likeness . . .

Romeo (*Coming downstage*) Oh, he will. He's so clever! Would you like to see a little sketch . . .

St Florimond Oh, no! Really!

Romeo Oh, yes! Look at this.

> (*He goes and gets the sketch from the sofa. Adrienne and Celestin remain upstage. The others come downstage in the following order: Mauricette (1), Dufoulay (2), Romeo (3), Camaret (4), Saint Florimond (5) and Angele (6)*)

Camaret (*Looking at the sketch*) Yes, very interesting. Especial the fat woman.

St Florimond Eh? . . . What fat woman?

Romeo (*Offended, taking the sketch and putting it back on the sofa, passing behind Dufoulay and Mauricette*) That's a mountain peak!

Camaret Ah, a mountain peak. Charming, charming! Well, Monsieur Champignol, that's all settled, so we'll come for a sitting on Friday.

St Florimond Friday . . . well . . .

Camaret You can't manage Friday? Thursday, then.

St Florimond No, no, no!

Camaret	Yes, yes, yes! Delighted to have met you, Monsieur Champignol . . . and your wife . . . I'm sorry to have to rush away, but I must catch the train for Clermont.
St Florimond	Of course you must.
Camaret	Come along Adrienne, Celestin.
Adrienne *Celestin*	} Goodbye.
Dufoulay	Captain, you won't forget . . .
Camaret	Of course not. (*He goes upstage after Adrienne and Celestin*)
Romeo	(*Following him*) We'll all see you out.
Mauricette	(*The same*) Captain, you will remember to take good care of him, won't you?
Camaret	Yes, yes . . .
Adrienne	Goodbye, Monsieur Champignol . . . Madame Champignol . . . and . . . (*The rest gets lost offstage*) (*They go out in the following order: Celestin and Adrienne, Camaret, Romeo, Dufoulay and Mauricette*)
St Florimond	(*Right of the door into the hall*) Well! This is the . . . A portrait! I've got to paint a portrait!
Angele	(*Left of the door*) What's going to happen when he comes back?
St Florimond	(*Coming downstage*) I don't know . . . I'll write to him . . . I'll say I'll go to him, instead of him coming to me.
Angele	(*Coming downstage*) But the portrait!
St Florimond	I'll paint it. I'll take lessons.
Angele	That will solve everything! . . . Oh, this is awful! (*Romeo enters with Mauricette and Dufoulay. He comes downstage between Saint Florimond and Angele, while Dufoulay and Mauricette come down to 1 and 2*)
Romeo	What a charming man! (*To Dufoulay*) You know, you are lucky to have a captain like that, he's really going to spoil you.

(*Clock strikes ten*)

Dufoulay (*At 2*) Ten o'clock already! We must say goodbye. We've only just time to catch the train for
Clermont.

Romeo (*At 4*) Of course. I'm so sorry we can't stay. (*He
goes to 3, passing behind Angele*) Now, Mauricette,
go and get our things.

Mauricette (*Going towards the left-hand door, passing behind the
sofa*) Yes, father.

Romeo (*In front of the sofa, to Saint Florimond and Angele*)
I'm so sorry . . .

St Florimond So are we. (*Pushing him towards the left-hand door,
passing in front of the sofa*) Do stay a little longer
. . . do.
(*Romeo goes out left, following Dufoulay and Mauricette*)

Angele (*At 1*) Phew! They've gone. Now it's your turn.
Go and get your coat. No, it's there, in my room.

St Florimond (*At 2*) Yes! I can't wait!
(*Saint Florimond goes out right*)

Angele (*Coming downstage right in front of the table*) Oh, what
a day! What a day!
(*Charlotte enters from the hall, followed by a police
sergeant and a policeman*)

Charlotte In here.

Angele The police!

Police Sgt (*Coming forward*) Where is Monsieur Champignol?
(*The policeman remains in the doorway*)

Angele Monsieur Champignol? What do you want him for?

Police Sgt (*Midstage*) My orders are to arrest Private
Champignol.

Angele My husband! . . . Arrest my husband!

Police Sgt Yes. He's a deserter.

Angele (*At 2*) This is too much!

Police Sgt (*At 1*) Where is he?

Angele He's not here. He's on a boat.

Charlotte (*Who has remained upstage right, coming downstage to 3*)
On a boat!

Angele Shut up, shut up.
(*Charlotte returns upstage and goes out*)

Police Sgt I'm very sorry, but in that case I'll have to search the flat.

Angele Search the flat!
(*Romeo enters left, followed by Mauricette and Dufoulay, carrying their baggage. He comes downstage to 3, in front of the sofa, while Mauricette comes down to 1 and Dufoulay to 2*)

Romeo What's all this? . . . The police?

Angele (*At 5*) It's all right, Uncle.

Police Sgt You must be Monsieur Champignol?

Romeo Me? Certainly not!

Police Sgt You're sure?

Romeo Of course I'm sure!
(*Saint Florimond enters right, fully dressed*)

Romeo (*Pointing to him*) There's Champignol!
(*Saint Florimond passes in front of the table and goes to 4*)

Police Sgt Right! (*To the policeman*) Seize that man.

All What!

't Florimond Me?

Police Sgt Don't answer back. (*To policeman*) Come along, get on with it.

Angele (*At 6*) No, no, you can't! It's a mistake!

Police Sgt Very sorry, but they're my orders. I've to take Private Champignol back to his unit. He should have been there three days ago.

Dufoulay You've been called up?

't Florimond No. No, I haven't.

Police Sgt What's all this? You're coming along with us!

t Florimond No, no, I'm not. (*He goes left, between Dufoulay and Romeo*)

    Police Sgt (*To policeman*) Go on, get hold of him.
         (*The policeman comes downstage and seizes Saint*
         Florimond)
    St Florimond Now look here . . .
    Police Sgt We'll be on our way to Clermont.
    All To Clermont!
         (*The police drag off Saint Florimond, struggling*)
    Romeo Goodbye, Angele. Oh, poor Champignol!
    Dufoulay Come along, we're late.
    Mauricette Goodbye, Angele.
         (*They go out in the following order: Dufoulay, Mauricette*
         and Romeo)
    Angele (*Coming downstage left*) Oh, this is the last straw!
         Arresting *him*, instead of my husband!
         (*Charlotte enters and comes downstage to 2*)
    Charlotte What does it all mean?
    Angele (*At 1*) It's no concern of yours. Go and get my
         hat and coat.
    Charlotte Very good, Madame.
         (*Charlotte goes out*)
    Angele Yes, there's only one thing to do. I must go to
         Clermont. My husband's not there. Perhaps I can
         avoid a scandal.
         (*Charlotte enters with Angele's hat and coat*)
    Charlotte Here's your hat and coat.
    Angele (*Putting them on*) Thank you. Now take a week's
         notice. And go tonight.
    Charlotte (*At 2*) You're getting rid of me! . . . Why? . . .
         What have I done?
    Angele (*Going upstage to the door*) It doesn't matter.
    Charlotte (*In tears, going extreme left*) It doesn't matter! What
         I did doesn't matter and I'm turned into the street!
         (*Joseph enters, wearing a cap. Seeing Angele dressed*
         for the street, he stands to the right of the door, to let
         her pass)

Joseph   You're going out, Madame?

Angele   Yes. Is my trunk downstairs?
      (*Joseph nods*)
      Good. I'm going to see my nephew in Nice.
      Don't wait up for me. (*Aside*) Oh, what a nightmare!
      (*Angele goes out*)

Joseph   (*At 2*) I've just heard the police have been to arrest
      Monsieur Champignol. Is that right?

Charlotte   (*At 1, downstage left. In tears*) How should I know?
      I don't care.

Joseph   (*Going towards her*) What's up with you?

Charlotte   (*Sobbing*) What's up with me is I've been sacked.

Joseph   Now, now! A lovely girl like you! (*He tries to put
      his arm round her waist*)

Charlotte   (*Slapping his face and crossing to 2*) Take your hands
      off me. You're not a millionaire, are you? Well,
      I shan't give myself to you. I'm going to pack
      my bags. And collect my eggs!
      (*Charlotte goes out in tears*)

Joseph   (*At 1*) Poor girl! Well, I don't care. Phew! The
      police here for Monsieur Champignol! They must
      have gone away empty handed. That's going to
      cause a spot of bother.

Champignol   (*Off*) Joseph! Joseph!

Joseph   Monsieur Champignol!
      (*Champignol enters, in travelling clothes, a small bag
      in one hand and, in the other, a paintbox, easel and
      camp-stool*)

Champignol   Phew! Home at last! Come on, Joseph, give me
      a hand.

Joseph   (*At 1, upstage, left of the door*) It's not worth it, sir.
      You must be off again at once.

Champignol   (*At 2*) Off again? What on earth for?

Joseph   Your military service. The police have just left.
      You're a deserter.

Champignol	What!
Joseph	(*Taking his bag, and giving him another one, which is upstage left*) Here are your things.
Champignol	Where's my wife?
Joseph	She's not here. Hurry up, sir, hurry.
Champignol	Where's my regiment?
Joseph	At Clermont, sir. The 75th.
Champignol	Right, I'll be going . . . Give me a canvas, in case I have time to paint.
Joseph	(*Taking one and sliding it under his arm*) Here you are, sir.
Champignol	Thank you. Ohhh! I was hoping for a little peace and quiet. Oh, what a nightmare!
	(*Champignol runs out*)

CURTAIN

Act II

(*Clermont: the entrance to the barracks. The next morning.*
Downstage right is a hut with a glass door. Midstage, immediately above this, is a gap, leading to the entrance to the barracks. Upstage of this is the guardroom, another hut, lying obliquely, parallel to the first, also with a door. At the back of the stage, facing the audience, is the canteen, a third hut, extending from the wings, right, to centre stage. The left-hand part of this hut forms an open shelter, containing tables and chairs.

*In the right-hand part is a glass door facing the
audience. An entrance between the canteen and the
guardroom.*

*Downstage left is the front of the Hotel du Cheval
Blanc, with a big entrance door in the centre, underneath
a window with a balcony, to which the hotel sign is
fixed. Upstage are two entrances to the stage, separated
by a clump of trees. At the back of the stage, between
the hotel and the canteen, is a backcloth, showing a
wooded mountainous landscape with a river winding
through it.*

*A bench in front of the canteen. Another bench on the
right, between the door of the first hut and the
entrance to the barracks.*

*When the curtain rises, the Reservists are standing in
two ranks facing the audience. They are wearing a wide
variety of clothes. The front row from left to right
consists of a Reservist, Lafauchette, Lavalanche, the
Prince of Valence and Badin, with five Reservists in the
rear rank.*

*Lieutenant Ledoux stands downstage with a list of
names in his hand, taking the roll call. Sergeant
Belouette stands immediately upstage of him)*

Ledoux   Dubois!

Reservist   Sir!

Ledoux   Planchet!

Reservist   Sir!

Ledoux   Champignol! (*Pause*) Well? Champignol!

Belouette   (*At 2*) Under arrest, sir!

Ledoux   Ah, yes. The deserter brought in by the police
yesterday. Benoit!

Reservist   Sir!

Ledoux   Pincon!

Reservist   Sir!

Ledoux   Lafauchette!

Lafauchette	(*Very urbane, elegantly dressed, with a bowler hat. Taking a step forward and saluting*) Here I am.
Ledoux	Here I am! What do you mean, here I am?
Lafauchette	I mean I'm here.
Ledoux	Don't be impertinent, you in the bowler hat! Didn't you hear everyone else say 'sir'?
Lafauchette	I thought . . .
Ledoux	You don't think, you say 'sir'!
	(*Lafauchette falls back into the ranks*)
	Dufoulay! (*Pause*) Dufoulay! Well, where is he?
Belouette	Dufoulay! Dufoulay!
	(*Mauricette runs out of the hotel, followed by Dufoulay, in civilian clothes, and Romeo*)
Mauricette	Oh heavens, the roll call! Hurry up, you'll be punished. (*She pushes Dufoulay past her*)
Dufoulay	(*Going to 3*) Coming! Coming!
Ledoux	Oh, you've arrived, have you?
Romeo	(*Going to 3*) Let me apologise for him. I'm his father-in-law.
Ledoux	(*Passing behind Romeo and going to 3*) Get to hell out of here.
Romeo	Very good, sir.
Mauricette	(*Embracing Dufoulay*) Goodbye, darling.
Dufoulay	Goodbye, angel.
Ledoux	Hey, you over there! Haven't you finished yet?
	(*Dufoulay falls in, between the Reservist and Lafauchette, in the front rank*)
Romeo	(*To Ledoux, pointing to Mauricette and Dufoulay*) They're lovebirds . . . lovebirds.
Ledoux	What did you say?
Romeo	(*Taken aback*) Nothing. (*Passing in front of Ledoux, Dufoulay and Mauricette, and going towards the hotel*) Come, Mauricette. That officer's not very polite. (*Romeo goes out into the hotel, followed by Mauricette. As she goes out, she blows a kiss to Dufoulay. Ledoux*

is facing her and thinks it's addressed to him. Flattered,
he salutes her, then turns round and finds himself face
to face with Dufoulay, who is also blowing a kiss,
which he receives)

Ledoux Try to restrain yourself a little! (*Pause*) You'd better start by being more punctual.

Dufoulay I was with my wife, sir.

Ledoux (*Still at 1, extreme left. Belouette is at the extreme right*) When you're a soldier, you haven't a wife. They're for civilians. Come along. Fall in! Lucky for you the Captain's not here!

Dufoulay The Captain won't say anything to me. We're great friends.

Ledoux Silence!

Dufoulay I was with him all yesterday.

Ledoux Silence, I said! How do I get men like this? (*Crossing to Belouette*) Three days ago we had the Territorials. Now we've the Reservists. Will it never end?

Dufoulay (*Aside to Lafauchette, who is next to him*) I'll get the Captain to deal with him.

Lafauchette A good job too!

Camaret (*Off*) Adjutant! . . . Where's the Adjutant?

Ledoux The Captain!

   (*Camaret enters midstage right from the barracks and goes to 2*)

Camaret (*To Ledoux*) Ah, there you are! I've just been round the barracks. The rooms aren't swept, the beds aren't made, the mess tins are filthy.

Ledoux (*To the Reservists*) Do you hear, you lot!

Camaret I don't want any 'you lot'. I'm talking to you, Adjutant!

Lafauchette (*Aside*) Good, it's his turn now.

Camaret (*To Lafauchette*) Stop laughing, you there, number 4. (*To Ledoux*) Don't let me have to tell you again, right?

Lafauchette (*Aside to Dufoulay*) The captain sounds a bit difficult.

Dufoulay No, a splendid fellow. I'll put in a word for you.

Lafauchette Thanks very much.

Camaret (*To Ledoux*) Ah! These are the reservists?

Ledoux Yes, sir.

Dufoulay (*Who has been signalling to the Captain. Aside*) Very odd! He doesn't seem to recognise me. (*He waves again and coughs to attract attention*)

Camaret You there, Tom Thumb, what's the matter with you?

Dufoulay I was just saying hullo, sir.

Camaret Ah, you were just saying hullo. (*To Ledoux*) Give that man two days C.B. for saying hullo to an officer.

Dufoulay (*Aside*) He doesn't recognise me. (*To Camaret*) Dufoulay!

Camaret Exactly. Dufoulay. Adjutant! This man's kind enough to give you his name: Dufoulay. Make it four days.

Dufoulay That's a bit tough.

Lafauchette (*Aside to Dufoulay*) Don't you put in a word for me.

Camaret (*To Ledoux*) What are you doing?

Ledoux Taking the roll call, sir.

Camaret Right. Carry on.

Ledoux Benoit!

Reservist Sir!

Ledoux Pincon!

Reservist Sir!

Ledoux Lafauchette!

Lafauchette Sir! (*He takes a step forward and salutes*)

Camaret Get back in the ranks. (*Going to Lafauchette*) He looks a cut above the others. Your job?

Lafauchette Stockbroker.

Camaret (*Scornfully*) A parasite! Pah!

(*He goes downstage left, near Ledoux, who is still at 2*)

Lafauchette (*Aside*) Parasite!

    Camaret (*To Ledoux*) Go on, get on with it.

    Ledoux Dufoulay!

    Dufoulay Sir!

    Ledoux Bloquet!

    Reservist Sir!

    Ledoux Valence!

    The Prince (*Taking off his hat*) Excuse me, Prince.

    Camaret Prince! What do you mean 'Prince'?

    The Prince Prince of Valence.

    Camaret You're a prince, are you? What do you do apart
from that?

    The Prince Nothing.

    Camaret Ah, you're a prince and you do nothing. (*To
Ledoux*) Well, we'll have to find something for this
prince to do. (*He comes downstage centre*)

    Ledoux Badin!

    Badin (*A fat man in an overcoat and top hat*) Sir!

    Camaret (*Turning round and going towards him*) Good God!
You look splendid, you do!

    Badin I'm fine, thank you, Captain. How are you?

    Camaret I'll show you how I am – in the guardroom! Your
job?

    Badin I sell tickets.

    Camaret What sort of tickets?

    Badin Er – all sorts of tickets.

    Camaret Ah, if it's impossible to get seats anywhere, you
make money, touting outside on the pavement.
Adjutant! Any trouble from him and we'll stick
him inside for a change.

    Ledoux Very good, sir. Lavalanche!

Lavalanche Sir!

    Camaret (*To Lavalanche, who is holding a bag*) Well, young man,
don't let me see you clutching your baggage again.
This is a parade ground, not a railway station.

Right, we'll cut the rest of the roll call. Form a circle!

> (*Reservists form a semicircle. Ledoux is at the extreme left, Belouette extreme right. Camaret is in the centre*)

We are destined to spend four weeks together. A lot of you, I'm sure, arrive with preconceived ideas; scared stiff. I'm here to tell you you're wrong. You must remember the regiment's just one big family. Your officers in effect are official fathers. The colonel's the father of his regiment, the captain, father of his company. In other words I shall be your father.

Lafauchette (*Aside*) Nice fellow!

Camaret (*In the same tone*) If you make a mistake at drill, you'll get two days C.B. If you answer back, three days. If you've a dirty uniform, you'll get two days in the guardroom. If you're drunk, a week. And so on.

> (*Everyone is thunderstruck*)

Now I rely on you not to cause me any trouble and you can rely on me to make your tour of duty as pleasant as possible.

Lafauchette (*Aside*) Splendid!

Camaret (*In the same tone*) Adjutant! Give that man two days in the guardroom, for not listening.

Ledoux Very good, sir.

Camaret Right. Carry on.

Ledoux In two ranks, fall in!

> (*The Reservists do so, upstage as before*)

Camaret (*To Ledoux*) See if the quartermaster's ready to issue uniforms.

Ledoux Very good, sir.

> (*Ledoux goes out upstage right, between canteen and guardroom, passing behind Camaret*)

Camaret	Stand easy!
	(*He signals to Belouette to join him and they talk quietly during the following lines*)
Dufoulay	Phew!
Lafauchette	Difficult chap, this captain of yours.
Dufoulay	Yes. But he's quite different socially.
Badin	(*Looking to the right*) Who's this NCO coming along now?
The Prince	He's a major.
	(*Belouette salutes Camaret and goes upstage right, in front of the Reservists. Fourrageot enters midstage right, from the barracks*)
Fourrageot	Where's Captain Camaret?
Camaret	Here, sir.
Fourrageot	(*Going to Camaret at 2*) Well, Captain, you've got all your reservists?
Camaret	Yes, sir.
Fourrageot	They haven't drawn their uniforms yet?
Camaret	I've just sent down to the quartermaster, sir.
Fourrageot	(*Passing in front of Camaret and going to 1*) Good, good, good.
	(*Ledoux enters upstage right, between guardroom and canteen and comes downstage*)
Camaret	(*To Ledoux*) Well?
Ledoux	All ready for them, sir.
Camaret	Very good. Take them along.
Fourrageot	(*To Camaret*) Right, I'll inspect them in an hour's time.
Camaret	Very good, sir.
	(*Fourrageot goes out midstage left, behind the hotel*)
Ledoux	Squad, shun! By the left, quick march!
	(*Reservists go out upstage right, between guardroom and canteen, Ledoux and Belouette marching alongside*)
Camaret	Left, right, left, right! Get into step, number five! My God, DuFOOLay! Get into step, will you!

> (*He follows them to the extreme right. Angele enters from the hotel*)

Angele Oh, I haven't slept a wink all night . . . All this excitement . . . I must see Saint Florimond . . . I couldn't send him a note, with those dreadful policemen . . . (*Noticing Camaret who is coming downstage*) Oh, Captain!

Camaret Madame Champignol! When I saw you in Paris yesterday, I never expected I'd have the pleasure of seeing you again today.

Angele Captain! I want to ask you a great favour.

Camaret I can guess. You're going to ask if you can see your husband.

Angele My husband! Exactly.

Camaret Actually, he's under arrest. How did he manage to forget about being called up?

Angele Oh, you know, Captain, artists are so absent-minded.

Camaret Of course . . . Of course . . . I must say, what you're asking is strictly illegal. Well, for you, I'll break the rules for once.

Angele Oh, thank you, Captain.

Camaret (*Looking to the right*) Here come the men under arrest. On fatigues. I'll get him for you. (*Going upstage right and calling*) Corporal Grosbon!

Grosbon (*Off*) Sir!

> (*Grosbon enters upstage right, between guardroom and canteen*)

Grosbon Yes, sir?

Camaret This lady would like to speak to her husband, Private Champignol . . . He's under arrest . . . Send him here.

Grosbon Very good, sir.

> (*Grosbon goes out right*)

Angele Oh, Captain, how kind of you!

Camaret (*Passing in front of Angele and going towards the hotel*)
I do apologise, but duty calls . . .

Angele Of course.

Camaret (*After saluting, as he goes into the hotel*) Get me a
vermouth.
    (*Grosbon enters upstage right, between guardroom and
    canteen*)

Grosbon Come along, get on with it. Quicker than that!
Why do I have to get saddled with a fool like this!
    (*Saint Florimond enters, wearing dirty ragged fatigues
    and a torn cap. He is painfully pulling a wheelbarrow*)

St Florimond All right, Corporal, all right. Angele!

Angele You!

St Florimond (*To Grosbon*) You might have told me not to bring
my barrow.

Grosbon This lady's asked for you, so I'll leave you here.
I'll come and collect you in a few minutes.

St Florimond Yes, yes. (*He sets down his barrow centre stage*)
    (*Grosbon goes out upstage right, between guardroom
    and canteen*)

Angele You! Dressed like this!

St Florimond (*Coming downstage to 2*) Yes. (*Aside*) Oh, it's
embarrassing to be seen like this by the woman
you love. (*Aloud*) Yes . . . these . . . these are
fatigues. You know, the last twenty-four hours
haven't been exactly funny!

Angele Do you think it's been funny for me? Anyway,
up to now, luckily, everything's all right.

St Florimond All right! Do you think I've been enjoying myself?
Dragged off by policemen like a pickpocket! Right
across Paris on foot, surrounded by jeering urchins!
I met friends from the Club, who said 'Oh' and
looked the other way. Do you think that's nice?
I couldn't explain to them. A crowd collected. One
wretched little man began telling everyone I'd been

	murdering children. I thought they were going to throw me in the river.
Angele	How dreadful!
St Florimond	Do you think it's any better here? I was vaccinated. Vaccinated! You know I can't stand a pinprick. It itched all night! Then they made me sleep on bare boards with a lot of men who'd been very badly brought up. I've been bitten all over.
	(*He rubs his sleeve. Angele recoils*)
	It's all right, they've gone now. Then this morning the most revolting fatigues. Now I've a wheelbarrow, but that's nothing. You don't know what Army latrines are like. I hope you never will. Oh, no! I've had enough. Enough! (*He goes upstage and sits down in the barrow*)
Angele	(*Going towards him*) Cheer up. Four weeks will go in a flash.
St Florimond	(*Rising, appalled*) Four weeks? You expect me to stay here for four weeks?
Angele	You made people think you were my husband. You must keep it up to the end.
St Florimond	No, I can't. I've other engagements. (*He comes downstage to 2*)
Angele	(*Following him at 1*) Nonsense! They're not important.
St Florimond	This evening there's Madame Rivolet's ball! I'm due to meet this girl with lots of money!
Angele	I won't stop you going to the Ball. It's here in Clermont, so if you can get leave . . . All I ask, no I insist, is that you do my husband's military service through to the end.
St Florimond	Ohhh! I'll never get caught again!
Angele	Nor will I. (*Laughter off*) Sh! Someone's coming.
	(*They go into the hotel doorway and talk there. Lavalanche, Lafauchette, The Prince, Badin and the*

other Reservists enter upstage right, between guardroom and canteen. They are all in uniform except Badin who is still in civilian clothes, complete with top hat)

Lavalanche *(The first to enter, pointing to Lafauchette who follows)* Take a look at this maternity dress! *(Pointing to the Prince who is next)* And the Prince is even worse!

The Prince *(Coming downstage right)* These uniforms are disgusting. Disgusting!

Lafauchette *(Noticing Angele who is still talking to Saint Florimond)* Look! A pretty woman! Prince!

The Prince Yes.

Lafauchette Do you know her?

The Prince Who? No, never seen her before. That surprises me. *(To Badin)* Do you know who that lady is?

Badin No. *(To Reservist)* Do you?

Reservist No.

(Dufoulay enters upstage right, between guardroom and canteen, wearing a uniform that is much too big for him. He comes downstage, passing through the group of Reservists)

Dufoulay Oh, what a uniform!

Lafauchette Hey, there! Perhaps you can tell us. Who's that pretty woman over there?

Dufoulay Where?

All *(Pointing to Angele)* There! There!

Dufoulay Talking to Champignol? Why, it's his wife!

All His wife!

Dufoulay She happens to be my cousin by marriage.

The Prince Introduce me.

All Introduce all of us.

Dufoulay *(Going towards Angele)* Good morning, Angele.

Angele
St Florimond } *(Aside)* Dufoulay!

Dufoulay *(To Saint Florimond)* Good morning. *(Introducing)* Angele . . . my comrades! Gentlemen, my cousin

	Madame Champignol and her husband!
Reservists	(*In a group, right, saluting*) Good morning.
St Florimond	(*Aside*) Ohhh! That man's a fool! A fool!
	(*Bugle call off. Belouette enters right and comes downstage centre*)
Belouette	Come on there, get back into barracks.
	(*The Reservists go out into the first hut, saluting Angele*)
	(*To Dufoulay*) Including you, Tom Thumb!
Dufoulay	(*Bumping into the barrow*) Coming, Sergeant, coming.
	(*To Saint Florimond and Angele*) See you later.
	(*He goes out into the first hut, followed by Belouette*)
Angele	(*To Saint Florimond in front of the hotel*) Then that's settled. I'll go back to Paris tonight, to be there when my husband comes home. I won't tell him he's been called up, you'll take his place and everything will be all right.
St Florimond	You twist me round your little finger.
Angele	Monsieur de Saint Florimond, you're a very gallant gentleman.
	(*She goes out into the hotel*)
St Florimond	(*Coming downstage*) A very gallant gentleman! Gallant, yes, but fed up! Oh, I'll never forget my affaire with Madame Champignol. (*He falls, sitting, into the barrow*)
	(*Grosbon enters upstage right, between guardroom and canteen*)
Grosbon	Hey! What are you up to? You were allowed to talk to your wife. Now it's over, get on your way!
St Florimond	Very good, Corporal. (*Going upstage, pulling the barrow*) Oh, what a life! What a life!
	(*Champignol enters quickly midstage left, behind the hotel. He is carrying a suitcase in one hand and, in the other, his painting equipment; a canvas, paint-box, easel and campstool*)

Champignol	Ah! Here at last! I must be posted as a deserter!
	(*He bumps into Saint Florimond, who is going upstage, pushing his barrow*)
St Florimond	Look where you're going, can't you!
Champignol	I am sorry.
Grosbon	Come along there!
St Florimond	Yes, Corporal.
	(*Saint Florimond goes out upstage right between guard-room and canteen, passing behind Grosbon*)
Champignol	(*Calling*) Excuse me, Corporal.
Grosbon	(*At 2*) What do *you* want?
Champignol	(*At 1, saluting*) Champignol, Corporal, Champignol!
Grosbon	Champignol? Under arrest.
	(*Grosbon goes out right, between guardroom and canteen*)
Champignol	(*Coming downstage*) Under arrest! I should have expected it. The whole thing's unbelievable. Maybe the first three days was partly my fault; I was away. I know that's none of their business. But I might have been here yesterday, if it hadn't been for the call-up papers. They tell me to report to Clermont. I've never heard of this Clermont, all I know is Clermont-Ferrand. So I went there. They might have given more details. I've been searching for the 75th Infantry all over Clermont-Ferrand. Ohhh! If I told them, they wouldn't believe me. They'd laugh. Now I'm overdue and under arrest. Under arrest! I'm finished!
	(*Ledoux enters from the first hut, right*)
Ledoux	What are you doing there?
Champignol	(*At 1. Aside*) An officer! (*Aloud*) I'm Champignol, sir.
Ledoux	Ah, you're Champignol! The deserter. Well, why aren't you in the Guardroom? You're under arrest.
Champignol	Under arrest! I'm finished. (*Louder*) Finished!
Ledoux	I didn't know it was finished. In that case, get

D

back into barracks. (*He passes behind Champignol and goes upstage left*)

Champignol What? . . . Very good, sir. (*Aside*) What did that Corporal mean? It doesn't matter. (*Going out*) I thought there'd be more trouble than this.

    (*Champignol goes out into the first hut*)

Ledoux (*Left*) He's pretty dense. Probably just a country bumpkin.

    (*Camaret enters and stands in the hotel doorway*)

Camaret Adjutant!

Ledoux Sir.

Camaret Are your men properly dressed now?

Ledoux Yes, sir.

Camaret Get them on parade. I'll inspect them.

Ledoux Very good, sir.

    (*Ledoux goes out upstage right, between guardroom and canteen. Camaret goes back into the hotel. A bell rings offstage. Belouette, Grosbon, and all the Reservists enter hurriedly from the first hut. They are in uniform except for Badin who is as before*)

Belouette Squad! Fall in! Get on with it!

    (*The Reservists fall in, facing the audience in two ranks. The front row, from left to right, consists of Corporal Grosbon, Dufoulay, Lafauchette, Lavalanche, Badin, the Prince. When they have fallen in, Camaret enters from the hotel*)

Camaret (*To Badin*) What the devil are you doing in civvies?

Badin They couldn't find clothes to fit me, sir.

Camaret Clothes! You don't wear clothes!

Badin Well, an outfit.

Camaret You don't wear outfits! What do you call it when everyone's dressed alike? When they're dressed uniformly, what do you call it?

Badin Er . . . Livery.

Camaret Livery! (*To Belouette, who is at 2, right*) Give that

man two days in the guardroom. If you're dressed
uniformly, you're wearing a uniform! Bloody fool!

Badin I can see I'm going to enjoy myself!

Belouette Company, shun!

(*Champignol enters from the first hut*)

Champignol (*Aside*) Ohhh! On parade already! (*To Belouette*)
Where do I go, Sergeant, where do I go?

Belouette Your usual place, of course!

Champignol My usual place! Oh, God!

(*He rushes into the squad, treading on the Prince's
toes. The Prince yells. Then he tries to take
Lavalanche's place*)

Lavalanche No, not here!

Champignol Oh, I see. (*He tries to take Dufoulay's place*)

Dufoulay You're not here!

Belouette Have you quite finished dancing around there?

Champignol (*Squeezing sideways into the ranks between Dufoulay
and Lafauchette*) All right, all right. You can carry
on now, Sergeant.

Belouette Squad, number!

(*The Squad starts to number: 1, 2, 3, 4*)

Champignol 4B.

Belouette Squad, open ranks, march!

Camaret (*Moving forward*) Everyone's on parade?

Belouette Yes, sir.

Camaret Let's have a look at them. (*He inspects them, starting
from the left. To the first man*) Your neckband goes
round twice, not once. (*He lifts up the next man's
jacket, and sees he is not wearing braces. The same with
Dufoulay*) You're not wearing braces. Weren't you
told to wear them?

Dufoulay Yes, sir, but they hurt me.

Camaret Oh, they hurt you. (*To Belouette, who is at 1*) Change
those four days C.B. to two days in the guardroom
for making subversive remarks.

Dufoulay But I thought . . .

Camaret You're not here to think. And shut up.

Dufoulay (*Aside*) He doesn't seem to like me.

Champignol This captain seems a bit strict.

Camaret Right! Now, Corporal, you can start drilling your squad.

Camaret (*To Belouette*) By the way, Sergeant, get me Private Champignol.

Champignol Me! (*He steps forward out of the ranks*) Sir!

Camaret (*At 3*) What's the matter with you?

Champignol But I . . .

Camaret You're not a Sergeant, are you? Well, get back in the ranks.

Champignol Oh! Very good, sir. (*Taking his place in the squad*) The man's mad!

Camaret Hurry up, Sergeant.
> (*Belouette goes out upstage right, between guardroom and canteen*)

Camaret (*Aside*) I've had an idea. I've got Champignol here, so I'll make him paint my portrait. (*Aloud*) Carry on, Corporal, I'm going to see if the barrack rooms look any better.
> (*Camaret goes out into the first hut*)

Grosbon (*Back to the audience*) Squad, shun! Form two ranks!
> (*They do so, finishing with, from left to right in the front rank, Champignol, Dufoulay, Lafauchette, Badin, Lavalanche, the Prince. The rear rank consists of six Reservists*)

Right dress!
> (*They do so, carefully leaving a little space between each, to allow freedom of movement*)

Grosbon Eyes front! Now remember you're not here to enjoy yourselves. Any nonsense and I'll have you in the guardroom. Squad, shun! Horizontal movement of the arms, keeping the elbows straight.

In two motions, like this. One, two! One, two!

Reservists (*Executing the movement*) One, two! One, two!

Grosbon All together. That's feeble . . .Feeble! (*To Champignol*) You there, you're feeble!

Champignol (*Aside*) If Mr Vanderbilt could see me now!

Grosbon Squad, halt! (*Running to Champignol*) Can't you hear me?

Champignol Sorry, Corporal. I didn't understand.

Grosbon Didn't understand? Is there something funny about the way I talk?

Champignol (*Aside*) It's too awful to be funny.

Grosbon You there, in civvies! You can't do this in a top hat!

Badin Very good, Corporal. (*He takes off his hat and, not knowing where to put it, keeps it in his right hand and carries on with the exercise*)

Grosbon Squad, shun! Horizontal and lateral movement of the arms, with elbows straight and knees bending. Like this. One, two! Begin!

Champignol (*As he does it*) This is ridiculous. God, this is ridiculous!

Reservists One, two! One, two!

(*Romeo enters from the hotel, followed by Mauricette. He has a fishing rod on his shoulder and a fisherman's basket hung round his body*)

Romeo Do come along, Mauricette.

Mauricette (*Coming downstage to 1*) Oh, Father . . . look at them.

Dufoulay (*Noticing her*) My wife!

Mauricette (*Signalling to Dufoulay*) Do look, Father. He's doing it much better than anyone else.

Dufoulay (*Aside*) God, how embarrassing doing this in front of one's wife!

Grosbon Squad, halt! (*Seeing Mauricette*) Oh, a pretty face! (*To the Reservists*) Come along, try to do it properly. You've got a gallery.

> *(Badin puts his hat down on the ground)*

Mauricette　Oh, Father, I want to kiss him.

Romeo　I shouldn't. This is not the moment.

Grosbon　Squad, left turn!

> *(They do so, except Dufoulay who turns right)*

Right turn!

> *(They turn back, facing the audience. Dufoulay turns the other way, finishing with his back to the audience)*

Just look at that idiot there.

Mauricette ⎫
Romeo ⎭ Oh!

> *(Dufoulay turns round, facing the audience)*

Grosbon　Don't you know your left from your right, you bloody fool?

Dufoulay　He calls me a bloody fool in front of my wife!

Mauricette　Oh! I won't have anyone talking to my husband like that!

Romeo　Keep out of this. Don't read the Riot Act to the Army.

Dufoulay　Let me tell you, Corporal . . .

Grosbon　'Let me tell you, Corporal'! Just look at him.
I advise you not to get married, no wife's going to stay faithful to you.

Dufoulay　Oh!

Mauricette ⎫
Romeo ⎭ Oh!

Grosbon　*(To Romeo, who is next to him)* Just look at him.
I've never seen such a fool.

Romeo　*(Stepping forward)* He's my son-in-law.

Grosbon　Oh! He's your . . . Hm . . . Squad, right turn! . . .
Quick march! . . . Double march!

> *(Badin picks up his hat and puts it on, then they all double out midstage left, behind the hotel)*

Mauricette　*(At 1)* Oh, Father! Did you hear how that awful man spoke to my husband?

Romeo	Don't worry. It doesn't mean a thing in the Army. They always talk like that. Well, you don't feel like coming fishing with me?
Mauricette	No. We've an introduction to a Madame Rivolet, I'll go and call on her. We have to stay here four weeks, we might as well get to know people.
Romeo	All right. Run along.
Mauricette	Goodbye, Father. (*She goes out left, behind the hotel*)
Romeo	The river's next to the hotel, I'll go and try a cast or two. I saw one or two pools this morning where I think I might catch something.
	(*Camaret enters from the first hut*)
Camaret	The barrack rooms are filthy. Where's the Sergeant?
Romeo	(*At 1*) Oh! The captain!
Camaret	(*Going downstage to 2*) Signor Romeo! Where are you going in that get-up?
Romeo	I'm going fishing. Perhaps I shall have an enormous tench.
Camaret	I'm sure you won't smell at all.
Romeo	Not enormous stench! Enormous tench!
Camaret	Oh, an enormous tench.
Romeo	That's what I said, enormous tench.
Camaret	Yes, yes, I see. By the way, you haven't seen your nephew, Champignol?
Romeo	No.
Camaret	(*Going upstage right*) Well, what's he doing? I sent for him.
	(*Saint Florimond enters midstage right, from the entrance to the barracks. He is now in ordinary uniform. Belouette enters with him*)
't Florimond	What does the Captain want me for?
Belouette	I don't know. He'll tell you. (*He points to Camaret*)
Camaret	Ah, there you are. Good.
Romeo	(*To Saint Florimond*) Hullo, prisoner!
't Florimond	(*Aside. Moving to 2*) Prisoner! (*Aloud*) Hullo, hullo!

Camaret	(*At 3, to Belouette who is at 4*) Sergeant! I've just been round the barrack rooms. They're almost the same as they were an hour ago. Filthy dirty and personal belongings all over the beds. You know I won't have that. Do something about it.
Belouette	Very good, sir.
	(*He goes out into the first hut. Romeo has been talking to Saint Florimond*)
Camaret	Champignol! Come here.
St Florimond	Sir . . .
Camaret	As you're not just anyone, I'm going to do you a great favour.
St Florimond	Me, sir?
Camaret	I'm excusing you all fatigues.
St Florimond	Oh, sir!
Camaret	Instead you're going to get your brushes and paint my portrait.
St Florimond	What!
Camaret	I said you're going to paint my portrait.
St Florimond	I thought you did. (*Aside*) That's the last straw!
Camaret	What are you waiting for?
St Florimond	I'm very honoured, sir, of course, but I can't. I can't.
Camaret	Why can't you?
St Florimond	Well . . .
Camaret	You refuse?
St Florimond	No, sir, no. I haven't any brushes. Or anything else. It's all in Paris.
Camaret	Damn! How infuriating!
St Florimond	Yes, sir, I'm terribly disappointed. Of course, if I had my things here . . . I'd be delighted . . . I'd start right away.
Camaret	Damn, damn, damn!
Romeo	Yes . . . it's a sad business (*pronounced peessiness*) . . . a sad peessiness.

(They slowly cross to extreme left in a line, still in the same order. Belouette enters from the first hut)

Belouette Everything's put away in the barrack rooms now, sir. This was all I could find. It seems to be a painter's things . . . a canvas, a paintbox, . . .
(He is also holding an easel and a campstool)

All What!

Camaret A paintbox!

Belouette *(At 4)* Yes, sir. It belongs to Champignol. His name's on it.

Camaret *(To Saint Florimond)* What an earth were you saying just now? *(To Belouette)* All right, leave it all here. Good. Now go and get someone to sweep out the rooms.

Belouette They're all on parade, sir.

Camaret Well, go and get one of them off parade.
(Belouette passes behind Camaret and goes out midstage left, behind the hotel)
What the devil were you talking about? You hadn't any . . .

St Florimond But, sir, I didn't know. I've no idea where all this came from. I didn't bring it. Perhaps my wife wanted to give me a surprise. Anyway, it's here, that's a fact, it is here.

Camaret Yes, that's the main thing. Now you can start work on my portrait.

Romeo *(To Saint Florimond)* Yes, isn't that lucky! You were so disappointed . . .
(Romeo passes in front of Saint Florimond and picks up the painting equipment, which he carries back to the left, passing again in front of Saint Florimond)

St Florimond Oh, do shut up.

Camaret *(At 3)* Right. Now get everything ready. *(He goes back upstage)*

St Florimond *(At 2, undoing the bag)* Ohhh! What a situation!

Romeo (*At 1, putting up the easel and setting out the stool*)
    I'll give you a hand.

St Florimond No, no. There's no hurry.

Camaret (*Coming downstage to 3*) What do you mean, 'No
    hurry'? Come along, how are you going to do me?

St Florimond (*Aside*) That's what I was wondering.

Camaret How shall I pose? Is this all right? (*He assumes
    a pose*)

St Florimond Hm . . . er . . . I think I'd prefer it if you were
    sitting.

Camaret Good idea! I'd prefer it too, from the posing point
    of view . . . Go and get me a chair.

St Florimond Right away, sir.
    (*Saint Florimond goes out into the hotel. Camaret and
    Romeo wait on the steps. Belouette enters midstage
    left, behind the hotel, with Champignol*)

Belouette Come along.

Champignol All right, Sergeant. What's all this about?
    (*Belouette goes out into the first hut*)
    Ah, an easel! . . . It's mine! These are my things!
    They're very free and easy here. (*He picks everything
    up, puts it under his arm and goes towards the first hut,
    right*)

Camaret (*Still on the steps*) Hey! What's the matter with you?
    Are you mad?

Champignol (*Turning back*) Well, sir . . .

Camaret Ah, it's our comedian. Trying to get yourself
    noticed. Put those things down.

Champignol But, sir . . .

Camaret I told you to put them down.
    (*Champignol, grumbling, puts them back where they
    were*)
    Now get to hell out of here.

Champignol This is tyranny. Tyranny!

Camaret How do we get hold of buffoons like this?

(Belouette enters from the first hut)

Belouette   Hey, you!

Champignol   Yes, sergeant.

Belouette   *(Genial)* You haven't eaten anything yet today, have you?

Champignol   No, Sergeant, no, I haven't.

Belouette   *(Taking a broom from inside the hut, and giving it to him)* Well, get a bellyful of this. Sweep out the hut.

Champignol   Me?

Belouette   Yes. Get a move on.

Champignol   Ohhh! If Mr Vanderbilt could see me now!

  (He passes in front of Belouette and goes out into the hut. Belouette follows him. Camaret and Romeo have been opening the paintbox, preparing brushes, etc. Saint Florimond enters from the hotel with a chair)

St Florimond   Here's the chair.

Camaret   Ah! Thank you.

St Florimond   *(Aside)* Oh, God! God! Inspire me.

  (Camaret sits down at 1, midstage, level with the hotel door. Saint Florimond sits on his stool at 2, with the easel in three quarters view, so that the canvas is visible to the audience. This canvas must be white and the actor must draw as best he can. Romeo stands behind him, still holding his fishing rod)

Camaret   *(Already seated, assuming a pose)* Like this? Full face?

St Florimond   Hm! No . . . In profile . . . *(Aside)* Now I've only half his face.

Camaret   I'd prefer it full face.

St Florimond   I'm not asking what you'd prefer. I prefer the profile.

Camaret   *(Showing his right profile)* This one?

St Florimond   No, the left . . . That's better. *(Aside)* Left out altogether would be better still.

Camaret   Right . . . Are you ready? . . . *(Giving an order)* Begin!

St Florimond	(*Settling down at the easel*) Ohhh! What am I going to do? (*Starting to sketch*) Sometimes desperation works miracles.
Romeo	(*Behind him*) Very good! . . . What's that?
St Florimond	His nose.
Romeo	I thought it was the peak of his cap.
St Florimond	Think what you like . . . but don't bother me. (*He goes on drawing. Aside*) Ohhh! He'll never believe it's a Champignol!
	(*Champignol enters from the first hut, sweeping away*)
Champignol	They're turning me into a charwoman! Oh, another painter! (*Coming down to 4*) Hm! He's not up to much.
Romeo	(*At 3, still behind Saint Florimond*) I say! What's that?
St Florimond	(*Impatiently*) His eye. Damn!
Romeo	Oh! His eye! (*To Champignol*) It's very interesting, watching someone painting. Not bad, eh?
Champignol	(*Making a face*) Yes. He looks like a primitive.
Romeo	Possibly, possibly.
Champignol	(*Shyly, approaching Saint Florimond, passing in front of Romeo*) I say . . . A bit too widely spaced . . . his eye and his ear.
St Florimond	What did you say?
Champignol	A bit too widely spaced . . . His eye and his ear.
Camaret	(*Posing*) What is it now? (*Turning his head*) You again! Tell the sergeant to mark you down for two days C.B.
Champignol	(*Aside*) Me! (*Passing in front of Romeo and going towards the first hut, right*) Whenever I say anything . . . Marvellous! . . . He always picks on me . . .
Camaret	Didn't you hear?
Champignol	Yes, sir. (*Going into the hut*) I won't open my mouth again.
	(*Champignol goes out into the first hut*)
Romeo	It's funny . . . to judge by his sketches you'd never think he could paint a pretty picture.

Camaret	Phew! . . . I'm getting a stiff neck . . . Are you nearly finished?
St Florimond	As you wish, sir.
Camaret	(*Rising, passing behind the easel and coming downstage to 2*) All right, that's enough for today. Let's have a look.
St Florimond	Ohhh! What's he going to say?
Camaret	(*Looking at the canvas on the easel*) That's me?
St Florimond	Yes . . . Yes . . . It's . . .
Camaret	(*Picking up the canvas and examining it*) Phew! If I look anything like that . . .
St Florimond	It's . . . It's . . . the first sketch. You know, simply a guide for the painter. It doesn't mean anything to anyone else.
Camaret	Is that so? I must say it doesn't mean anything to me.
St Florimond	You won't see this eventually.
Camaret	Right. You can put your things away.
	(*Saint Florimond does so during the next few lines*)
Romeo	I think it's going to be very good.
Camaret	I hope so, because at the moment . . .
Romeo	Now . . . I'm going fishing . . . (*To Camaret*) You're not coming?
Camaret	No . . . Thank you.
Romeo	Then I'll see you later.
	(*Romeo goes out upstage left. Camaret goes out with him for a moment. Saint Florimond puts his things away, picks them up in one hand and, with the other, collects the chair and goes out into the hotel. Reservists enter midstage right from the barracks*)
Reservists	Ah, a break at last. (*Etc.*)
	(*Reservists go towards the first hut*)
Grosbon	Hey, steady there! Not so fast! Who's coming with me to get the potatoes?
Reservist	(*At 3*) I will, Corporal, if you like.

Grosbon (*At 2*) What's your job?

Reservist Unloading vegetable carts.

Grosbon Then stay here. (*To the Prince*) What about you?

The Prince (*At 1*) I'm the Prince of Valence.

Grosbon A prince?... Go and get the potatoes.
> (*The Prince goes out midstage left, behind the hotel. The others remain in a group upstage. Saint Florimond enters from the hotel, carrying his things. Camaret enters upstage left*)

St Florimond I'll be going now, sir. (*He crosses to the right*)

Camaret Right. By the way, your hair's too long. Get it cut.

St Florimond (*Aside*) What a life! (*Aloud*) Very good, sir.
> (*Saint Florimond goes out midstage right, into the barracks. Ledoux enters from the first hut*)

Camaret Adjutant! Private Champignol's hair's too long. Get it cut.

Ledoux Very good, sir.

Camaret Right away!
> (*Camaret goes out into the hotel*)

Ledoux Where is Champignol?
> (*Champignol enters from the first hut*)

Ah, there he is! (*To Belouette*) Sergeant! Get that man's hair cut.

Champignol (*At 2*) Me?

Belouette (*At 3*) Very good, sir.
> (*Ledoux goes upstage left*)

Champignol But, Sergeant, my doctor won't allow it.

Belouette I didn't ask for your opinion.
> (*Grosbon enters from the first hut*)

Corporal! Get that man's hair cut.
> (*Belouette goes out downstage right*)

Grosbon Very good, Sergeant. (*Calling*) Barber!

Champignol But, Corporal...

Grosbon Shut up.
> (*The Barber enters from the first hut*)

Barber   Corporal?

Grosbon   Cut that man's hair.

    (*Grosbon goes upstage left*)

Barber   Very good, Corporal. (*To Champignol*) Come along
    then.

Champignol   This is awful. Awful!

    (*Champignol goes out into the first hut, followed by
    the Barber. The Prince enters midstage left with an
    enormous sack of potatoes on his back*)

Grosbon   Come along, you prince there, get moving.

The Prince   (*Crossing the stage*) Ohhh! I feel as though the whole
    of Society's staring at me.

Grosbon   Put it down there.

    (*The Prince does so, downstage right*)

    Now everyone, get into those potatoes.

    (*The Reservists gather round the sack and start peeling
    the potatoes*)

Ledoux   (*Left*) I'm going to smoke a cigarette. (*He goes upstage
    left*) Oh, a fisherman! He'll never catch anything.
    I'll go and have a look. (*Ledoux goes out upstage left*)

    (*Chatter from Reservists, gradually dominated by:*)

Lavalanche   (*Singing to the tune of Alouette*)

    Oh, potatoes,

    We all peel potatoes.

    Peel potatoes

    Every bloody day.

    I will pluck out all the eyes

All   We will pluck out all the eyes. (*Etc.*)

    (*A shout, off. Ledoux re-enters and comes downstage*)

Ledoux   Help! Help! Quickly! Help!

Reservists   What is it?

Ledoux   That fisherman's fallen in the river! Hurry! Hurry!

Dufoulay   I bet it's my father-in-law.

Lavalanche   A man in the river! Good! That's finished potato
    peeling.

Reservists	Hurry! Hurry!
	(*Reservists rush out*)
The Prince	(*Downstage. Not moving*) Hurry! Hurry!
	(*Camaret enters from the hotel*)
Camaret	What's happened? What's all this shouting?
The Prince	(*Still downstage. Very calmly*) A fisherman's fallen in the river.
Camaret	What! And you stand there! Run and help! Where is this fisherman? Where is he?
	(*Romeo enters upstage left, supported by Dufoulay and surrounded by Ledoux and the Reservists. He is soaked to the skin and sneezing, as though he has swallowed a lot of water*)
Ledoux	Come along. This way. This way.
Dufoulay	Come along, Father.
Camaret	(*At 1*) Signor Romeo!
Romeo	(*At 2. Sneezing*) Atchoo! Atchoo! I'm drowned! I'm drowned!
Camaret	It's really you, Signor Romeo?
Romeo	Captain! Oh, Captain! What a plunge! Let me tell you all about it.
Camaret	No, you can do that later. You can't stay like this. You're soaked. (*To Reservists*) Take him into barracks and rub him down. (*To Romeo*) Would you like a drink?
Romeo	Yes. Something hot and strong.
Ledoux	I'll go and get it for you.
	(*Ledoux goes out into the canteen*)
Dufoulay	Come along, Father.
Romeo	(*Going out midstage right, into the barracks*) Oh, what a plunge! What a plunge!
	(*Romeo goes out, sneezing*)
Camaret	Phew! A fine state he's in!
	(*Saint Florimond enters upstage right, between guardroom and canteen*)

	Ah, there you are! Just in time! Your uncle's fallen in the river.
St Florimond	(*Coming downstage to 2*) My uncle? I haven't an uncle.
Camaret	What! You haven't an uncle! . . . Signor Romeo!
St Florimond	Oh, Romeo! . . . He's . . . He's my wife's uncle. That's why I . . . Oh, he's fallen in the river. Well, well, well! (*Pause. Unconcerned*) Is he dead?
Camaret	What! Is he dead? A fine nephew you are! No, he's not dead, just soaked to the skin. So hurry up, will you!
St Florimond	Yes, yes, yes.
Camaret	Good god, your hair! Is that how they've cut it?
St Florimond	(*Taking off his cap*) No, they haven't yet.
Camaret	What! Not yet!
St Florimond	Oh, poor uncle! Fallen in the river! Well, well, well! (*Saint Florimond goes out into the first hut*)
Camaret	They haven't cut his hair yet! This is too much. I'll deal with that adjutant.
	(*Ledoux enters from the canteen and comes down to 2*)
Ledoux	Here's the drink.
Camaret	Adjutant! I thought I told you to get Private Champignol's hair cut.
Ledoux	Yes, sir . . . It's being done now.
Camaret	Bloody lies! Take two days C.B. for not obeying my orders.
Ledoux	But, sir . . .
Camaret	Be quiet! . . . That's enough!
	(*Camaret goes out into the hotel*)
Ledoux	Damn you, Champignol! Right! Just you wait! (*Champignol enters from the first hut and comes downstage to 2. His hair is slightly shorter*)
Champignol	Phew! They've just cut my hair!
Ledoux	So there you are! I told you to get your hair cut!
Champignol	(*Taking off his cap*) It's just been done, sir.
Ledoux	Bloody lies! To start with, you've just got me

E

confined to barracks. Take two days C.B. (*Crossing to midstage and calling*) Sergeant!
> (*Belouette enters from the first hut*)

Belouette (*At 3*) Sir!

Ledoux I thought I told you to get this man's hair cut!

Belouette It's just been done, sir.

Ledoux Bloody lies! Take three days C.B. for not obeying my orders.
> (*Ledoux passes behind Champignol and goes out downstage left*)

Belouette Ah, you get me confined to barracks, do you? Take three days C.B. Just a moment. Corporal Grosbon!
> (*Grosbon enters from the first hut and comes downstage to 3*)

Grosbon Sergeant!

Belouette I thought I told you to get that man's hair cut!

Grosbon It's just been done, Sergeant.

Belouette Bloody lies! Take four days C.B. for not obeying my orders.
> (*Belouette goes out upstage right*)

Grosbon (*Passing to 2*) Ah, you get me confined to barracks, do you? Take four days C.B.

Champignol (*Aside*) That makes nine.

Grosbon Just a moment. Barber!
> (*The Barber enters from the first hut*)

Barber Corporal! (*He comes downstage to 3*)

Grosbon I thought I told you to get that man's hair cut!

Barber I've just done it, Corporal.

Grosbon Bloody lies! Take four days C.B. for not obeying my orders.

Barber Oh! (*Aside*) That's a bit steep.

Grosbon Go and crop that man's head. Now!
> (*Grosbon goes out*)

Barber (*At 2*) Well! That's pretty mean of you. Getting a pal into trouble!

Champignol A pity he can't give me any C.B. I was beginning to get used to it.

Barber Come along then.

> (*The Barber goes out into the first hut, followed by Champignol. Dufoulay enters midstage right, from the barracks, with Romeo, Lafauchette and the Prince*)

Dufoulay Well, Father, are you all right now?

Romeo (*In uniform. Coming downstage to 2*) Ah, that's better. It's very good of you all to lend me these clothes.

All Not at all.

Dufoulay I've taken yours to the cookhouse to dry out.

Romeo These don't seem to fit very well.

Dufoulay You look like a very new recruit!

Romeo It was a silly business (*peessiness*) falling in the river like that.

Dufoulay How did it happen?

Romeo (*Sitting down on the bench. Everyone gathers round him*) Well, I was on the river bank. But you can't cast very far from there. Then I saw a tree trunk sticking out of the water. I jumped onto it and splash! I fell in!

> (*Everyone laughs. Grosbon enters midstage right, from the barracks, running*)

Grosbon The C.O. . . . The C.O.! Hurry up, you lot! Get back into barracks!

All The C.O.! Oh!

> (*Reservists rush out into the first hut, jostling Romeo. Grosbon follows them. An uproar can be heard inside*)

Romeo (*Midstage*) What was all that? Well, I don't care. It's nice here. The sun's coming out. Just right after a swim. (*He lies down on the bench in front of the canteen*)

> (*Fourrageot enters from the barracks, a cigar in his mouth, and comes downstage right*)

Fourrageot Nobody here! Damn this cigar, it keeps on going out. Extraordinary! The Colonel gave it me. (*He takes a box of matches out of his pocket and lights his cigar*)

Romeo (*Singing*) 'O sole mio . . .'

Fourrageot (*Turning round*) What the devil's that?

Romeo (*Singing*) La, la, la, la, la.

(*Fourrageot sees Romeo and goes slowly up to him. Romeo goes on singing. Fourrageot stands firmly in front of him*)

Fourrageot A reservist! What are you doing there?

Romeo (*At 1*) Hullo, hullo!

Fourrageot (*At 2*) Hullo! He says hullo to me! What the devil are you doing? Who do you think you're talking to? Who do you think you're talking to?

Romeo Hullo, hullo!

Fourrageot Are you deaf, man? Are you saying hullo to me?

Romeo Hullo! Yes.

Fourrageot You lout, you! Will you stop this nonsense!

Romeo Who is this extraordinary man?

Fourrageot Stand up! Have you ever seen a man lying down in front of his commanding officer? Come on, stand up!

(*Romeo shrugs his shoulders, lies down again and goes on singing. Fourrageot, furious, takes him by the collar and drags him downstage right to 2*)

Will you stand up!

Romeo Really! Do leave me alone.

Fourrageot What did you say? Do you realise I'm going to put you in prison?

Romeo Don't talk rubbish.

Fourrageot You're not back in your farmyard now, you peasant. Trying to be clever, eh? You don't know me. I'll tame you.

Romeo Now, now, now! I'll tell you what happened. (*As he talks, he takes a bit of fluff off Fourrageot's uniform*)

Fourrageot	Stand to attention! (*He slaps his hand*)
Romeo	(*Crossing to 1*) Oh, really! This man's so rough! There's no talking to you. You will keep on yelling all the time.
Fourrageot	Sergeant! Who the devil's this man?
	(*Belouette enters midstage right, from the barracks and comes downstage to 3*)
Belouette	I don't know, sir. He must be a reservist arrived this morning.
Fourrageot	Ah, that's it! Nothing military about him! You've never been a soldier of France, have you?
Romeo	No, I'm Italian.
Fourrageot	Ice-cream wallah! I'm not surprised. What's your name?
Romeo	Romeo.
Fourrageot	Sergeant, put Romeo down for four days C.B.
Romeo	Me?
Fourrageot	Detail a corporal to take this man and read the Manual of Discipline to him for the next hour.
Belouette	Very good, sir.
Fourrageot	(*Going towards the first hut*) You don't know me, you lout. I'll tame you.
	(*Fourrageot, still muttering, goes out into the hut*)
Grosbon	(*Off*) Squad, shun!
Romeo	(*At 1*) That sergeant seems rather rude.
Belouette	(*At 2*) Silence!
	(*Ledoux enters midstage right, from the barracks*)
	Wait here while I speak to the Adjutant.
	(*He goes behind Romeo towards Ledoux*)
Ledoux	(*Coming downstage to 1, a letter in his hand*) Just my luck! My little milliner's free tonight and thanks to Champignol, damn him, I'm confined to barracks.
Belouette	(*Coming downstage to 2*) Sir! One of the men on guard is ill. I need a replacement.
Ledoux	(*Passing to 2*) A replacement! Take Champignol.

Belouette	(*Passing behind Ledoux and going towards* Romeo) Champignol. Very good, sir.
Ledoux	I'll make him pay for this.
Belouette	(*To Romeo*) Come along, you.
Romeo	Where?
Belouette	You'll see.

(They go out midstage right, into the barracks)

Ledoux	(*Coming downstage*) After all, at night the adjutant's in command. I'll do my C.B. at my milliner's house.

(Champignol enters from the first hut and comes downstage to 2. His hair is cropped close)

Champignol	Phew! I've certainly been cropped all right.
Ledoux	Ah, there you are. Have you had your hair cut?
Champignol	Oh, yes, sir. (*Taking off his cap*) Is that all right now?
Ledoux	That will do. Now go and get changed. You're on guard.
Champignol	Me?
Ledoux	(*Passing behind him and going towards the hut*) Yes, you! Hurry up.

(Ledoux goes out)

Champignol	It never rains but it pours!

(He follows Ledoux into the hut. Romeo enters midstage right, from the barracks, followed by Grosbon)

Romeo	For heaven's sake! What's it all got to do with me? Leave me in peace.
Grosbon	(*Reading*) 'If any other rank . . .
Romeo	(*Coming downstage to 2*) Ohhh!
Grosbon	(*At 1. Continuing*) . . . 'wishes to speak to an officer when carrying a rifle, he will salute in accordance with the Small Arms Manual.'
Romeo	(*In desperation shrugging his shoulders, raising his eyes to heaven and starting to hum*) La, la, la, la.
Grosbon	You don't seem to be listening to what I'm saying.
Romeo	Yes, yes.

Grosbon You're carrying a rifle, an officer passes . . . what do you do?

Romeo Hm. Well . . . I fire.

Grosbon You fire! Is that how you listen?

Romeo What? No. How do I know? (*Passing to 1*) You stand there jabbering away. I'm not interested. Leave me in peace.

    (*Mauricette enters midstage left, behind the hotel*)

Mauricette Father! Where are you?

Romeo Mauricette!

Mauricette (*Coming downstage to 1*) Father! You're in uniform!

Romeo You see, I fell in the river.

Mauricette You fell in the river!

Romeo Yes, but everything's all right now.

Grosbon (*Ignoring the conversation and going on reading*) 'If an other rank speaks to an officer and is not carrying a rifle . . .'

Romeo I was standing on the bank . . .

Grosbon ⎫ '. . . he springs smartly to attention . . .'

Romeo ⎬ I saw a tree stump sticking out of the water . . .

Grosbon ⎭ '. . . and salutes in the usual manner.'

Romeo Oh, for heavens sake! For heavens sake! I can't hear myself speak!

Grosbon I was told to read you the Regulations.

    (*Dufoulay enters from the first hut, carrying Romeo's clothes. He comes downstage to 4*)

Dufoulay Here are your clothes, Father. They're dry now.

Romeo My clothes! There! You can see I'm not a soldier!

Grosbon These are the Sergeant's orders.

Dufoulay Well, the Adjutant's orders are that he's to change into civvies.

Grosbon Oh, if it's the Adjutant . . .

    (*Grosbon goes out upstage right, between guardroom and canteen*)

Romeo Have you been to Madame Rivolet?

Mauricette	I left our cards and the letter.
Romeo	Good, good. Come along then, children.
	(*They go out into the hotel. Immediately before they go out, Belouette enters midstage right, from the barracks, followed by Saint Florimond in dress uniform, the chinstrap of his cap underneath his chin*)
St Florimond	I have to go on guard?
Belouette	You're Champignol, aren't you? The Adjutant said 'Put Champignol on guard'.
St Florimond	What a damned nuisance! Sergeant!
Belouette	Well? What is it?
St Florimond	Do I have to stay here?
Belouette	Of course you have to stay here.
St Florimond	No, I mean where is my beat?
Belouette	From there to there. (*He points to the whole depth of the stage from the first hut to the canteen*) And from there to there. (*He points to the area from the canteen to the wings, right*)
St Florimond	Very good, Sergeant.
	(*Belouette goes out into the guardroom. Saint Florimond mounts guard, first across the width of the stage, then disappearing between guardroom and canteen. Ledoux enters from the first hut, followed by Champignol, dressed for guard duty*)
Ledoux	Are you ready, Champignol? Right. You can go on sentry duty straight away.
Champignol	Where, sir?
Ledoux	Here of course.
	(*Ledoux goes out midstage left*)
Champignol	Very odd! . . . I've only just arrived . . . And on guard already! (*He marches up and down from the first hut to the canteen. As he goes back the second time, he comes face to face with Saint Florimond who is coming back downstage*) Another sentry!
St Florimond	Another sentry!

Champignol	What are you doing?
St Florimond	They've put me on guard.
Champignol	Me too.
St Florimond	Oh . . . How funny!
Champignol	Very funny!
	(*They march up and down the stage from front to back in opposite directions*)
St Florimond	You're a Reservist?
Champignol	Yes? And you?
St Florimond	Me too.
Champignol	How do you do?
St Florimond	How do you do?
	(*They shake hands, then resume their beat*)
Champignol	I say . . . Weren't you painting the Captain's portrait just now?
St Florimond	Yes. I was.
Champignol	You're an artist then?
St Florimond	No, I'm not. I've never held a brush in my life. That's what's so awful.
Champignol	How is that?
St Florimond	It's like a novel.
Champignol	A novel? (*Taking his arm*) I like a good story. (*They continue their beat, arm in arm, their rifles at the slope*)
St Florimond	Well . . you see . . . It's very serious . . . An intrigue with a married woman . . . and professional discretion . . .
Champignol	Go on, go on. I won't tell anyone.
St Florimond	I won't mention the lady's name . . . Well . . . you see . . . (*Going upstage arm in arm as before*) For several weeks I've been pursuing a married woman.
Champignol	Pretty?
St Florimond	Enchanting! . . . But there's absolutely nothing between us.
Champignol	That's what people always say.

St Florimond No, I promise you.

  Champignol (*As they come downstage*) Oh, come on! All right, we'll say nothing happened.

St Florimond Oh, it did.

  Champignol There! You see!
        (*They both halt arm in arm, facing the audience, Saint Florimond still at 1, Champignol at 2*)

St Florimond No, you don't understand. What happened was I was mistaken for the husband. I'm here in the Army instead of him.

  Champignol No! How terribly funny! Some husbands have all the luck! It's never happened to me! But tell me, why were you painting the Captain's portrait, if you've never held a brush before?

St Florimond Oh, I haven't told you. The lady's husband . . .

  Champignol Well?

St Florimond He's a painter.

  Champignol Another painter? How amusing!

St Florimond Another painter?

  Champignol Of course! You don't know me. I'm Champignol.

St Florimond (*Jumping in the air and going into bayonet drill*) In! Out! On guard! (*Falling terrified on the bench in front of the canteen*) It's him! Him! (*Turning it into a cough*) Ahim! Ahim!

  Champignol Bad cough you have, old man! (*Slapping him on the back, then sitting next to him*) Well . . . what about you?

St Florimond Me? . . . What?

  Champignol What's your name?

St Florimond Er . . . Augustus.

  Champignol Augustus . . . what?

St Florimond Augustus . . . nothing. Illegitimate!

  Champignol My dear fellow, I am sorry. But don't let that worry you. Look at the Roman Emperor . . . he was just Augustus, like you. But that didn't affect his career.

St Florimond	No, it didn't.
Champignol	(*Rising*) Augustus! Go on . . . tell me. This painter . . . well? . . . In confidence . . . what's his name?
St Florimond	(*Rising*) Oh, no! No! I can't!
Champignol	(*Taking his arm*) Come on. I'm longing to know.
	(*They continue their beat, arm in arm as before*)
St Florimond	Oh, you say that . . . !
Champignol	I'm not just being inquisitive, I may know him.
	(*They halt downstage*)
St Florimond	Well . . . it's . . . Raphael.
Champignol	(*Laughing*) Nonsense! He's been dead for over three hundred years.
St Florimond	Wait. You won't let me finish. Raphael Potard!
Champignol	Raphael Potard! Extraordinary! A painter . . . called Potard. Never heard of him.
St Florimond	Oh, he's not well known. Not at all well known. (*Going upstage with Champignol*) He married a mulatto . . . a mulatto . . . She had negro blood.
Champignol	(*Coming downstage*) Naturally.
St Florimond	Well, this mulatto . . .
	(*Fourrageot enters from the first hut, as they come downstage arm in arm*)
Fourrageot	What! What the blazes is this? What do you two think you're doing?
Champignol (*At 1*) *St Florimond* (*At 2*)	(*Halting*) Sir?
Fourrageot	Where have you ever seen anyone mount guard like that? And present arms when you see me!
	(*Fourrageot passes to the left (1). Champignol and Saint Florimond turn face to face and present arms*)
	Not like that!
	(*Champignol does a half turn. They then find themselves one behind the other and present arms like that*)
	Where do they find these men? Why are there two of you?

St Florimond	I don't know, sir . . . They detailed us . . .
Champignol	Yes, Augustus and me . . .
Fourrageot	Augustus! . . . Sergeant!

    (Belouette enters from the guardroom and comes downstage to 4)

	Who are these men? Why are there two of them?
Belouette	*(Dumbfounded)* I don't know, sir. I only detailed this one. *(He points to Saint Florimond)*
Fourrageot	*(To Champignol)* Well, what do you think you're doing?

    (Belouette goes upstage in front of the canteen)

Champignol	I don't know, sir. I was detailed by the Adjutant.
Fourrageot	The Adjutant! . . . Get back into barracks!
Champignol	*(Aside)* Delighted!
Fourrageot	And don't let me catch you at it again.
Champignol	*(Aside)* He seems to think I did it for pleasure. *(Aloud)* Goodbye, Augustus.

    (Champignol goes out into the first hut)

Fourrageot	*(To Saint Florimond)* As for you, try to behave a bit better when you're on guard. What's your name?
St Florimond	*(At 2)* Me? I don't know any more.
Belouette	*(Coming downstage between them)* He's Private Champignol, sir.
Fourrageot	Champignol. *(To Belouette)* Keep an eye on this man when he's on guard. Right, dismiss!

    (Belouette salutes and goes out into the guardroom)

    (To Saint Florimond) Take your cap off.

    (Saint Florimond does so)

    Your hair's too long.

St Florimond	I've been told so already, sir.
Fourrageot	Well, get it cut then!
St Florimond	*(Going upstage and resuming his beat)* Very good, sir. Ohhh! Her husband here! Her husband!

    (Saint Florimond goes out upstage right, between

    guardroom and canteen, still on sentry duty. Ledoux
    enters midstage right, from the barracks)

Fourrageot Adjutant!

 Ledoux (*Coming downstage to 1*) Sir!

Fourrageot (*At 2*) Get Champignol's hair cut.

 Ledoux (*Dumbfounded*) Shorter?

Fourrageot Naturally. Not longer! Don't make silly remarks.
    (*He passes to 1*)

 Ledoux (*At 2*) Yes, sir.

Fourrageot You understand, eh?
    (*Fourrageot goes out midstage right, into the barracks*)

 Ledoux Why is everybody making such a fuss about
    Champignol's hair? Well, why should I bother?
    (*Champignol enters from the first hut with the barber.*
    He has got rid of his pack and rifle)

Champignol Come along. I'll give you a drink for all the trouble
    I've caused you.

 Ledoux (*At 1*) Ah, Champignol! Come here.

Champignol (*At 2*) Sir! (*Aside*) What is it now?

 Ledoux Let's see your hair.
    (*Champignol takes his cap off*)
    Right! Barber! Go and cut Champignol's hair.

Champignol Again!

 Barber (*At 3*) But, sir, I've put the clippers all over his
    head!

 Ledoux Well shave it then. I'm not going to have any more
    trouble. Go on, take him away.
    (*Ledoux goes out midstage right, into the barracks*)

Champignol (*Upset*) Oh . . .

 Barber Come on, you.

Champignol I'm being disfigured! Disfigured! I won't have a
    hair left.
    (*He goes out into the first hut with the barber. Saint*
    Florimond, still on duty, enters upstage right, between
    guardroom and canteen and comes downstage right)

St Florimond Her husband! That's the final blessing!
(*Ledoux enters. Saint Florimond ignores him*)

Ledoux (*At 1*) Sentry! What do you do when you see me?

St Florimond (*At 2, presenting arms*) Is this right?

Ledoux No, that's presenting arms. But it will do.
(*Ledoux passes in front of Saint Florimond and goes out into the first hut*)

St Florimond What's going to happen? Oh, I know. A scandal. An appalling scandal! There's only one thing to do. Champignol's here. So let them sort it out. I've this ball tonight. As soon as my guard's finished, I'll vanish.
(*Celestin enters left*)

Celestin I say, Sentry, where's Captain Camaret?

St Florimond (*Midstage at 2*) I haven't seen him, sir.

Celestin (*Coming downstage to 1*) If I'm not mistaken . . . Monsieur Champignol!

St Florimond The Captain's nephew!

Celestin What a surprise!
(*They shake hands. Camaret enters from the hotel*)

Camaret What! Go on, Sentry, make yourself at home.

Celestin Uncle!

Camaret (*Coming downstage to 1*) Oh, it's you!

Celestin Yes. I was just asking Monsieur Champignol . . .

Camaret Champignol on guard! You're under arrest! What are you doing on guard?

St Florimond I don't know, sir.

Camaret Sergeant!
(*Belouette enters from the guardroom*)

Belouette Sir! (*He comes down to 4*)

Camaret Sergeant! What's the meaning of this? Men don't go on guard, if they're under arrest! I let him off fatigues, that's all. Relieve him at once and lock him up.

Belouette Very good, sir. (*To Saint Florimond*) Come along, you.

St Florimond (*Going upstage*) Lock me up! (*Aside*) How shall I
get to the ball? (*To Belouette*) All right, I'm coming.
I know the way.

> (*Saint Florimond goes out into the guardroom with
> Belouette*)

Celestin (*At 1*) Poor Monsieur Champignol!

Camaret (*At 2*) Pah! Well, what's brought you here?

Celestin Mother wants you to come early this evening.
With Adrienne.

Camaret Why is that?

Celestin The ball. Adrienne will have to be the hostess.
Mother's ill.

Camaret Very well. What's the matter with her?

Celestin Oh, nothing serious. A bout of gout.

Camaret What?

Celestin Her gout. She's had another bout of it.

Camaret She's rather stout for gout. But there's a lot of it
about.

Celestin No doubt.

> (*Camaret goes upstage with Celestin. Champignol enters*)

Champignol How dare they mutilate anyone like this!
(*He takes off his cap, wraps his head in his handkerchief,
and puts his cap back on top*)

Camaret (*Upstage left*) What! What the devil's that man
doing with a bald head? Hey, you there!

Champignol (*Reaching midstage*) Sir?

Camaret (*Coming downstage to 2, while Celestin comes down to 1*)
Show me your head.

Champignol (*Taking off his cap*) Look. Would you believe it?

Camaret Would I believe it! Oh, it's our funny man.

Champignol (*Proudly*) He's recognised me.

Camaret How dare you have your hair cut like that! Do
you think you've the right to turn your head into
a marble?

Champignol But sir . . .

Camaret Take two days in the guardroom. That will teach you not to make yourself grotesque.

Champignol Oh, no! This caps everything.

Camaret Dismiss. Get back into barracks. And stay there till your hair's grown again.

Champignol Yes, sir. (*Aside*) I've had enough of this. Oh, they'll drive me mad. First they shave my head, then they throw me in prison.

    (*Champignol goes out into the first hut*)

Camaret That's typical. Leave them alone for one moment and all they think about is making themselves ridiculous. (*He passes in front of Celestin and goes to 1*)

    (*Angele enters from the hotel*)

Angele (*Speaking into the wings*) Yes, do, please.

Celestin Madame Champignol!

Angele (*Coming downstage to 1*) Excuse me, Captain, but could you tell me where I can find out the times of the trains?

Celestin (*Saluting*) Good afternoon.

Angele Oh, forgive me, I didn't recognise you.

Camaret They must have a timetable in the hotel. You really mean to leave us?

Angele Yes. I'm going back to Paris this evening.

Celestin Why don't you stay one more day? My mother, and all of us, would be delighted if you'd come to our ball tonight.

Angele Your mother?

Camaret Yes, Madame Rivolet. My sister.

Angele (*Aside*) His sister!

Camaret She's giving a small dance . . . for my daughter Adrienne. They're going to introduce her to a suitor – a Monsieur de Saint Florimond.

Angele (*Aside*) Saint Florimond! And the Captain's daughter! Oh! Poor man!

Celestin   Can't you really come?

Angele   Oh no, impossible! Absolutely impossible!

Celestin   I am sorry.

Camaret   So am I. I hope you have a good journey.
(*He salutes and goes upstage left with Celestin*)

Angele   (*Aside*) I've got to see Saint Florimond. If he goes
to this ball, everything's ruined. (*Aloud*) Captain . . .

Camaret   Yes?

Angele   I must ask you for yet another favour. Before I go,
I'd like to say goodbye to my husband.

Camaret   (*Upstage*) Of course.
(*Ledoux enters upstage right, between guardroom and
canteen*)
Adjutant!

Ledoux   Sir!

Camaret   Go and get Champignol and tell him his wife's
asking for him.

Ledoux   (*Going out*) Very good, sir.
(*Ledoux goes out right*)

Camaret   (*Saluting*) Now I must be going . . .

Celestin   (*Bowing*) Good afternoon . . .

Angele   Goodbye. Goodbye, Captain; thank you.
(*Camaret goes out midstage left, behind the hotel, with
Celestin*)
Oh, thank heavens I was warned in time!
(*Dinnertime is sounded on the bugle. The Reservists
enter, running, from the first hut and disappear upstage
right, between the guardroom and canteen*)

Reservists   Dinner's ready. About time too. (*Etc.*)
(*Ledoux enters midstage right, from the barracks and
is jostled by the Reservists*)

Ledoux   Look where you're going! (*To Angele*) Here's
Private Champignol.

Angele   Thank you so much.

Ledoux   (*To Champignol, off*) Come along then.

F

        (*Champignol enters midstage right, from the barracks.*
        Ledoux goes out)

Champignol A lady's asking for me?

Angele (*At 1*) My husband!

Champignol (*Coming downstage to 2*) My wife! You're here!
Angele, darling! How good of you to come!

Angele Yes. I thought . . . They said . . . (*Aside*) Oh, I
feel faint.

Champignol I was going to write . . . Why are you staring at
me like that? . . . Oh, my hair? (*Taking off his cap*)
Could you believe they'd do this to me? I'm bald,
darling, I'm bald!

Angele (*With a forced laugh*) How funny! (*Aside*) He's going
to learn the truth.

        (*During this scene the Reservists have returned one by
        one with their mess tins. Some sit down on the benches
        upstage, others go back into the hut*)

Champignol Angele, darling . . . Let me kiss you.

Lavalanche (*On one of the canteen benches*) Just look at that. A
soldier's kissing Madame Champignol.

Reservists (*Crowded upstage*) Oh!

Badin Phew! What about her husband?

        (*Saint Florimond enters midstage right, from the
        barracks*)

St Florimond Done it! There was a flimsy wooden door and I
broke it down. I've escaped.

Reservists Here he is.

Angele (*Aside*) Saint Florimond!

Lavalanche (*Going to Saint Florimond*) Hey! Who's that fellow
talking to your wife?

St Florimond I don't know him.

Lavalanche You don't know him! . . . He's kissing your wife!

St Florimond Ah, he . . . Well, well, well! He . . . he must be . . .
a relation of hers.

Lavalanche (*To the Reservists*) He's a relation of hers!

Reservists	(*Sarcastically*) Oh!
Champignol	(*To Angele*) Where are you staying? The hotel?
Angele	Yes. There!
Champignol	Good. (*To the Reservists*) I say, we don't have to sleep in barracks, do we?
Reservists	No, no.
Champignol	Splendid. Because of course I'd rather spend the night with Madame Champignol.
All	Oh!
Florimond	(*Falling onto the right-hand bench*) Ohhh!
Angele	Ohhh!
Champignol	Come along, darling . . . Take me to your room. (*Reservists laugh*)
Angele	This way. (*Aside*) What a nightmare! (*Angele and Champignol go out into the hotel*)
Florimond	(*Rising and going midstage, followed by the Reservists*) Well, who am I meant to be? Who am I meant to be?
Lavalanche	Well? . . . Did you hear? . . . She's taking him up to her room!
Florimond	(*At 2*) Yes. Yes.
Lavalanche	(*At 3*) You don't say anything?
Florimond	Oh! Oh! That man has certain rights. The fact is, he's . . .
Lavalanche	The fact is he's your wife's lover, dammit. That's obvious.
Florimond	My wife's lover!
Lavalanche	You've got it, old man, you've got it. (*The Reservists go upstage, laughing*)
Florimond	I've got it! I've got it! (*Aside*) Champignol's getting on my nerves. He's making me look a fool. I seem to be the deceived husband. No, that's silly, because it's as Champignol . . . so he's the one . . . He's deceiving himself! Ah well, I don't care. I'll get into my own clothes and when I'm seen again, it won't matter.

> (*Saint Florimond goes out into the first hut*)

Lavalanche (*Upstage*) Look, he's going. Watch out.

Badin He's amazing.

All (*Laughing*) Marvellous! (*Etc.*)

> (*Lafauchette, the Prince and other Reservists enter midstage right, from the barracks, carrying their mess tins*)

Lavalanche Come here. You don't know what we've just seen!

Reservists No. What?

Lavalanche Champignol. You know, Champignol . . . he's under arrest. Well! His wife's sleeping with another man!

Reservists No!

Lavalanche Yes! One of us!

> (*Laughter*)
>
> Come on, Badin, Pincon, let's go and tell everybody
>
> (*They go out midstage right, into the barracks*)

Reservists (*Laughing*) Marvellous!

> (*Champignol enters from the hotel*)

Champignol (*Coming downstage to 1*) What's the joke?

Lafauchette (*At 2*) We've just heard a wonderful story. You know Champignol?

Champignol Champignol?

Lafauchette His wife's sleeping with another man!

Champignol What!

The Prince (*At 3, roaring with laughter*) One of us reservists!

Champignol (*Furious*) Where is this man? Where is he?

> (*Saint Florimond, in civilian clothes, enters from the first hut*)

St Florimond Ah, I'm ready now.

The Prince Look. There he is!

Champignol What! Augustus! . . . Ha! So I was Potard! (*Falling on him*) And you're my wife's lover!

St Florimond (*At 2*) Let go of me.

Champignol (*At 1*) You'll pay for this!

Reservists What does he mean?

> (*Romeo appears on the hotel balcony with Mauricette and Dufoulay*)

Romeo A battle!

All Separate them.

> (*Angele enters from the hotel and comes downstage*)

Angele Heavens! My husband and Saint Florimond!

> (*They separate Saint Florimond and Champignol*)

Champignol I'll find you again. I'll find you.

St Florimond Yes . . . In the meantime, I'm getting out of here.

> (*Saint Florimond runs out upstage right, between guard-room and canteen*)

Champignol Catch him. Catch him.

Angele Robert!

Champignol Get out of my way.

All (*Surrounding Champignol*) Keep calm. Keep calm.

> (*From the moment the fight started, the dialogue is only just distinguishable above the general hubbub. Grosbon runs in from the guardroom and comes downstage to 3*)

Grosbon Where is he? Where is he?

> (*Ledoux enters from the first hut*)

Ledoux What's happening? What's all this noise about? What do you want, Corporal?

Grosbon Private Champignol, sir. He's escaped.

Ledoux Escaped?

Grosbon Yes, he broke the door down. (*To the Reservists*) Has anyone seen Champignol?

Champignol (*Advancing*) Champignol? What do you want with Champignol? What are you saying about Champignol? I am Champignol!

Grosbon You are? Well, back to the guardroom!

Champignol Me?

All The guardroom!

> (*General tumult. Champignol is dragged off, right*)

CURTAIN

Act III

(Madame Rivolet's House. The same evening.
A small drawing-room, with a door in the back wall,
leading into the hall. Downstage right, another door.
Midstage, a door at an angle, leading into other
reception rooms. Downstage left, a door leading into
Madame Rivolet's room. Midstage, a table laid with
glasses, etc., for the reception, placed at an angle.
Behind the table, a door leading into the kitchen. A
chandelier upstage.
When the curtain rises, the Prince of Valence, still in
uniform, is mounted on a pair of steps, arranging
the chandelier. The steps are placed in such a way that
the chandelier masks his face and only his legs can be
seen. Jerome stands between the steps and the table,
watching him.
Celestin, in a dinner jacket, enters midstage right)

Celestin   Jerome! Really! Jerome!

Jerome   (*At 1*) Sir?

Celestin   (*At 2*) What is going on?

Jerome   (*Pointing to the Prince*) The orderly the Captain sent
is arranging the chandelier.

Celestin   Ah, good! Where are the drinks?

Jerome   (*Passing behind the table, which he sets out during the*
following dialogue) I'm getting them ready, sir.

Celestin   (*Going to the table*) Well, hurry up. Everybody's
asking for them.

(Adrienne enters in evening dress, midstage right and
comes downstage to 3, between the steps and the table)

Adrienne   Celestin! Do tell them to serve the drinks.
Everyone's dying of thirst.

Celestin   I was just telling Jerome.

(Camaret, in tails, enters midstage right)

Camaret Celestin! Aren't we getting anything to drink? Everybody's tongue's hanging out.

Celestin Yes, Uncle, I was just . . .

Camaret (*To Jerome, going towards the table and passing under the steps*) Well, hurry up, we're dying of thirst. (*When he gets under the steps, he stops*) Has that orderly arrived?

Jerome Yes, sir. He's arranging the chandelier. (*He points*)

Camaret (*Raising his head*) Ah! Good! Don't hesitate to use him for washing glasses . . . any odd jobs about the kitchen. (*To the Prince*) Eh, orderly?

The Prince (*On the steps*) Sir?

Camaret What's your name?

The Prince Prince of Valence.

Camaret Of course. Well, Prince of Valence, you'll stay in the kitchen, right? Under command of the butler.

The Prince Very good, sir. (*Aside*) Highly honoured!

Camaret You'll help wash the glasses. Do you know how to wash glasses?

The Prince (*Coming down the steps*) I regret I have never been taught to, sir.

Camaret Well, they'll show you. Run along.

The Prince What decadence!

(*The Prince goes out upstage, carrying the steps*)

Camaret (*To Jerome*) Come on. Take the drinks in.

Jerome Right, sir. (*He passes behind Camaret and goes towards the right with his tray*)

Camaret Hey, not so fast! (*Jerome stops at 4. Camaret takes a glass*) It's not like the Gospel here. The first . . . shall be first!

(*Jerome goes out, midstage right*)

Camaret (*To Celestin*) Phew! It's beginning to get hot in there.

Celestin (*Passing behind Adrienne to 2*) Well, the whole town's here.

Camaret Including that Saint Florimond of yours?

Celestin I must say he's not in much of a hurry for a suitor.

Adrienne (*Aside*) Does he want him to come?

Camaret Do you know this Saint Florimond?

Celestin No, nobody does, except Mother. And she can't get about. With her gout. So I'll have to introduce him. But I don't know what he looks like.

Camaret You'll recognise him . . . by his name! I'm going back into the cauldron. Call me, when he arrives.

Celestin Yes, Uncle.

     (*Camaret goes out midstage right*)

Adrienne (*Downstage centre, aside*) To think he'll let me marry! . . . And will never know!

Celestin (*Going behind Adrienne to the table and pouring a glass of champagne*) Won't you join me, Adrienne? A little champagne?

Adrienne I'd love some. (*Celestin gives her a glass; she drinks a little*)

Celestin (*Watching her; aside*) How pretty she is!

Adrienne Why are you looking at me like that?

Celestin You know . . . I did admire you just now. It was wonderful the way you took your mother's place.

Adrienne (*Giving him her glass*) Oh, was that why?

Celestin (*Holding the glass*) You'd be a marvellous hostess!

Adrienne I'd better be, as I'm going to be married.

Celestin I'm sorry Monsieur de Saint Florimond wasn't here to see you.

Adrienne (*Offended*) Oh, you're sorry! He'll have time enough to find out, if I marry him.

Celestin Of course. Of course. (*Not knowing what to say, he puts Adrienne's glass to his lips, thinking it is his own*)

Adrienne (*Quickly*) That's my glass! I've just drunk from it.

Celestin Oh, I'm sorry. (*He puts it back on the table*)

Adrienne (*Offended*) That's something Monsieur de Saint Florimond would not have done.

Celestin What is?

Adrienne Not drink from a glass because my lips touched it.

Celestin Now look! *I* can't do anything right. But Monsieur de Saint Florimond . . . the so-called suitor . . . the so-called lover . . .

Adrienne But you're not in love. I suppose that's what you mean?

Celestin I mean I'm not your suitor.

Adrienne Precisely.

Celestin (*Aside, looking at her*) How pretty she is! (*Aloud*) You know, if you weren't my cousin, I would be your suitor.

Adrienne Then I'm sorry we're cousins.

Celestin You're laughing at me. Monsieur de Saint Florimond can be proud of having a wonderful wife. You can trust me to sing your praises.

Adrienne You're too kind.

Celestin Apparently he's a charming man.

Adrienne Oh!

Celestin Yes. He's rich – that doesn't matter, you are too – and he has a great name. You'll be the Countess de Saint Florimond. That sounds splendid. Countess de Saint Florimond.

Adrienne Yes, yes. That does sound splendid.

Celestin He's so distinguished and intelligent.

Adrienne (*Impatiently*) Oh, for heaven's sake, that's enough! You make me want to marry him right away!

Celestin If he's everything he's said to be, that wouldn't be so bad. Just think. A husband who's young, handsome, intelligent. He'll be so kind and loving . . .

Adrienne (*Tapping her foot*) Please, please! That's enough!

Celestin What's the matter?

Adrienne You do carry on about Monsieur de Saint Florimond's virtues. If you were a marriage broker you couldn't do better.

Celestin   But Adrienne . . . What I said . . .

Adrienne   What you said! I may become his wife! Does that mean nothing to you?

Celestin   Well, you'll marry somebody some day.

Adrienne   You're right. So it might as well be him as anyone else. As you're so insistent, I'll marry your Saint Florimond!

Celestin   Adrienne, what is it? Are you angry?

Adrienne   Oh Celestin, Celestin! I didn't expect this of you.

Celestin   Great heavens! What's the matter with her? Adrienne!

Adrienne   (*In tears*) When we were children and promised to be husband and wife . . . was it only a game?

Celestin   What! This can't be true!

Adrienne   I thought it was in earnest. I've always said to myself: That's the man you must love, because he will be your husband.

Celestin   Adrienne! Don't say another word. Unless you want me to throw Saint Florimond out of the window as soon as he enters this house.

Adrienne   Really? You'd do that for me?

Celestin   Of course I would. Don't you realise I haven't forgotten either? You've been saying: That's the man I must love, because he'll be my husband. I've been saying: That's the girl I must not love, because she can't be my wife.

Adrienne   Why?

Celestin   Why? Because you're so rich . . .

Adrienne   (*Joyfully*) Was that why? Oh, you're so stupid!

Celestin   Yes, I am stupid . . . But that was why.

Adrienne   Oh, it was . . . You're going to marry me immediately!

Celestin   Me?

Adrienne   Yes, you! And as you feel so guilty about it, I'll tell Father he can keep his sixty thousand francs a year. There!

Celestin You know, I think I can forget about your fortune.

Adrienne Now you are going to apologise.

Celestin Adrienne!

Adrienne No, not like that. (*Giving a military order*) Down on your knees!

Celestin (*Kneeling*) Very good, my commanding officer.

Adrienne (*Embracing him*) My husband.
  (*Camaret enters midstage right*)

Camaret Well! I must say! What a way to carry on! What are you two up to?

Adrienne (*At 2*) Father!
  (*Celestin quickly gets to his feet*)

Camaret (*At 3*) Don't let me disturb you. (*He passes behind Adrienne and stands between her and Celestin at 2*) Is this how you behave when you're about to meet a suitor? . . . But I'm sorry Monsieur de Saint Florimond isn't here.

Adrienne (*At 3*) Oh, Father! Monsieur de Saint Florimond doesn't matter any more. You said you'd never stand in the way of my true feelings. Well, the man I love and am going to marry . . . is here.
  (*She points to Celestin*)

Camaret (*Bursting out laughing*) Eh? Him? Extraordinary! This young rascal! Why . . . I've known him since he was so high.

Celestin I've grown since then, Uncle.

Camaret No, I'll never stand in the way of your true feelings. But, good God, why didn't you tell me sooner? You let your aunt hunt for suitors, organise a party . . .

Adrienne Never mind . . . It will be our engagement party.

Camaret Ah well . . . I like things to be done in a regular military manner . . . You love each other, you can get married.

Celestin Oh! Uncle!

Camaret Go on. Give her a kiss.

Adrienne That's what he was doing when you came in.

Camaret Carry on then. Last time it was illegal. Now it's official. (*He passes behind Adrienne and comes down to 3*)

Adrienne (*To Celestin*) Now . . . shun! (*She offers her cheek*)

Celestin (*Kissing her*) I preferred it when it was illegal.
(*A carriage is heard*)

Camaret Damn! That must be Saint Florimond.

Adrienne (*Quickly giving her arm to Celestin*) Saint Florimond!

Celestin Let's get out of here.
(*They run off right. Camaret follows them upstage to try to stop them and disappears for a moment. Jerome enters from the hall*)

Jerome Madame Champignol!
(*Angele enters, in evening dress, with a cloak, and comes downstage left. Jerome goes out*)

Angele I'm being very daring, but you can often escape danger by going to meet it.
(*Camaret enters midstage right*)
Captain!

Camaret Madame Champignol! It wasn't you I was expecting.

Angele Who was it then?

Camaret Nobody important. A man who wants to marry my daughter.

Angele Oh!

Camaret Yes, no one you'd know. A Monsieur de Saint Florimond.

Angele Saint Florimond! (*Aside*) He hasn't arrived yet. It may still be all right.

Camaret It is kind of you to come, you gave me so little hope . . .

Angele I managed to postpone my return to Paris.

Camaret How very charming! Would you like to take off your . . . what's its name . . . greatcoat?

Angele My evening wrap.

Camaret Yes, I don't know the right name for that sort of thing.

      (*Jerome enters from the hall*)

      Ah, Jerome! Get . . . whoever's in charge of the stores.

Jerome In charge of the stores?

Camaret Yes. For the lady's wrap.

Jerome Oh, the woman in charge of the cloakroom! That's the maid, sir. You have to ring twice . . . (*He points to the bell, which is on the left of the door into the hall*)

Camaret Go on then, ring.

Jerome (*Going to the bell, ringing it and coming downstage to 3*) She doesn't know the house yet, sir. She only arrived this morning.

      (*Jerome goes out, downstage right. Charlotte enters from the hall*)

Charlotte Did somebody ring for me?

Angele (*Aside*) Charlotte here!

Charlotte (*Coming downstage to 2*) Madame Champignol! What a surprise!

Camaret Ah! If I'm not mistaken . . . that's the maid you had in Paris.

Angele No . . . Yes. Yes. It is.

Charlotte Yes, Madame Champignol had the honour of having me as a maid.

Camaret All right, all right. Stop chattering. Come on, be off with it.

      (*Angele takes off her cloak*)

Charlotte Very good, sir. (*She passes in front of Camaret and goes towards the door, downstage right*)

Camaret Where are you going?

Charlotte (*At 3*) Back to the cloakroom, sir. You said: Be off with you.

Camaret (*Aside*) The girl's an idiot. (*Aloud*) I said: Be off with *it*. The lady's wrap!

Charlotte (*Passing in front of Camaret towards Angele*) You
should speak more clearly.

Angele (*At 1, giving her the cloak*) Here it is.

Camaret Be careful with it. (*Passing in front of Charlotte and
going to Angele*) Now, if you will allow me to offer
you my arm . . .

Angele (*Taking his arm*) Captain!

Camaret This way . . . (*As he passes in front of Charlotte*) Be
careful you don't crease it.
(*Camaret and Angele go out midstage right*)

Charlotte (*Coming downstage*) Crease it! I wouldn't crease a
beautiful coat like this. A wrap they call it! If I
gave myself to a banker (*She puts her hand on her
stomach*) I might carry the rap! Let's try it on.
(*She does so*) It suits me.
(*The Prince enters downstage right, with a tray*)

The Prince (*Talking into the wings*) On the table? Right. (*Aside*)
A lady!

Charlotte (*At 1, aside*) A soldier!

The Prince (*At 2, aside*) She must be one of the local aristocracy.

Charlotte (*Laughing affectedly*) Ha ha ha!

The Prince (*Aside*) Is that for me? (*Laughing with embarrassment*)
Ho ho ho! (*Aside*) This tray embarrasses me.
(*Putting it under his arm*) I may be in uniform, but
I'm not what you think I am.

Charlotte Would you like to know something? Me neither.
I'm not what you think I am.

The Prince I am the Prince of Valence.

Charlotte Yes? I'm the maid.

The Prince The maid?

Charlotte (*Showing Angele's cloak*) I'm taking this to the
cloakroom.
(*Camaret enters midstage right*)

Camaret (*Seeing Charlotte from behind*) A lady!

Charlotte The captain!

Camaret (*Passing behind the Prince towards Charlotte*) The maid!
Make yourself at home. That's Madame
Champignol's evening wrap.

Charlotte I'm giving it an airing. So it won't get creased.

Camaret Yes. All right. Go and put it away. As for you,
Orderly, go back to the kitchen and don't let me
catch you chasing after the maids again.

The Prince Me! Chase after maids! I don't chase after maids!

Camaret What did you say?

The Prince I said I don't chase after maids!

Camaret Shut up.

The Prince (*Going towards the door, downstage right*) All right!
But I don't chase after maids!

Camaret I told you to shut up!

The Prince (*As he disappears*) All right! But I don't chase after
maids!
(*The Prince goes out downstage right*)

Camaret What! I'll give you 'I don't chase after maids'!
I'll teach you!
(*Camaret goes out, after the Prince*)

Charlotte That soldier's going to get into trouble.
(*Romeo enters from the hall, followed by Mauricette.
He is in tails, she in evening dress*)

Romeo Come along, Mauricette.

Mauricette Yes, Father. (*She passes in front of him to 1*)

Romeo (*At 2*) Where's your husband?

Mauricette He's handing in our coats.

Romeo Ah, good. (*To Charlotte, who has remained upstage,
folding Angele's cloak*) Where is Madame Rivolet?
You see, she doesn't know us.

Charlotte In bed, sir. (*Voices off, right*) But here's her brother.
(*Charlotte goes out into the hall. Camaret enters
downstage right*)

Camaret I'll wring that man's neck for him! I'll wring his
neck!

Mauricette⎫
Romeo⎭ The Captain!

Camaret (*Coming downstage to 3*) Madame Dufoulay! . . . Signor Romeo!

Mauricette (*Aside*) Heavens! My husband's meant to be under arrest.

Camaret What a delightful surprise!

Romeo Yes, Madame Rivolet was kind enough to ask us.

Mauricette I gather she's ill.

Camaret Yes, a bout of gout.

Romeo What a terrible business (*peessiness*)! What a terrible business!

Camaret I'm happy to welcome you in her place. I'm only sorry your husband couldn't come with you. But he's under arrest.

Mauricette Yes, yes, so he is. (*Aside*) Oh dear!

Romeo (*Passing in front of Mauricette to 1*) My son-in-law is going to enjoy himself!
(*Adrienne and Celestin enter right, laughing, arm in arm*)

Camaret What's the matter with you two young things?

Adrienne (*Coming downstage right*) We've been dancing madly. Oh! Madame Dufoulay and Signor Romeo!

Camaret (*At 3*) Let me introduce you to an engaged couple.

Romeo Oh!

Mauricette This is something new?

Camaret It's ten minutes old.

Mauricette (*Passing in front of Camaret to 3*) Congratulations!

Adrienne I told you I had an idea of my own. This is who it was.

Camaret Now, Celestin, give Madame Dufoulay your arm.
(*Celestin passes in front of Adrienne and offers his arm to Mauricette; together they go upstage right*)

Mauricette (*Aside*) Oh heavens! My husband's going to arrive!

Romeo Come, Mauricette . . .

> (*Romeo goes out midstage right after Celestin and Mauricette*)

Adrienne Well, Father, aren't you coming in?

Camaret No, I can't stand ovens. There are too many people in there. There's no air left.

> (*Jerome enters from the hall*)

Jerome Monsieur Dufoulay!

Camaret What!

> (*Dufoulay enters in very new tails, putting on his gloves*)

Dufoulay Good evening. (*Coming downstage to 2 and finding himself face to face with Camaret*) The captain!

Camaret You!

Dufoulay (*Very embarrassed*) No. No.

Camaret What do you mean, no!

Dufoulay Hm! Yes. Yes.

Camaret What are you doing here? Why aren't you in the guardroom?

Dufoulay I . . . I . . .

Camaret What do you mean: I? What reason can you give me for coming to this ball?

Dufoulay Er . . . I didn't expect to find *you* here, Captain.

Camaret Is that why?

Dufoulay Yes. Yes.

Camaret Outrageous! Never mind. In this house you are our guest. Give my daughter your arm.

Dufoulay (*Giving Adrienne his arm*) Oh, Captain . . .

Camaret And when you get back to barracks tomorrow, add two days to your punishment.

Dufoulay What!

Camaret Be off with you.

Dufoulay (*Dumbfounded*) Very good, sir. (*To Adrienne as they go towards the door midstage right*) Delightful party this is . . .

> (*Adrienne and Dufoulay go out*)

Camaret (*Going to the table*) Poor fellow, I must say it's bad

luck finding me here. I have to be strict, though
I've nothing against him. (*Drinking a glass of
champagne*) I remember, before I was an officer,
I was once confined to barracks. I went to a ball
and had the same bad luck. I ran into my captain.
He said: 'I know your face, aren't you in my
company?' I replied: 'I'm Saint Florentin'. There
wasn't any Saint Florentin in the company, but it
went off as smoothly as posting a letter. Talking of
Saint Florentin, Monsieur de Saint Florimond's still
not arrived. But perhaps it's for the best, he's no
reason to now.
 (*Jerome enters from the hall*)

Jerome	Monsieur de Saint Florimond!
Camaret	Talk of the devil!

 (*Saint Florimond enters, in tails*)

St Florimond	(*Coming downstage to 2*) I'm a little late.
Camaret	Monsieur Champignol!
St Florimond	The Captain!
Camaret	You! You here!
St Florimond	No. No.
Camaret	What do you mean, No. No! They all say No. No.
St Florimond	Yes. Yes.
Camaret	Has the whole battalion decided to come here?
St Florimond	(*Aside*) Too bad, the scandal's broken. Her husband knows everything, I've no need to hide now. (*Aloud*) Captain, I am not Champignol.
Camaret	(*Joking*) Well, well! Ha-ha! You aren't . . . Really! He's another of them! Who are you then, may I ask?
St Florimond	You've just heard. I am Monsieur de Saint Florimond.
Camaret	Saint Florimond! Oh, no. That's the limit. No. You're pretty impudent, I must say!
St Florimond	I swear . . .

Camaret	No, I tell you, no! I know that one. I invented it.
St Florimond	Invented what?
Camaret	Yes, if you meet your captain, you give a false name. Yes. But to bring it off, the Captain mustn't know you as well as I do.
St Florimond	I can't explain, but I swear I am Saint Florimond.
Camaret	Now, look. I've been to your studio. I've had you in my regiment, you started my portrait. And now you're trying to make me believe you're not Champignol, the painter Champignol, the reservist in my company.
St Florimond	I am not Champignol.
Camaret	But you are Saint Florimond.
St Florimond	(*Passing to 1*) Exactly.
Camaret	My dear fellow, you've no luck with the name you've chosen. You thought you'd picked one out of the air. Well, Saint Florimond exists and we're expecting him this evening. That's a shock for you, eh?
St Florimond	No.
Camaret	He's coming here to marry my daughter.
Florimond	(*Aside*) She's his daughter!
Camaret	Though he's on a wild goose chase. She's engaged already.
St Florimond	Engaged!
Camaret	Well, what have you to say to that, eh?
St Florimond	I have to say there's been a mistake. I am Saint Florimond, I am not Champignol. If you have a Champignol in your company, he's still there.
Camaret	(*Aside*) Really! There can't be two men as alike as this. Though . . . twins . . . (*Aloud*) Right, I'll confirm what you say. (*He goes to the door, midstage right*)
St Florimond	What's he going to do?
Camaret	Orderly!

>>> *(The Prince enters midstage right and remains in the
doorway)*

The Prince *(Saluting, then noticing Saint Florimond)* Champignol!

Camaret *(At 2)* There! You see! I didn't make him say it.
Orderly, run back to barracks and tell them to send
along Private Champignol, now under arrest.

St Florimond What!

The Prince *(Dumbfounded)* Private Champignol!

Camaret Yes. I understand your surprise, but do as I say.

The Prince Very good, sir. *(Aside, going towards the door)* The
captain's going mad . . . mad!

>>> *(The Prince goes out into the hall)*

Camaret Now we shall learn the truth.

St Florimond Yes. *(Aside)* Ohhh! They're going to bring the
husband here!

Camaret Do you still insist you're not Champignol?

St Florimond Definitely.

>>> *(Charlotte enters upstage right, with a tray)*

Charlotte Oh! Monsieur Champignol!

Camaret Look. Look. Your own maid!

St Florimond *(At 1)* Ha, the maid! What does a maid know?

Charlotte *(Passing in front of Camaret to 2)* How are you,
Monsieur Champignol?

St Florimond *(Pushing her away to 1)* Go away.

>>> *(Charlotte goes out into the hall. Dufoulay and
Mauricette enter downstage right)*

Dufoulay Hullo! Champignol!

Mauricette Monsieur Champignol!

Camaret The family too! Do you disown your family?

St Florimond Ohhh!

>>> *(Romeo enters downstage right)*

Romeo Hullo! Champignol!

Camaret There!

Romeo *(Coming downstage to 3)* How are you?

St Florimond Oh, go to hell.

Romeo	What's the matter with him?
Camaret	He's trying to make me believe he's not Champignol.
Romeo	(*Laughing, passing to 2*) That's marvellous. Clever, eh? Because you're under arrest!
St Florimond	(*Furious*) I told you to shut up.
Romeo	Pah!
	(*Angele enters midstage right*)
Camaret	Ah! Here's a witness who'll be more convincing than any of them.
Angele	(*Aside*) Saint Florimond . . . Here!
Camaret	(*To Angele*) You can help us. (*Pointing to Saint Florimond*) Who is this man?
Angele	(*At 4*) Why . . . it's Monsieur Champignol, my husband.
Camaret	Ah! There!
St Florimond	Her as well!
Camaret	For the last hour he's been insisting he's Monsieur de Saint Florimond.
Angele	Really? How awful! He's had another attack.
All	Attack?
St Florimond	What does she mean, attack?
Angele	Oh, Captain, if you only knew! Every now and then his mind wanders; he thinks he's someone else.
St Florimond	Eh? What's she saying?
Angele	Only the other day . . . He thought he was President . . . he kept on making speeches.
St Florimond	Me?
Romeo	Yes, that does happen. I once heard about a man who always stood like this. (*He puts his left hand on his hip, with his right arm stretched out horizontally, the hand gently curved downwards*)
All	Why?
Romeo	He thought he was a teapot.
Angele	There you are! Exactly the same! Oh, dear! Oh, dear!

St Florimond	(*Aside*) They're trying to get me certified. Certified!
Camaret	Yes, this is serious. Would you like me to send for the MO?
Angele	You needn't worry. It never lasts long.
St Florimond	(*Furiously striding up and down in front of the others, who retreat terrified upstage, forming a semicircle*) Attacks! I don't have attacks! It's all a joke!
All	Yes, yes, a joke!
St Florimond	(*Back to the audience*) But it is a joke! It is! I told you I am Saint Florimond.
All	Yes, yes, you are Saint Florimond.
St Florimond	(*Coming downstage to the left, at 1*) Oh, they're getting on my nerves!
Camaret	(*To Angele*) If only I'd thought of you earlier, I needn't have sent an orderly back to barracks to get the real Champignol.
Angele	(*Aside, leaving the group upstage and coming down to 2*) They're bringing my husband here!
Camaret	(*Coming down to 3*) We'll leave you alone with Monsieur Champignol. In this situation a wife can do more good than strangers.
Angele	I'm very grateful.
Romeo	(*Who has remained upstage with Mauricette and Dufoulay*) Come along.
Mauricette	Poor Monsieur Champignol!
Romeo	What a terrible business!
	(*They all go out except Angele and Saint Florimond*)
St Florimond	They're driving me mad!
Angele	Look what you've done. It's your fault they've gone to get my husband.
St Florimond	Thank heavens! Let him come. It's time someone put an end to this outrageous situation I've been floundering in for the last twenty-four hours.
Angele	Then you're going to ruin me? You want a scandal?
St Florimond	If there's any scandal, it's your husband's fault.

I'd have done anything to avoid it. Now he knows everything and is shouting it all over the rooftops, why should I go on playing this ridiculous part?

Angele   What's going to happen to me? What do I become? A dishonoured woman, rejected by my husband! Your mistress, which I've never been! All because of you!

St Florimond   (*Passing to 2*) Ah well, Angele! It's fate.

Angele   (*At 1*) Fate! You mean your clumsiness. But you don't care. When my husband kills you, you won't give a thought to me.

St Florimond   What! Kill me?

Angele   Don't you deserve it?

(*The Prince enters from the hall*)

The Prince   (*Talking into the wings*) Come on, Champignol. Come on in.

St Florimond   He's coming! Let's get out of here.

(*Saint Florimond runs out downstage right*)

Angele   That's typical. He runs away.

(*Champignol enters upstage*)

The Prince   Stay here. I'll tell the Captain.

(*The Prince goes out midstage right*)

Angele   My husband! Well, it's for the best.

Champignol   (*Coming downstage to 2*) Angele! . . . Darling! . . . You, Madame!

Angele   (*At 1*) Robert . . . Let me explain . . .

Champignol   Stand back. (*Passing to 1*) This is the woman I married! Not only did I marry her, I gave her my name! She was a Chapouillet, I made her a Champignol!

Angele   Robert, don't be angry with me.

Champignol   (*Passing behind Angele and coming downstage to 2*) I'm appalled! Appalled!

Angele   Robert . . .

Champignol   (*Going upstage and furiously throwing his cap on the*

	ground) No! When I think about it, my hair stands on end.
Angele	(*At 1*) Appearances are against me, but I'm not guilty.
Champignol	Nonsense! You're not going to tell me he's not your lover!
Angele	Who?
Champignol	Augustus.
Angele	Augustus?
Champignol	Augustus. The natural son of the Roman Emperor.
Angele	What?
Champignol	He's doing Potard's service for him. You know Potard. That's him!
Angele	What's he saying?
Champignol	(*Tearing his hair, which he hasn't got*) Oh, I'm appalled! Appalled!
Angele	Robert, you must be confused. You mean Monsieur de Saint Florimond.
Champignol	Saint Florimond? He told me Augustus. Never mind. Do you dare to say he's not your lover?
Angele	My lover? Never.
Champignol	Nonsense! He admitted it.
Angele	It isn't true.
Champignol	He said: 'There's never been anything between this woman and me'. Never! Do you hear?
Angele	Exactly. Well?
Champignol	Exactly. You're not going to tell me that if a man says that about a woman, there never has been anything between them!
Angele	What's he to say when it's true?
Champignol	(*Taken aback*) That's right.
Angele	Robert, let me explain.
Champignol	(*Dramatically*) Very well, then!
Angele	Everything I've done was for your sake.
Champignol	Nonsense! For my . . . I never expected that!

Angele It was for you. There has never been anything between Monsieur de Saint Florimond and me. I swear it . . . on your head.

Champignol No, please . . . leave my head alone.

Angele All right. On my mother's head.

Champignol That's better. On my mother-in-law's head.

Angele You were away and he was pursuing me. He was there when the police came to arrest you as a deserter. So I thought I'd teach him a lesson he won't forget. I said to the police: 'You're looking for Monsieur Champignol. Here he is.'

Champignol What! Is that true?

Angele I did it for the honour of your name.

Champignol (*Laughing*) For the honour . . . What a joke! What a joke!

Angele That's why he was brought here instead of you.

Champignol Now I understand. What a joke! I'm delighted. Delighted!

Angele Well, are you satisfied?

Champignol Yes, I am. Mademoiselle Chapouillet, you are worthy of the name of Champignol.

Angele (*Rushing into his arms*) Robert! . . . What are we going to do?

Champignol What?

Angele The Captain's convinced Saint Florimond is Champignol.

Champignol He is, is he? Don't worry. I've an idea . . .

Angele But . . .

Champignol Yes, yes. I'm going to get my own back on Saint Florimond. Augustus!

Angele (*At 1*) Here he is.

    (*Camaret enters midstage right with Saint Florimond and the others*)

Camaret They've found Champignol in barracks?

St Florimond I told you, Captain . . .

Camaret	(*Seeing Champignol and coming downstage to 3*) This man! Nonsense, you're quite different! (*To everybody*) You all know him, is he Champignol?
All	No. No.
St Florimond	Yes! All right, ask him.
Camaret	(*To Champignol*) Come here. What's your name?
Champignol	(*Aside*) You wait! You wait, Augustus! (*Aloud*) My name is Saint Florimond.
St Florimond	(*Dumbfounded*) What!
Camaret	There! I knew it!
St Florimond	This is too much. *I* am!
Camaret	Not again!
Angele	It's another attack, Captain. (*She goes upstage with Camaret*)
All	(*Also going upstage*) Another attack! (*During the following two lines, Angele, Camaret and Romeo talk quietly together upstage. Dufoulay and Mauricette pass behind them and come downstage to 1 and 2*)
St Florimond	(*Whispering to Champignol*) You dare to say . . .
Champignol	(*Sharply*) Exactly. And I forbid you to deny it, Augustus!
Camaret	(*Coming downstage between Champignol and Saint Florimond. To Saint Florimond*) Well, are you better now? Do you still maintain you're Saint Florimond?
Florimond	You're right, Captain, I am Champignol.
Camaret	(*Triumphant*) There! You see!
Angele	(*Pretending to be overjoyed and coming downstage to 3*) His attack's over at last. (*Romeo comes down to 7*)
Camaret	(*To Champignol*) Oh! . . . Saint Florimond, Saint Florimond! Extraordinary! I haven't got a Saint Florimond in my company.
Champignol	The fact is I'm not a soldier. This uniform was lent to me, because I fell in the river.

Romeo	What!
Camaret	He did too.
Champignol	I was fishing from the bank.
Romeo	You didn't try to jump onto a tree stump that was covered with mud?
Champignol	Exactly. And splash! I fell in.
Romeo	You'll never believe it, but exactly the same thing happened to me.
Champignol	Really?
Romeo	Word of honour!
Camaret	I'll have to do something about that tree stump.

(*Adrienne enters downstage right with Celestin*)

Adrienne	What are you all plotting about?
Camaret	Ah! Good! Here's Adrienne.

(*Adrienne comes downstage to 7, Celestin to 8*)
(*Pointing to Champignol*) Let me introduce Monsieur de Saint Florimond.

Adrienne	(*Aside*) They wanted me to marry him! He's bald!
Camaret	My dear Monsieur de Saint Florimond, I'm sorry to tell you my daughter is engaged to her cousin Celestin.
Champignol	Never mind, Captain, I'm delighted to hear it.
Camaret	Oh! Ah, he's making the best of it. (*To Saint Florimond*) As for you, Champignol, get back to barracks.
St Florimond	(*Aside*) So I've got to take his place for the next month. It's the last time I'll get caught pursuing married women.
Camaret	And don't let me have to tell you again. Your hair's too long. Get it cut.
Champignol	Yes, give him a close shave. That's what I've had.

CURTAIN

Sauce for the Goose
Le Dindon

Translator's Note

This translation was commissioned by the BBC for broadcasting, but I have here ignored my radio adaptation and reverted to the original text. Feydeau's stage directions frequently include the relative positions of the characters, which are numbered from left to right, so that, for example, 1 is always left of 2 but may be anywhere on the stage. Maggie from England has become Heidi from Berlin, to permit the misunderstandings which are essential to the development of the plot in Act II and I am grateful to the BBC for providing the necessary German lines. I have also lightened the tone of the last scenes of Act III, so that, for example, Vatelin does not have to burst into tears.

This translation was first broadcast on 28 August 1972 with the following cast:

Lucienne	*Jill Bennett*
Pontagnac	*John Moffatt*
Vatelin	*Derek Godfrey*
Jean	*Lewis Stringer*
Rédillon	*Basil Moss*
Mme de Pontagnac	*Patricia Routledge*
Heidi	*Eleanor Bron*
Soldignac	*Wilfred Carter*
Armandine	*Adrienne Posta*
Victor	*Christopher Good*
Hotel Manager	*William Sleigh*
Pinchard	*Aubrey Woods*
Clara	*Olwen Griffiths*
Mme Pinchard	*Betty Baskcomb*
Inspector	*Brian Haines*
Gerome	*Rolf Lefebvre*

Produced by Glyn Dearman

Characters
In Order of Appearance

LUCIENNE	*Vatelin's wife*
PONTAGNAC	
VATELIN	
JEAN	*Vatelin's manservant*
REDILLON	
MADAME DE PONTAGNAC	
HEIDI	*Soldignac's wife*
SOLDIGNAC	
ARMANDINE	*A cocotte*
VICTOR	*Pageboy at the Hotel Ultimus*
HOTEL MANAGER	
CLARA	*Chambermaid at the Hotel Ultimus*
PINCHARD	*An Army doctor*
MADAME PINCHARD	*His wife*
1ST POLICE INSPECTOR	
2ND POLICE INSPECTOR	
GEROME	*Rédillon's manservant*
A WAITER, TWO POLICEMEN, HOTEL GUESTS	

ACT I   The Vatelin's flat
ACT II Room 39 at the Hotel Ultimus. That night
ACT III Rédillon's flat. The next morning
        Paris in the Nineties

Act I

(The Vatelins' drawing-room in Paris.
An elegant room with a door in the rear wall, two
doors on the right and two on the left.
When the curtain rises, the stage remains empty for
a moment. Then a noise is heard offstage rear.
Lucienne bursts into the room, terrified. She is wearing
outdoor clothes, with her hat askew. She closes the door
behind her, but not quickly enough to prevent a walking-
stick being thrust through by someone outside)

Lucienne Oh! Heavens! Go away . . . Go away.

Pontagnac *(Off. Trying to push the door open, as Lucienne each*
time manages to push it back) Please! . . . Please!
Do listen . . .

Lucienne Certainly not! . . . How dare you! *(Calling, as she*
struggles with the door) Jean, Jean! . . . Augustine!
Where is everyone?

Pontagnac *(Off)* Please! Please!

Lucienne No! No!

     (Pontagnac finally succeeds in entering)

Pontagnac Do please listen to me.

Lucienne This is outrageous! . . . How dare you! . . . Leave
this house.

Pontagnac Don't be afraid, I won't do you any harm. My
intentions may not be pure, but they're certainly
not hostile . . . Just the opposite. *(He goes towards*
her)

Lucienne *(Backing away)* You must be mad!

Pontagnac *(Pursuing her)* Yes, I am. Mad about you. I know
I'm being very daring, but I don't care. All I know
is I love you and I'll do anything to be with you.

Lucienne *(Stopping)* I won't listen to another word. Leave
this house.

Pontagnac Oh no, anything else but not that! I tell you I love you! (*Pursuing her again*) One look and it was love at first sight. For a week I've followed you everywhere. You must have noticed.

Lucienne (*Stopping in front of the table*) No, no, I haven't.

Pontagnac Yes, you have. A woman always notices when she's being followed.

Lucienne Oh! What nonsense!

Pontagnac It's not nonsense, it's observation.

Lucienne But really, I don't know you.

Pontagnac I don't know you. And it worries me so much, I must do something about it . . . Oh, Madame!

Lucienne Monsieur!

Pontagnac Oh, Marguerite!

Lucienne (*Forgetting*) My name's Lucienne.

Pontagnac Thank you. Oh, Lucienne!

Lucienne What! . . . How dare you!

Pontagnac You've just told me your name.

Lucienne What do you take me for? I'm a respectable woman.

Pontagnac I adore respectable women.

Lucienne I warn you. I wanted to avoid a scandal, but if you refuse to go, I shall call my husband.

Pontagnac Oh! You've a husband?

Lucienne Precisely.

Pontagnac All right! Now let's forget that idiot.

Lucienne Idiot! My husband!

Pontagnac Husbands of attractive women are always idiots.

Lucienne (*Going upstage*) Very well. You'll see how this idiot deals with you. You refuse to go?

Pontagnac More than ever, now.

Lucienne Very well. (*Calling to the right*) Crépin!

Pontagnac What a hideous name!

Lucienne Crépin!

        (*Vatelin enters*)

Vatelin You called me, darling?

Pontagnac (*Aside*) Vatelin! Damnation!

Vatelin (*Recognising him*) Pontagnac! How good to see you!

Lucienne What!

Pontagnac My dear fellow!

Vatelin How are you?

Pontagnac Fine. Fine.

Lucienne (*Aside*) He knows him! (*She goes downstage left, takes off her hat and puts it on the sofa*)

Pontagnac Well! This is a surprise!

Vatelin Surprise? You're in my house, you must have expected to see me.

Pontagnac Eh? . . . No . . . I mean what a surprise for you!

Vatelin Yes, it certainly is.

Lucienne This is going too far. (*To Vatelin*) You mean you know him?

Vatelin Of course I know him.

Pontagnac (*Panic-stricken*) Yes . . . Yes, he . . . (*Losing his head, he takes a coin from his pocket and puts it into Lucienne's hand*) Here, take this; don't breathe a word.

Lucienne (*Appalled*) He gives me twenty francs!

Vatelin (*Not having seen it*) Well, what's the matter with you?

Pontagnac Me? Nothing. What do you think's the matter?
(*Vatelin moves upstage*)

Lucienne (*Quietly*) Take this back. What do you expect me to do with twenty francs?

Pontagnac Oh, I'm terribly sorry. (*Aside*) I don't know what I'm doing. I'm going out of my mind.

Vatelin My dear old friend! You can't imagine how delighted I am. I'd given up all hope of ever seeing you here. You've promised so often, but . . .

Lucienne Yes, you can't thank him enough.
(*Pontagnac bows repeatedly, in a useless attempt to disguise his anxiety*)

Vatelin I know. It's so good of him to come, especially like this.

Lucienne Yes, especially like this! (*She goes to the fireplace*)

Pontagnac You're so kind, both of you. (*Aside*) She doesn't give a damn for me.

Vatelin I was forgetting, you don't know my wife . . . (*Introducing*) Lucienne darling, a great friend of mine, Monsieur de Pontagnac . . . My wife.

Pontagnac How do you do.

Vatelin On second thoughts I don't know if it's very wise to introduce you to him.

Pontagnac Why is that?

Vatelin He's a monster. He can't see a woman without pursuing her. He has to have them all.

Lucienne (*Mockingly*) All! Oh! That's not very flattering for any one of them.

Pontagnac (*To Lucienne*) He's exaggerating. (*Aside*) What a fool to tell her that!

Lucienne (*In front of the fireplace*) How disappointing for the poor woman who thinks she's a special selection and discovers she's only part of a collection!

Pontagnac (*To Lucienne*) I tell you it's quite untrue.

Lucienne I must say, if I were one of these ladies, I wouldn't be exactly proud . . . Won't you sit down? (*She sits in an armchair near the fireplace*)

Pontagnac (*Aside, as he sits on the sofa*) I was right. She's laughing at me.

Vatelin (*Sitting near them*) I don't think she approves of you.

Pontagnac I don't think she does.

Lucienne You men must have a very poor opinion of us, to judge by the way you treat us. If a man pays court to us, he is . . . a courtier. That does imply a certain respect. But men who hope to take us by assault and follow us in the street!

Pontagnac (*Aside*) Oh! Here she goes again!

Vatelin Oh, men who follow you in the street are what? Gigolos, lunatics, dirty old men?

Lucienne (*Very sweetly to Pontagnac*) You tell me.

Pontagnac (*Embarrassed*) I don't know why you ask me . . .

Vatelin Oh, my wife was speaking in general.

Lucienne Naturally.

Pontagnac Oh! Good. (*Aside*) It's amazing what unfortunate conversation some people have.

Lucienne I don't know what you think, but if I were a man, I can't believe I'd want that sort of conquest. Either the woman would turn me down and I'd have wasted my time. Or she'd accept me and I'd immediately lose all desire for her.

Pontagnac (*Embarrassed*) Yes, of course . . . (*Aside*) How much longer are they going on chattering!

Lucienne Yes, but apparently all men don't think that. To judge by the man who keeps following me.

Pontagnac (*Aside*) Oh! She's going too far.

Vatelin (*Rising and going towards his wife*) A man's been following you?

Lucienne The whole time.

Pontagnac (*Rising and coming downstage*) I say, why don't we talk about something else! This conversation's . . .

Vatelin (*Going towards him*) Nonsense, this is interesting. Would you believe it, a man dares to follow my wife!

Pontagnac Oh, very discreetly.

Vatelin How do you know? If a man follows a woman, of course it's not discreetly. (*To Lucienne*) Why didn't you tell me before?

Lucienne There was no need to. He's not at all dangerous.

Pontagnac (*Aside*) Thanks very much!

Vatelin You should have tried to get rid of him. It must be maddening to have someone at your heels the whole time.

Lucienne Oh, maddening!

Vatelin Besides, it's humiliating for me. You should, I don't know, take a cab . . . go into a shop.

Lucienne I did. I went into a cakeshop. He came in after me.

Vatelin If a man's following you, you don't go into a cakeshop, you find a jeweller's. Why didn't you think of a jeweller?

Lucienne I did. He waited outside the door.

Pontagnac (*Aside*) For heaven's sake!

Vatelin Did he? . . . Patient! And practical! (*To Pontagnac*) My dear fellow, would you ever have believed such ill-mannered people exist in Paris?

Pontagnac No. Oh, ill-mannered's rather . . . Hm . . . Let's talk about something else . . .

Vatelin I must say, if a husband can't let his wife leave the house without her being exposed to the advances of a stinking, dirty-minded . . .

(*Lucienne rises and almost immediately goes and sits on the pouffe*)

Pontagnac (*Furious*) Vatelin!

Vatelin Yes?

Pontagnac (*Containing himself*) You're going too far!

Vatelin Nonsense, I couldn't! . . . Oh, I'd like to lay my hands on the swine.

Lucienne (*On the pouffe*) Yes. Well, that's easy, isn't it, Monsieur de Pontagnac?

Pontagnac Well, I . . . Hm . . . What time is it?

Vatelin What! He knows him?

Lucienne Better than anyone! . . . Hm, Monsieur de Pontagnac, tell us his name.

Pontagnac (*In trouble*) Well, I, er, how should I . . . ?

Lucienne Oh yes, oh yes . . . His name is . . . Pon . . . ta . . . let me see, Pontawhat?

Pontagnac Pontawhat. It could be.

Lucienne Pontagnac!

Vatelin Pontagnac! You!

Pontagnac (*With a forced laugh*) Actually, yes . . . It was me. Ha-ha! It was me.

Vatelin (*Roaring with laughter*) You old rogue!
    (*Lucienne rises and goes towards the fireplace*)

Pontagnac Oh, but you see I knew all the time . . .I knew it was your wife, so I thought: Ah! I'll puzzle her a little, I'll pretend to follow her . . .

Lucienne (*Aside*) Oh! I like 'Pretend to'! (*She remains in front of the fireplace*)

Pontagnac . . . and she'll be amazed when we meet face to face in her own house.

Vatelin Yes . . . Rubbish! You knew nothing of the sort. Well, that will teach you to follow women in the street. You find the wife of a friend of yours and you've wasted your time . . . Let that be a lesson to you.

Pontagnac All right. I admit it. You're not angry with me?

Vatelin Of course not . . . You're a friend of mine . . . When this sort of thing happens, what annoys me – because I trust my wife – is I must look a fool. A man follows my wife and I think: he might know who she is. Then he meets me and thinks: oh, that's her husband! And I do look a fool. But now you know I know. I know you know I know. We both know we know we know. So I don't care, I don't look a fool.

Pontagnac Obviously.

Vatelin If anyone could be embarrassed, you could.

Pontagnac Me?

Vatelin Yes, you. It's always embarrassing to make this sort of mistake.

Pontagnac Not this time, because I've had the pleasure of meeting you.

Vatelin A mutual pleasure I assure you.

Pontagnac You're too kind.

Vatelin Not at all.

Lucienne (*Aside*) How very touching, the pair of them!

(*Aloud*) I'm delighted I'm a bond between you.
(*She sits on the sofa*)

Vatelin There's one other thing you have to do: apologise to my wife.

Pontagnac (*To Lucienne*) Forgive me. I'm very much to blame. (*He goes to the fireplace*)

Lucienne Oh, you're all the same, you bachelors!

Vatelin Bachelor! He's married!

Lucienne No!

Vatelin Yes!

Lucienne Married! You're married!

Pontagnac (*Embarrassed*) Yes . . . Slightly . . .

Lucienne But that's dreadful!

Pontagnac Do you think so?

Lucienne It's terrible! . . . How can you . . .

Pontagnac Oh well, you know how it is . . . One fine day you meet in a registry office . . . I don't know, force of circumstances . . . You're asked questions . . . You say 'yes', because everyone expects you to. Then when they've gone, you find you're married. For life!

Lucienne Really! You've no excuse!

Pontagnac (*Sitting in the armchair*) For being married?

Lucienne No, for behaving as you do, when you are married. What does your wife say?

Pontagnac Frankly, I don't keep her informed.

Lucienne Do you think that's an honourable way to behave?

Pontagnac Oh! Oh!

Lucienne Of course. You'd think it wrong to spend the slightest part of your wife's money, but her only other possession, marital fidelity, you hold very cheap. 'Roll up, roll up, what lady would like a taste? Roll up, roll up, there's enough for everyone!' You waste it away. Waste it away. You don't care, your wife pays. Do you think that's honourable?

Pontagnac Really! If it's admitted I'm rich enough to satisfy all marital demands, I think I . . .

Lucienne Really!

Pontagnac Now look, when Rothschild . . .

Lucienne Yes, look! In the first place you're not Rothschild . . . or if you have been, you'd better begin to stop.

Pontagnac What do you know about that?

Vatelin (*Standing next to Lucienne*) She's hard on you.

Lucienne And even if you still are? This is something that isn't yours any more. It's your wife's. You've no right to spend capital you've given to her.

Pontagnac I'm not touching the capital. That remains intact. I'm spending a little of the income. I've placed most of the capital in long-dated stocks; you can't object to my speculating a little with the rest.

Lucienne When you're married, you should invest everything in the family business.

Pontagnac You're talking like a mother-in-law.

Lucienne I'd like to hear what you'd say if your wife did the same.

Pontagnac Oh, that's quite different.

Lucienne (*Rising and coming downstage*) Of course it's quite different. Men always say that. Your wife should lose everything you both have at roulette or twenty-one.

Vatelin (*Coming downstage*) Be careful, Lucienne. Pontagnac's not going to like you, if you go on lecturing him like this.

Lucienne I'm not just talking to him. It applies to you, if you ever decide to follow his example.

Vatelin Me? Oh!

Lucienne You'd be unfortunate if you ever did stray. I wouldn't wait a moment.

Vatelin (*Nodding his head*) Roulette or twenty-one!

Lucienne No need of twenty-one. A single one would be enough.

Pontagnac (*Barely concealing his joy*) Really?

Vatelin That seems to make you happy!

Pontagnac Me? Not at all. I said 'really', meaning 'impossible'.

Lucienne I don't know your wife, but I feel sorry for her.

Pontagnac You needn't tell me that. Every time I'm unfaithful, I feel sorry for her.

Lucienne You must spend a lot of time feeling sorry.

Vatelin Anyway, now you've found your way here, I hope you'll bring your wife. We'd love to meet her.

Pontagnac (*Aside*) My wife! Oh, no! (*Aloud*) Yes, of course, I'd be delighted; and she would too. Unfortunately it's out of the question.

Lucienne Why is that?

Pontagnac Her rheumatism. She's crippled with rheumatism ...

Vatelin Really?

Pontagnac She never goes out. Or if she does, it's in a wheelchair.

Vatelin I'd no idea.

Lucienne How very sad!

Pontagnac Indeed it is.

Vatelin What a pity! Oh! We could go and see her, if you'll let us.

Pontagnac Of course. Certainly.

Vatelin Where does she live?

Pontagnac Bordeaux.

Vatelin That is rather far.

Pontagnac There are fast trains ... Ah well, the South is recommended for her health.

Vatelin We'll have to abandon the idea.

Lucienne I am sorry.

(*Jean enters upstage*)

Jean (*Upstage*) Sir, a picture dealer's arrived with a painting.

Vatelin Ah, my Corot! I bought a Corot yesterday.

Pontagnac Yes?

Vatelin Six hundred francs!

Pontagnac That's not much. It's signed?

  (*Lucienne goes and sits to the right of the desk*)

Vatelin It's signed. It's signed Poitevin, but the dealer guarantees the signature's false.

Pontagnac Is that so?

Vatelin I'll remove Poitevin and be left with the Corot . . . (*To Jean*) I won't be a moment. Show him into the sitting-room . . .

  (*Jean goes out*)

  Forgive me, I shan't be long. I'll have a word with him and then I'll be free. I'll show you my pictures. You're a connoisseur, you can tell me what you think of them.

  (*Vatelin goes out midstage right*)

Lucienne Sit down.

Pontagnac You're not afraid of me any more?

Lucienne You see!

Pontagnac (*Sitting*) I must have seemed ridiculous.

Lucienne (*Smiling*) You think so?

Pontagnac You're laughing at me.

Lucienne Well . . . Tell me, what were you hoping for, when you followed me like that?

Pontagnac What every man hopes for when he follows a woman he doesn't know.

Lucienne You're very frank.

Pontagnac I must say, if I said I followed you to discover your opinion of Voltaire, you probably wouldn't believe me.

Lucienne You rather amuse me. Does this little scheme ever succeed? Are there really women who . . .

Pontagnac Are there . . . Thirty-three and a third per cent!

Lucienne (*Bowing*) Aha! Well, this time you're unlucky, you've met one of the sixty-six and two-thirds.

  (*She rises. He puts down his hat and stick and also rises*)

Pontagnac Please don't say another word about it. If you knew how sad I am!

Lucienne Sad? Are you sure the first letter's correct?

Pontagnac You mean bad? No, I'm not really. I'm just unlucky to be like this. I can't help it. Women are in my blood.

Lucienne Well, the marriage ceremony provided you with one.

Pontagnac My wife, yes. Oh, of course she's charming. But for me she's been charming for so long. She's a book I know from cover to cover.

Lucienne Yes. And it can't be easy to turn the pages now.

Pontagnac Why is that?

Lucienne Her rheumatism.

Pontagnac Since when?

Lucienne You've just told us . . .

Pontagnac (*Quickly*) Oh, my wife, yes, yes . . . At Bordeaux . . . Exactly . . . Yes. Eh?

Lucienne Oh yes . . .

Pontagnac And you say I've no excuse. So when heaven puts in my path a divine, enchanting creature . . .

Lucienne (*Passing to the left*) That's quite enough. I think you've made a sufficient apology.

Pontagnac Go on, admit it. You love another man.

Lucienne This is too impertinent! You won't admit that any woman can be a faithful wife. She only resists you because she loves another man. That's the only possible reason. What kind of women do you mix with?

Pontagnac Listen. Will you promise not to tell anyone what I'm going to say?

Lucienne (*Sitting in the armchair*) Not even my husband.

Pontagnac (*Sitting on the pouffe*) That's all I want. Well . . . I can't believe you really love him.

Lucienne Really! No, go further away.

    (*Pontagnac moves the pouffe towards her*)
    No! I said further away!

Pontagnac (*Moving the pouffe back*) Oh, I'm sorry . . . Of course he's an excellent fellow. I'm very fond of him.

Lucienne I saw that right away.

Pontagnac But frankly he's not a man to inspire passion.

Lucienne (*Severely*) He's my husband.

Pontagnac There, you agree with me.

Lucienne I do not!

Pontagnac Oh yes, you do! If you loved him – and I mean love, not affection – you wouldn't need a reason. When a woman loves, she says 'I love, because I love', not 'Because he's my husband'. Love's a cause not a consequence. It only exists as itself.

Lucienne You're very eloquent.

Pontagnac Being a husband doesn't prove anything. Anyone can be a husband. He needs the same qualifications as a clerk. (*He sits on the pouffe*) But for a lover you need something more. You need passion. The lover's the artist; the husband's a mere craftsman.

Lucienne So you've come here as an artist . . .

Pontagnac Oh, yes . . .

Lucienne Oh, no! No! You may think I'm ridiculous, but I'm happy with a husband who's both craftsman and artist.

Pontagnac That's rare.

Lucienne So I don't desire anything more. As long as he doesn't spread his artistic qualities abroad . . .

Pontagnac Oh? Really, if he ever . . .

Lucienne (*Rising*) That would be a different matter. What's sauce for the goose is sauce for the gander. I'd stop at nothing.

Pontagnac (*Rising*) Oh, thank you.

Lucienne Not at all. I'll never be the first . . . but if ever he . . . Then immediately! . . . As I was saying just now to . . .

Pontagnac (*Seeing she has stopped*) To?

B

Lucienne A niece of mine. She insisted on knowing if I ever
             might one day.

Pontagnac (*Incredulous*) A niece!
             (*Jean enters*)

Jean (*Announcing*) Monsieur Rédillon.
             (*Rédillon enters. Jean goes out*)

Lucienne Come in. Come in. You can help me. (*Introducing*)
             Monsieur Ernest Rédillon, Monsieur de Pontagnac,
             friends of my husband . . . mutually.
             (*The two men bow to each other*)
             Now, you know me, tell this gentleman I'm a model
             wife and I'll never be unfaithful to my husband
             unless he sets me an example.

Rédillon What! Why do you ask me that?

Lucienne Please. This gentleman would like to know.

Rédillon (*Stiffly*) This gentleman? Oh, this gentleman would
             like to . . . A charming conversation, I must say!
             It makes me wonder if I'm not intruding.

Lucienne Of course not. I'm asking for your help.

Pontagnac We were just chatting.

Rédillon Oh, were you? This gentleman is no doubt an old
             friend . . . a close friend, though I've never
             seen him in the house before.

Lucienne Him? I've only known him twenty minutes.

Rédillon Better still! I'm sorry I can't answer your question,
             but I've too much respect for women to discuss
             certain subjects which I'd consider out of place . . .
             in my mouth. (*He goes upstage right*)

Pontagnac (*Aside*) This fellow seems to be trying to teach me
             a lesson.

Rédillon Your husband's not here?

Lucienne Yes, he's having a tête-à-tête with a Corot. I'll go
             and make sure he hasn't got lost in the landscape.
             I've introduced you, now you know each other.
             I'll leave you alone together.

> *(Pontagnac and Rédillon bow. Lucienne goes out right.*
> *The two men secretly size each other up. A pause)*

Pontagnac (*Aside*) That man must be the niece!

> *(Pause. The two men go upstage and look at the*
> *pictures. They come slowly downstage, still looking at*
> *the pictures, one on the right, the other on the left.*
> *From time to time they steal a look, sizing each other*
> *up, but pretending to be indifferent when their eyes*
> *meet. Rédillon reaches the sofa, sits down and starts*
> *whistling)*
>
> (*Seated near the table*) What?

Rédillon Yes?

Pontagnac I thought you said something.

Rédillon No, I didn't.

Pontagnac I'm sorry.

Rédillon Not at all.

> *(Rédillon starts whistling again. Pause. Pontagnac,*
> *irritated, starts to hum a different tune. Rédillon has*
> *taken a newspaper from his pocket and, seated on the*
> *sofa, turns his back on Pontagnac and begins to read*
> *it. Pontagnac sees a magazine on the table and begins*
> *to glance through it. Lucienne enters)*

Lucienne I'm sorry to interrupt your conversation . . .

> *(The two men put down their newspaper and magazine*
> *and rise)*
>
> . . . but my husband is asking for you, Monsieur
> de Pontagnac. He wants to show you his Corot.

Pontagnac Oh! He wants to . . .

Lucienne Through there. Straight ahead.

Pontagnac (*Going in that direction, unenthusiastically*) Through
there?

Lucienne Yes. Well, go on.

Pontagnac (*Picking up his hat and stick which he'd put down on the*
table) Yes, yes . . . (*A pause. To Rédillon*) You
wouldn't like to come with me?

Rédillon   Me?

Lucienne   No, he doesn't like pictures.

Pontagnac   Oh! . . . Oh! . . . Well! (*As he goes out*) I hate leaving them alone together.
> (*Pontagnac goes out midstage right. Rédillon walks angrily up and down the stage*)

Lucienne   (*Charmingly*) Do sit down.

Rédillon   (*Having reached the right*) No, thank you. I came here in my carriage, I need exercise.

Lucienne   (*Going to the fireplace*) What's the matter with you?

Rédillon   Nothing. Do I look as though something's the matter?

Lucienne   (*At the fireplace*) You look like a bear in a cage. Are you angry because he's here?

Rédillon   Me? Ha, what's it to me? Do you think I care about him?

Lucienne   Oh! . . . I thought . . .

Rédillon   Oh! . . . Ha, do I care about . . . (*A pause*) Who the devil is he?

Lucienne   But you don't care!

Rédillon   Oh! Forgive me if I'm being indiscreet.

Lucienne   I forgive you.

Rédillon   Thank you. (*A pause*) Is he pursuing you?

Lucienne   Yes.

Rédillon   How disgusting!

Lucienne   Is it your exclusive privilege?

Rédillon   That's different. I love you.

Lucienne   He might say the same.

Rédillon   For heaven's sake! He's only known you ten minutes!

Lucienne   Twenty.

Rédillon   Oh, ten, twenty, I'm not a stopwatch!

Lucienne   It's true he was . . . introduced twenty minutes ago. But I've known him much longer by sight. For the last week he's been following me in the street.

Rédillon No!

Lucienne Yes!

Rédillon The swine!

Lucienne (*At the fireplace*) Thank you. On his behalf.

Rédillon And your husband thought it amusing to introduce
you!
> (*Lucienne smiles, spreading out her arms, as if to
> confirm it*)

Charming! Oh, husbands! You'd think they do it
on purpose to make their life more difficult.

Lucienne Now look . . .

Rédillon Oh, I'm expressing my thoughts. Then when what
can happen . . . does happen, they start complaining.
Why on earth does he have to bring strange men
into the house? Wasn't he happy with the three of
us on our own? (*He sees that Lucienne is laughing*)
It's a fact. I can't see a man hovering round you
without getting furious. (*One knee on the pouffe*)
But I can't tell your husband that.

Lucienne (*Going to him*) Now stop worrying.

Rédillon Oh, I knew something dreadful would happen
today.
> (*They come downstage*)

I dreamt all my teeth fell out . . . and I'd already
lost forty-five. Whenever I dream my teeth fall out,
something always happens. Last time someone stole
a dog I adored. Now someone's trying to steal my
mistress.

Lucienne I'm not your mistress!

Rédillon You're the mistress of my heart . . . and even you
can't prevent that.

Lucienne Provided you relieve me of all responsibility!

Rédillon Oh, swear you'll never love that man.

Lucienne You're out of your mind! . . . I hardly know him.
I've never even looked at him.

Rédillon Ah, thank you. Have you noticed how unattractive
he is? And his nose! No man with a nose like that
is capable of loving.

Lucienne Oh!

Rédillon I have the right nose. I have the nose for love.

Lucienne How do you know?

Rédillon Everyone's always told me.

Lucienne Oh! In that case . . .

Rédillon Oh, Lucienne, don't forget you promised you'd
never belong to anyone but me.

Lucienne (*Correcting him*) I'm sorry . . . If I ever have to
belong to someone! But for that, I'm afraid, there
would have to be very special circumstances.
(*She sits, right of the table*)

Rédillon (*With a sigh*) Oh, yes. If your husband's unfaithful!
Oh, well! (*Aside*) Then what on earth's that man
waiting for? Has he no feelings, damn him!
(*Aloud*) Don't you realise how you're torturing me?
It's like continually giving a man aperitifs and never
any dinner.

Lucienne I'm sorry, but . . . go and dine somewhere else.

Rédillon I'll have to. What do you expect, I'm made of flesh
and blood! I'm starving, starving . . .

Lucienne Oh, you're so ugly when you start screaming famine.

Rédillon You're laughing at me! (*He goes and sits on the pouffe*)

Lucienne Do you want me to cry? Especially now I know
you're indulging in side dishes. (*She rises*)

Rédillon Oh, my side dishes are stupendous! You can have
them! Oh, if you'd agree, I shouldn't have any.
But you won't. So what do you expect? It's your
misfortune, they reap the benefit.

Lucienne (*Leaning back on the table*) Good. I hope they enjoy it.

Rédillon (*Smugly*) I'll answer for that!

Lucienne (*Going upstage*) And this is the man who's just said
he loves me.

Rédillon   Of course. What difference does that make? It's
             not my fault if besides love there is . . . the beast
             in me.

Lucienne   Ah, yes. Of course. I was surprised you hadn't
             mentioned that. Well, can't you make up your mind
             to kill . . . the beast?

Rédillon   I hate cruelty to animals.

Lucienne   I always knew there was a gay dog in you. Well,
             keep it on a lead.

Rédillon   I do. But it's stronger than I am. It drags me along
             behind. So when I have to, I give in. (*Rising*) I take
             it for a walk. (*He reaches the right*)

Lucienne   Oh, men! Poor Ernest! What's her name? (*She
             sits on the sofa*)

Rédillon   Who?

Lucienne   The object of your walk.

Rédillon   Pluplu . . . short for Pluchette.

Lucienne   Enchanting!

Rédillon   (*Going to her*) Oh, my heart's not involved, you
             know that. Pluplu doesn't mean anything to me.
             There's only one woman in my life, only one. And
             that's you. I may burn incense before other altars;
             the burnt offering is only for you.

Lucienne   What an elegant thought!

Rédillon   My body, my me is with Pluplu but my thoughts
             are with you. When I'm with her, I try to imagine
             it's you. When I put my arms around her, I think
             I'm holding you. I tell her to shut up, so I can't
             hear her voice. I close my eyes and call her Lucienne.

Lucienne   That's false impersonation, I won't have it!
             Doesn't she object?

Rédillon   Pluplu? Certainly not. She feels she has to follow
             suit. She closes her eyes and calls me Clément.

Lucienne   (*Rising and passing to midstage*) Oh! How delightful!
             It's like a play performed by understudies.

Rédillon (*In a burst of passion*) Oh, Lucienne, Lucienne! When will you end this torture? When will you say 'Rédillon, I'm yours. Take me.'?

Lucienne What! If you please!

Rédillon (*Kneeling before her*) Oh, Lucienne, Lucienne, I love you . . .

Lucienne Will you get up! . . . My husband might come in. He's found you on your knees like this twice already.

Rédillon I don't care! Let him come in! Let him see me!

Lucienne Certainly not! I won't have it! What nonsense!
(*She pushes him away so that she can get up, but it makes him fall to the ground in a sitting position. She moves away and sits at the table. Vatelin enters with Pontagnac*)

Vatelin (*Stopping, as he sees Rédillon sitting on the ground*) Well, well, well! Here you are on the floor again!

Rédillon Yes, I am, yes . . . Hm! How are you?

Vatelin Quite well, thank you. It's a complex, is it? (*To Pontagnac*) You'd never believe it, my dear fellow, but there is my friend Rédillon! (*Introducing*) Monsieur Rédillon, Monsieur de Pontagnac.

Pontagnac You needn't bother, it's been done.

Vatelin Has it? I've never seen anyone else like this. It's not as if we're short of chairs, but every time he waits for me in this room, I find him sitting on the floor.

Pontagnac (*Caustically*) Oh!

Rédillon Let me explain . . . Ever since I was a child, I've loved turning somersaults. So whenever I get the chance . . .

Vatelin How extraordinary! I don't believe it. Your grandmother was frightened by a beggar without any legs!

Rédillon (*Getting up*) Ha-ha! Very funny! That's very funny!

Pontagnac	(*Between his teeth, looking at Vatelin*) The man must be blind!
Lucienne	(*Who has risen*) Well, Monsieur de Pontagnac, you've seen my husband's pictures?
Vatelin	Indeed he has. He was enchanted. He said 'No museum has anything like this'. (*To Pontagnac*) Didn't you?
Pontagnac	Yes, yes. (*Aside*) Luckily for them! (*The bell rings*)
Vatelin	(*Pointing upstage left*) I've some more in there . . . if you'd like to . . .
Pontagnac	No, no. Not too many delights on one day! I'd rather keep some for another time.
Vatelin	What a pity your wife's so ill, I'd have been proud to show her my collection.
Pontagnac	Yes, there we are . . . her rheumatism . . . in Bordeaux.
Vatelin	Her wheelchair, yes, yes. Oh, poor thing!
All	(*With a sigh*) Oh, yes. (*Jean enters upstage*)
Jean	(*Announcing*) Madame de Pontagnac.
All	What!
Pontagnac	(*Leaping in the air, aside*) Oh, no! My wife!
All	Your wife!
Pontagnac	Eh? . . . Yes! . . . No! . . . Apparently!
Lucienne	I thought she was in Bordeaux.
Vatelin	Because of her rheumatism.
Pontagnac	Well, yes . . . I don't know . . . She must have been cured! . . . (*To Jean*) We're out! . . . Say we're out!
Lucienne	Of course not. Show her in. (*Jean goes out*)
Pontagnac	Yes, that's what I said. Show her in. (*Aside*) Oh dear, oh dear, oh dear!
All	(*Aside*) What's the matter with him?

Rédillon (*Aside*) The little man doesn't seem very happy.

Pontagnac (*Aside*) Oh, now I'm for it! (*Aloud*) Please, all of you, I'll explain why later, but if my wife asks questions, not a word . . . No, no . . . I mean, say whatever I say, eh? Say what I say!

(*Madame de Pontagnac enters*)

Mme Pont. (*As she enters*) Do forgive me . . .

Pontagnac (*Running to her*) Ah, darling, here you are! What a delightful surprise! . . . I was just leaving. So say goodbye and let's go. Come along, let's go.

All What!

Mme Pont. Certainly not! What an extraordinary idea!

Pontagnac Yes, yes!

Mme Pont. No, no!

Lucienne Now stop it, please.

Pontagnac All right, I'll stop. (*Aside*) Oh dear, oh dear, oh dear!

Mme Pont. (*Sitting on a chair which Vatelin moves forward for her. To Lucienne*) Do forgive me for coming to your house like this, without being introduced.

Lucienne (*Seated*) No, we're delighted to . . .

Vatelin (*One knee on the pouffe*) Of course . . .

Mme Pont. But my husband's talked about you for so long . . .

Vatelin Really? . . . Ah, Pontagnac, how nice of you!

Mme Pont. So I said to myself: 'Things can't go on like this. Two such close friends! And their wives don't know each other!'

Vatelin Close friends!

Mme Pont. Oh, my husband's so fond of you, I was beginning to get jealous. Every day the same story! 'Where are you going?' . . . 'To the Vatelins.' And at night: 'Where are you going?' . . . 'To the Vatelins.' The Vatelins all the time!

Vatelin What do you mean?

Pontagnac Yes, naturally, yes! Eh? Why are you so surprised?

	(*Sharply to his wife*) You haven't seen his pictures, have you? Come and see his pictures. They're marvellous! Come and see his pictures.
Mme Pont.	No, no! . . . What is the matter with you?
Pontagnac	Me? Oh, nothing. What do you think's the matter?
Vatelin	What does all this mean?
Rédillon	(*Seated in the armchair. Aside*) I'm enjoying this. I'm really enjoying this.
Mme Pont.	Ah-ha! You seem very anxious . . . Would you by any chance . . .
Pontagnac	Me? Anxious? Anxious? I'm not anxious . . . But you keep on telling the Vatelins I come here every day. They know I come here every day!
Lucienne	(*Aside*) Ah-ha!
Vatelin	(*Aside*) Ah! I understand.
Pontagnac	(*To Vatelin, signalling to him all the time*) Well, Vatelin, you know I come here every day, don't you?
Vatelin	Yes. Yes. Yes. Yes. Yes.
Pontagnac	There, you see!
Rédillon	(*Rising and intervening ironically*) I've met him here too.
Pontagnac	(*Astonished. Aside*) Eh? . . . (*Quietly*) Thank you very much.
Rédillon	(*Quietly*) Not at all. (*He sits down again*)
Pontagnac	There! Are you convinced now?
Mme Pont.	(*Doubtfully as she rises*) Yes. Yes. Yes. (*She moves to the left*)
Pontagnac	Well, really!
Vatelin	(*Aside*) Poor Pontagnac, I feel sorry for him. (*Quietly*) I'll get you out of this.
Pontagnac	Oh! Yes!
Vatelin	(*To Mme de Pontagnac*) When your husband's here, he talks about you so much.
Mme Pont.	Oh, really!

Pontagnac	(*Aside*) That's it! Fine!
Vatelin	I'd have asked him to introduce us a long time ago, if you hadn't been in Bordeaux.
Mme Pont.	Bordeaux?
Pontagnac	(*Aside*) Enough of this. (*Aloud, as he twirls Vatelin round to put himself between him and his wife*) No! No! Bordeaux? Where's Bordeaux? What are you up to with Bordeaux?
Vatelin	What am I up to with . . .?
Pontagnac	Yes, yes! Whoever mentioned Bordeaux?
Vatelin	(*Trying to put things right*) No, Bordeaux . . . I said Bordeaux . . . I mean . . . If I'd known you were . . . you were . . .
Pontagnac	Nowhere!
Vatelin	(*Completely lost*) Exactly. That you were nowhere.
Pontagnac	Of course, of course! (*Aside*) Do shut up.
Vatelin	With pleasure. I don't know what I'm saying. (*They go upstage*)
Rédillon	(*Aside*) What a mess they're in!
Mme Pont.	(*Aside*) I'm beginning to believe my suspicions were right. (*Aloud*) Oh, Monsieur Vatelin, don't apologise. I didn't expect you to call, my husband's told me about your condition.
Pontagnac	(*Aside*) Here we go again!
Vatelin	My condition?
Mme Pont.	Yes. Crippled with rheumatism.
Vatelin	I know you are.
Mme Pont.	Me? No, you! You're confined to a wheelchair!
Vatelin	I'm sorry, but you are!
Mme Pont.	No, you are!
Pontagnac	(*Going to Vatelin*) Of course you are, old man! There's no need to pretend in front of my wife.
Vatelin	Oh, I am! . . . Yes, yes! . . . I am too!
Pontagnac	No, no, you aren't too! (*Dragging Vatelin to the left*) Look, come and show me your pictures . . . I

	haven't seen them all . . . I haven't seen them all.
Vatelin	Ah! Delighted! Let's go and see the pictures.
Mme Pont.	Edmond! Stay here!
	(*Lucienne rises*)
Pontagnac	I won't be long! I won't be long!
Vatelin	We won't be long! We won't be long!
	(*Vatelin and Pontagnac go out left*)
Mme Pont.	Oh, this is too much! Tell me the truth. They're trying to make a fool of me?
Lucienne	Well, yes, they are.
	(*Mme de Pontagnac collapses into the chair next to the pouffe*)
	Men support each other so faithfully, we women should do the same. Yes, they are trying to make a fool of you. (*She sits*)
Mme Pont.	Oh, I knew it!
Lucienne	Our husbands are not close friends, they belong to the same club, that's all. Your husband's never set foot in this house before today. You've only found him here now because he came to see a woman he'd followed in the street.
Mme Pont.	A woman!
Lucienne	Yes, me.
Mme Pont.	No!
Lucienne	He followed me as outrageously as a . . .
Rédillon	(*In his armchair*) Skunk!
Mme Pont.	Oh! Yes!
Lucienne	Then he was disappointed to find I was the wife of one of his friends. It was bad luck. But never mind. Your husband's lied to you. His imaginary visits here were just an alibi for his love affaires.
Mme Pont.	Oh! The swine!
Rédillon	Precisely.
Lucienne	(*Rising*) Forgive me for speaking so brutally, but you asked me to be frank with you.

Mme Pont. (*Rising*) You were quite right. I'm very grateful.

Lucienne I've spoken to you as I'd hope anyone would speak to me if ever my husband . . .

Rédillon (*Despondently*) Oh, yes! But he never will.

Lucienne Fortunately, you should add.

Mme Pont. Now I understand. My suspicions were right. Oh! Now I know what I wanted to know. It's war between us. I'll say nothing, I'll spy on him, I'll have him followed, I'll catch him redhanded and then . . . (*She comes downstage*)

Lucienne And then?

Mme Pont. (*Picking up the chair and taking it upstage near the sofa*) Ah-ha, I leave that to your imagination!

Lucienne Retaliation in kind?

Mme Pont. Precisely.

Rédillon (*Rising*) Bravo!

Lucienne (*Getting excited, following Mme de Pontagnac's example*) Oh! So would I! If ever my husband . . .

Rédillon Yes! Yes!

Mme Pont. Why shouldn't I? I'm young, I'm pretty!

Lucienne So am I!

Mme Pont. Though it may not be modest to say so.

Rédillon Never mind, when you're angry, there's no need to be modest.

Mme Pont. After all, I'd find lots of men who'd be delighted . . .

Rédillon (*Enthusiastically*) Yes! Yes!

Lucienne So would I! Wouldn't I, Rédillon?

Rédillon Oh, you! Yes, yes, yes!

Mme Pont. And don't think I'd be particular. Just the opposite! That would prevent me really savouring my revenge. No! Anybody! The first poor fool I saw!

Rédillon That's right!

Mme Pont. (*To Rédillon*) You! If you like! (*She goes upstage*)

Rédillon Me? Oh, Madame . . .

Lucienne I agree. Me, too!

Rédillon Oh, Lucienne!

Mme Pont. (*Coming downstage*) What's your name? And address?

Rédillon Rédillon, 17 Rue Caumartin.

Mme Pont. Rédillon, 17 Rue Caumartin. Good! Well, Monsieur Rédillon, when I catch my husband, I'll come straight to you and say: Monsieur Rédillon, take me, I'm yours! (*She falls into his arms*)

Lucienne (*Doing the same*) So will I, Rédillon! I'm yours! Yours!

Rédillon (*Both women in his arms*) Oh, ladies! . . . (*Aside*) It's amazing how my opportunities always have conditions attached.

    (*Voices off*)

Mme Pont. Our husbands! Not a word!

    (*Vatelin and Pontagnac enter apprehensively and stand in the doorway with a woeful look*)

    Come in, come in. Why do you stand there in the doorway?

Vatelin No reason. No reason at all.

Mme Pont. Well, you've seen the pictures? You liked them?

Pontagnac Enormously. Enormously. (*Aside, reassured*) Mme Vatelin hasn't said anything. (*Aloud*) There are some paintings . . . Oh! . . . Such paintings! Related to great masters! . . .

Vatelin Oh, yes!

Pontagnac There's one by Corot's son. And another by Poussin's cousin. It's really not worth having the masters themselves.

Vatelin That's what I say. They're just as well painted. Usually much more carefully.

Rédillon And much cheaper!

Mme Pont. Well, in the meantime I've been getting to know Mme Vatelin. We've been talking about you.

Pontagnac (*Anxious*) Oh?

Mme Pont. This gentleman was saying how often he'd met

you here. And how much he liked you.

Pontagnac No! He said that? (*To Rédillon*) Thank you. (*Aside*) And I thought he . . . (*Aloud*) Darling . . . Monsieur Dodillon.

Rédillon Rédillon! Ré! Ré!

Pontagnac Oh, I'm sorry . . . Rédillon . . . Do, ré, mi, what's the difference! Monsieur Rédillon, Mme de Pontagnac.

Mme Pont. We've had time to get to know each other.
(*She goes upstage of the table with Lucienne*)

Pontagnac Have you? Good! . . . (*To Rédillon*) My dear fellow, my wife's at home every Friday, if you'd care to honour us . . .

Rédillon How delightful! (*Aside*) Marvellous! A moment ago he was the lover and cold-shouldered me. His wife arrives, so he becomes the husband and issues invitations. They're all alike!
(*Jean enters*)

Jean A lady's asking for you, sir.

Vatelin (*Going upstage and putting the chair in its place*) For me? Who is it?

Jean I don't know. I've never seen her before.

Lucienne A lady? What does she want?

Vatelin (*With the gesture of a man who doesn't want to know any more*) Oh, my dear . . . (*To Jean*) You should have asked her name.

Lucienne (*To Jean*) Is she pretty?

Jean (*Making a face*) Mmmm!

Vatelin Jean, really! Please, darling, it's not the servants' business to express opinions about our visitors.
(*To Jean*) You said I was in?

Jean Yes. She's waiting in the sitting-room.

Vatelin All right, let her wait. I'll see her in a moment.
(*Jean goes out upstage*)

Mme Pont. Well, Monsieur Vatelin, I see you're busy, I won't

	waste your time . . . especially as you have to see a lady!
Vatelin	Oh, she must be a client . . . There's no hurry. She's obviously come to see the lawyer, not the man.
Lucienne	So I should hope!
Mme Pont.	Goodbye, Madame Vatelin . . . So happy to have met you. And Monsieur . . . er . . .
Pontagnac	Rédillon.
Rédillon	17 Rue Caumartin, exactly.
Mme Pont.	Of course. (*To Pontagnac*) Make a note of that, dear.
Rédillon	It's in the Directory.
Pontagnac	Never mind, I always write it down.
Rédillon	I'll come with you. I've some shopping to do. (*To Lucienne*) Goodbye, Madame. (*Whispering*) Goodbye, Lucienne darling. . . . (*To Vatelin*) Goodbye, old man.
Pontagnac	Come along, let's go . . . (*He shakes Vatelin's hand, then Lucienne's. Aside, quickly*) I'll take my wife home. Then I'll come back and explain.
Mme Pont.	You're coming?
Pontagnac	Yes. Yes.
Mme Pont.	(*Aside*) Now, you be careful!
	(*Pontagnac and Mme de Pontagnac go out*)
Vatelin	Will you leave me for a moment, darling, while I get rid of this woman. (*He rings the bell*)
Lucienne	Very well . . .Don't be long.
	(*Lucienne takes her hat from the sofa and goes out left. Jean enters*)
Jean	You rang, sir?
Vatelin	Yes. Show the lady in.
	(*Jean shows in Heidi midstage right, then goes out. Vatelin is seated at the table, trying to appear busy sorting his papers. He does not look up*)
	If you'll take a chair . . .

C

Heidi (*Coming from behind and giving him two big kisses on his eyes. Strong German accent*) Ach! Mein Liebling!

Vatelin (*Rising, dumbfounded*) What! (*Recognising her*) Madame Soldignac! Heidi! Ho! You!

Heidi In person!

Vatelin You! Here! You're out of your mind!

Heidi Why?

Vatelin Well . . . Berlin?

Heidi I've left it.

Vatelin And your husband?

Heidi I've brought him with me. He's in Paris on business.

Vatelin (*Falling back into his chair*) Well! . . . What have you come for?

Heidi Really! What have I come for! Ach, du undankbarer Kerl! Wie kannst du das von mir verlangen? Ich habe alles für dich aufgegeben . . . meinen Gatten betrogen . . .

Vatelin (*Rising and trying to interrupt her*) Yes . . . Yes . . . (*He goes and listens at his wife's door*)

Heidi (*Reaching the right*) Ich fahre weg von Berlin! Ich komme über die Grenze! Um bei dir zu sein! Und wenn ich dich endlich finde, dann fragst du mich warum bist du gekommen!

Vatelin (*Coming downstage*) Yes . . . I'm not asking that! You're talking German and I can't understand a word. How are you here? Why? What do you want?

Heidi (*Behind the table*) What do I want? He asks me what I want! I want . . . you!

Vatelin Me?

Heidi Yes. Because I love you still. Oh! To find you, I left Berlin, I crossed the frontier. Trains make me so ill. . . . I was trainsick . . . I brought up . . . brought up . . . what's the word . . .

Vatelin Yes, yes, never mind, what happened next?

Heidi . . . brought up my whole life before my eyes.
I said I'm going to see him . . . and here I am. For
seven days! (*She sits*)

Vatelin (*Falling into a chair*) Seven days! . . . A week! . . .
You're here for a week!

Heidi Yes, a week, just for you . . . Oh, tell me you still
love me . . . Why haven't you answered my
letters? . . . I thought 'My Crépin doesn't love me
any more' . . . Oh yes, you love me! . . . Oh,
Crépin, sag mir dass du mich liebst!

Vatelin (*Rising*) Yes, of course. Of course.

Heidi (*Rising and coming downstage*) When I arrived this
morning, I wrote to you at once . . . and then,
then . . . I didn't send the letter . . . I thought you
might not answer . . . so I threw it in the waste
paper basket . . . I took a cab . . . Oh, it's so difficult
. . . finding the street . . . I don't know, the driver
couldn't understand . . . he wouldn't bring me!

Vatelin (*Aside*) Sensible fellow!

Heidi I said 'Driver, Rue Tremol!' He said 'Never heard
of it!'

Vatelin Rue Tremol! Yes, yes . . . Now if you'd said Rue
La Trémoille . . .

Heidi That's what I did say, 'Rue Tremol'.

Vatelin I see.

Heidi Oh, Crépin, Crépin, I'm so happy! You will come
and see me this evening, won't you?

Vatelin Eh? Now look . . .

Heidi Oh, don't say nein. This morning I found a little
furnished flat, as I said in the letter I threw in the
waste paper basket . . . 6 und 20 Rue Roquépein.

Vatelin You're staying in the Rue Roquépein?

Heidi Oh no, with my husband at the Hotel Chatham.
The flat's for us! I've leased it. You'll come this
evening, eh?

Vatelin (*Releasing himself and crossing to 2*) Me! Oh, no! No!

Heidi Nein? Why nein?

Vatelin Because . . . Because I can't . . . I'm not free. I've a wife. I'm married.

Heidi You're married!

Vatelin Of course I am!

Heidi Oh! But in Berlin you said you had no vife alife!

Vatelin Well, in Berlin I had no vife alife.

Heidi What do you mean?

Vatelin I have one in Paris!

Heidi Then . . . Then . . . it's all finished between us?

Vatelin Now look, Heidi, be sensible.

Heidi And you'll never love me again . . . ever?

Vatelin Yes, next time I'm in Berlin. There!

Heidi (*Bursting into tears and crossing to 2*) Oh! Crépin doesn't love me any more! Crépin doesn't love me!

Vatelin (*Running to Lucienne's door*) Do be quiet! My wife might hear you!

Heidi I don't care!

Vatelin (*Coming downstage*) Yes, but I do! Now look, please try to be sensible. I'm very touched, of course, but our affaire in Berlin couldn't possibly last for ever. We met on the train. You were trainsick. I was trainsick. We were so ill, we were destined to understand each other. And we did. In Berlin you came to my hotel every day, I met your husband, he became a friend of mine, what had to happen did happen. Well! Let's be happy with the memory of those wonderful days, without trying to start all over again. Besides, here I've no right to . . . there I had an excuse. There are things you can do on one side of a frontier, you can't do on the other . . . The Rhine stood between my wife and me. Here it doesn't. So follow my example . . . Make

a sacrifice . . . Forget me. There are other attractive
men in Berlin.

Heidi Oh, no! No, I couldn't . . . I'm a faithful wife . . .
I've had one lover, I shan't have others.

Vatelin Of course. Yes, faithful . . . yes, up to a certain
point, because after all . . . your husband . . .

Heidi It is ever the same!

Vatelin Splendid!

Heidi Nein, nein! Only one husband! Only one lover!

Vatelin All right. If it's a principle!

Heidi (*Suddenly*) Oh, Crépin . . . Crépin! You don't want
me any more?

Vatelin Now look . . . You must understand!

Heidi Jawohl! . . . Goodbye, Crépin.

Vatelin (*Going to open the door upstage*) Goodbye, goodbye.
This way.

Heidi (*Falling into a chair*) Oh, I suspected this! When you
didn't answer my letters . . . So I wrote my husband
a note. Now I'll send it to him.

Vatelin Ah-ha?

Heidi (*Producing a letter and reading it*) Leb wohl mein
Geliebter, vergiss mich. Ich bin eine schuldige
Frau und für mich gibt es nichts mehr als der Tod.
Ich war die Geliebte von Monsieur Vatelin, 8 und 40
Tremol Strasse, der mich verlassen hat. Und jetzt
werde ich mir das leben nehmen.

Vatelin Yes, well that's fine. You send it to him . . . What
does it say?

Heidi You don't understand? Oh! (*Translating*) Goodbye
darling, forget me. I am a guilty woman. Nothing
remains but death. . .

Vatelin Eh?

Heidi I have been the mistress of Monsieur Vatelin,
8 und 40 Rue Tremol . . .

Vatelin What! My name! You can't! My address too!

Heidi   He has . . . He has . . . what's the word? . . .
      ditched me. I am killing myself.

Vatelin   (*Coming downstage to her*) You're out of your mind!
      You're not going to send him that?

Heidi   Ach! Ja!

Vatelin   I won't let you! . . . Kill yourself! And with my
      name and address . . . 48 Rue . . .

Heidi   Tremol . . .

Vatelin   Tremol, yes . . . Oh, what a mess! Heidi, Heidi,
      darling . . .

Heidi   (*Rising and passing to the left*) It's not Heidi darling
      any more.

Vatelin   This is ridiculous. Heidi, you won't do it!

Heidi   Then come this evening, 6 und 20 Rue Roquépein.

Vatelin   I keep on telling you I can't! What excuse can I
      give my wife?

Heidi   Nein? Very well, I'll kill myself.

Vatelin   Ohhh! Well, yes, all right, I will!

Heidi   Ja? Ah! So you'll love me again?

Vatelin   So I'll love you again, all right! (*Aside, furiously*)
      Ohhh!

Heidi   Oh, I'm so happy! Crépin, I love you!
      (*Bell rings*)

Vatelin   (*Aside*) Oh, what a leech! Why can't she stay in
      Berlin?
      (*Jean enters upstage*)

Jean   A gentleman's asking for you, sir.

Vatelin   Who is it?

Jean   Herr Soldignac.

Heidi   My husband!

Vatelin   Oh no! (*To Jean*) All right, I'll be free in a
      moment.
      (*Jean goes out*)
      What has he come for?

Heidi   I don't know. To say hullo, as he's in Paris.

Vatelin   Anyway he mustn't see you! Go out this way. (*He points to the door downstage right and shows her towards it*)

Heidi   All right. This evening then.

Vatelin   Yes, yes.

Heidi   6 und 20 Rue Roquépein.

Vatelin   Rue Roquépein. Do go. . . .

Heidi   I'm going . . . I'm going . . . Oh, you wicked boy! Ich liebe dich.
     (*Heidi goes out right*)

Vatelin   Oh, all this from one small slip! . . . The only time since I've been married . . . and the frontier was a reason . . . Ah well, there we are!
     (*Lucienne enters*)

Lucienne   The lady's gone?

Vatelin   Yes, yes.

Lucienne   Who's that at the door?

Vatelin   A man I knew in Berlin.
     (*Jean enters*)

Jean   Herr Soldignac.
     (*Soldignac enters. He has a German accent. Jean goes out*)

Soldignac   Well, hullo! How are you!

Vatelin   (*Shaking his hand*) I'm fine. What a nice surprise!
     (*Soldignac bows to Lucienne*)
     Darling, Herr Soldignac.

Lucienne   How do you do.

Soldignac   Your wife, I presume. Oh, fine, fine! (*Sitting*) My dear fellow, I've only looked in for a moment. I'm so rushed, you know, an evening, if you like, I could spare, but during the day . . . business is business, geschäft ist geschäft, as we say in Germany. (*Rising*) So I've just come to say hullo. And about my wife.

Vatelin   (*Seated at his desk*) Your wife's well?

Soldignac Very well, thank you. She asked me to do so many things . . . But it's because of her I'm here! My dear fellow, you'll never believe it, but I've discovered I'm a cuckoo.

Vatelin Cuckwhat?

Soldignac Not cuckwhat, cuckoo . . . My wife's unfaithful!

Vatelin Oh, a cuckold. What!

Lucienne (*Rising*) I'm sorry, I must be in the way. I'll leave you two alone.

Soldignac Oh no, I don't mind, I'm very philosophical. But I'm in a hurry, I've so much to do . . . (*Sitting*) Well, this morning I discovered the truth. I found this letter in my wife's wastepaper basket.

Vatelin (*Aside*) Oh no! The letter she wrote me! If only I'm not mentioned!

Soldignac 'Mein Herz . . .'

Vatelin (*Aside, reassured*) Herz! . . . It's someone else.

Soldignac 'I'm in Paris . . . So we can love each other again.' You understand?

Vatelin Yes, yes.

Soldignac 'Tonight my husband . . .' That's me. '. . . will be working late. I'm alone, come to me, 26 Rue Roquépein . . . I'll be waiting for you. Heidi.' What do you make of that?

Vatelin Well, you know, you mustn't make too much of it . . . at first sight . . . Perhaps it doesn't really mean anything.

Soldignac (*Rising*) Nonsense! Well, we shall see. I've been to the police station . . . And tonight, I don't know who her Herz is, but I'll catch the pair of them, her and her Herz, at 26 Rue Roquépein.

Vatelin (*Aside*) Oh no! Well, thank heavens he's warned me!

Soldignac (*To Lucienne*) Don't you agree?

Lucienne (*Rising*) Well, really, I must say . . .

Soldignac Yes. And then I'll divorce her.

Vatelin (*Rising*) Divorce her?

Soldignac Oh, yes . . . I shan't be sorry. She gets on my nerves. She has such a temper, I can't attend to my business. So I've come to see you as a lawyer, to ask you to start preparing my divorce.

Vatelin Me!

Soldignac (*Going upstage and taking his hat*) Yes. Because I'm in a hurry.

Vatelin It's nothing to do with me . . . How can I . . . You must do it in Berlin.

Soldignac Why Berlin? I'm not really from Berlin.

Vatelin Oh?

Soldignac Nein, I'm from Marseilles.

Vatelin
Lucienne } Marseilles?

Soldignac Yes, Marius Soldignac from Marseilles, but I was brought up in Germany and I've lived there ever since for my business. I was married at the French Consulate there, so you can deal with the divorce.

Vatelin Oh! So you want me . . .

Soldignac Of course. Because I'm French!

Vatelin Yes, yes, yes . . . (*Aside*) I have to . . . Oh, this is the limit!

Soldignac That's settled then? . . . I'm sorry, but I'm in a hurry.

Vatelin (*Aside*) After all, what do I risk? (*Aloud*) All right, that's settled, but on one condition . . . you must catch your wife with her lover.

Soldignac Of course. I will tonight at 26 Rue Roquépein.

Vatelin (*Aside*) Yes, but you won't catch me there!

Soldignac And when I lay my hands on him, I look forward to giving him a little boxing lesson.

Vatelin Oh, you're an expert in . . .

Soldignac Me? Very expert . . . My wife is too. I taught

	her . . . I once fought the German champion. I hit him so hard, he went straight over the frontier.
Lucienne	Oh, oh, oh!
Soldignac	It's a fact . . . On the next train.
Vatelin	Oh, I see.
Lucienne	You have such a Mediterranean way of exaggerating.
Soldignac	Well, I may have to eat sauerkraut, but I spice it full of garlic.
Lucienne	How poetical!
Soldignac	(*Changing his tone*) Nein, I've no time, I'm in a hurry, Geschäft ist Geschäft, as we say in Berlin. Goodbye . . . And as for this man tonight . . . (*Making a boxing movement*) . . . Aha! Goodbye.
	(*He goes upstage and bumps into Pontagnac who enters*)
Pontagnac	Oh! I'm sorry.
Soldignac	Yes, hullo . . . I'm in a hurry.
Vatelin	Pontagnac, just in time! . . . (*To Lucienne*) Will you take Herr Soldignac to the door, I must have a word with Pontagnac.
Lucienne	Of course.
	(*Lucienne and Soldignac go out*)
Pontagnac	Who's that little bundle of energy?
Vatelin	No one. A German from Marseilles. My dear fellow, I'm delighted to see you. You can do something for me.
Pontagnac	Me?
Vatelin	Yes. As man to man . . . Tonight I've a rendezvous with a lady.
Pontagnac	You have! I don't believe it!
Vatelin	That's the way it is.
Pontagnac	You're being unfaithful to your wife?
Vatelin	Circumstances sometimes force a husband to . . .
Pontagnac	(*Aside, delighted*) He's unfaithful to his wife and he confides in me!
Vatelin	Well . . . we had a rendezvous and there are pressing

	reasons why we can't go there. Now you know these things, could you tell me some hotel where I could . . .
Pontagnac	Of course, of course . . . The Continental, the Grand Hotel. Ah, the Ultimus! That's where I always go. Very convenient, several exits . . . Send them a telegram and book a room for this evening.
Vatelin	Thank you, my dear fellow, thank you. I'll send one right away . . . and to the lady to tell her the room's in my name.
Pontagnac	That's right. Is your wife going away?
Vatelin	Oh, that's no worry. I often have to leave Paris on business. I'll say I'm called to the country for a will, a contract, anything.
Pontagnac	Splendid, splendid!
Vatelin	Excuse me, I'll go and send the telegram.
	(*Vatelin goes out right*)
Pontagnac	He's going to be unfaithful! This is marvellous!
	(*Lucienne enters upstage*)
Lucienne	Extraordinary man, that German!
Pontagnac	Oh, Lucienne! . . . I'm sorry . . . Madame Vatelin! Come here, quickly!
Lucienne	Why, what is it?
Pontagnac	Well, you see . . . (*Aside*) Oh, no, no, I can't!
Lucienne	Well, you see . . . Is that all?
Pontagnac	(*Aside*) Well, after all, why not? . . . I don't owe him anything. He's no friend of mine. Besides, love comes first.
Lucienne	Well, you see . . . ?
Pontagnac	You always keep your word, don't you? You really did say 'I'll never be the first to be unfaithful, but if my husband ever starts, I'll do the same. Without hesitation.'
Lucienne	Yes, of course I said that.

Pontagnac You really mean it? You'll be unfaithful as soon as you have the evidence?

Lucienne Indeed I will. Immediately.

Pontagnac Marvellous! Well, I have the evidence. Tonight at the Hotel Ultimus, your husband and another woman . . .

Lucienne No, no, you're lying!

Pontagnac Lying? . . . He's about to come in here and tell you he's had a telegram calling him into the country. For a will or a contract.

Lucienne It can't be true. Crépin! No!

Pontagnac Crépin! Yes!

Lucienne It could be. Oh, if you can prove it! If you can prove it!

Pontagnac Tonight I'll wait till he goes out, then I'll collect you and take you to the scene of the crime. The Hotel Ultimus. Agreed?

Lucienne (*Passing to the left*) Oh yes! Oh yes!

Pontagnac Here he comes. Keep calm. (*He reaches the right*) (*Vatelin enters*)

Vatelin Ah, darling, there you are. A maddening thing's happened.

Lucienne Oh, really? What is that?

Pontagnac (*Aside*) Go on, my boy, go on.

Vatelin A telegram, just imagine, a telegram! I must leave Paris tonight by the eight o'clock train.

Lucienne (*Aside*) It *was* true!

Vatelin To go to Amiens for the reading of a will.

Lucienne (*Aside*) Oh, the brute! (*Aloud*) Can't one of your clerks go instead?

Vatelin Oh, no. Impossible. They want me to go myself.

Lucienne Very well, dear. You must go. Geschäft ist Geschäft, as your German friend says.

Vatelin Yes, I know. Oh, I'm furious.

Lucienne (*Aside*) Yes, you hypocrite!

Vatelin   Excuse me, I must send some telegrams.
            (*Vatelin goes out right*)
Pontagnac Well? Are you satisfied?
Lucienne Oh! . . . I see it all! . . . Oh, the brute! . . . I
            thought he was one of those rare faithful husbands.
            And now! Like all the rest! Right, Monsieur de
            Pontagnac, I'll expect you this evening and, if what
            you say is true, oh I promise you, yes, I promise
            you . . . I'll be revenged. Within the hour. Sauce
            for the goose!
Pontagnac Oh, thank you . . . (*Aside*) I am playing a dirty
            trick . . . But I have an excuse. To get his wife!
            (*Aloud*) I'll see you this evening.
                (*Pontagnac goes out quickly upstage*)
Lucienne (*Going towards her room*) This evening!

CURTAIN

Act II

(*Room 39 at the Hotel Ultimus.*
A large room, comfortably furnished. In the back wall,
a bed in an alcove, with the door into the corridor on
the left. Downstage left a door into Room 38. A
fireplace midstage left. Upstage right a door into the
bathroom. A table in the centre of the stage.
When the curtain rises, Armandine is standing at the
table, closing a travelling bag. There is a knock at
the door)

Armandine Come in!
> (*Victor enters. He is 17; pageboy's uniform*)
> Ah, there you are! Did you do as I said?

Victor Oh, yes. The manager's coming up right away.

Armandine You explained about changing my room?

Victor Yes, yes. Anyway he knew, the chambermaid had told him.

Armandine Good. Thank you. (*Aside*) He's rather sweet! (*Aloud*) Come over here.

Victor Yes?

Armandine How old are you?

Victor Seventeen.

Armandine Seventeen! You know, you're rather sweet!

Victor (*Blushing and looking at the ground*) Oh!

Armandine Does that make you blush? I think you like it.

Victor Oh! . . . Yes! . . . From you! (*He closes his eyes, not daring to say any more*)

Armandine (*Patting his face*) Well, I won't deny it, you're very sweet!
> (*As Armandine's hand passes across his mouth, he loses his head, seizes her hand in both of his and kisses it frantically*)
> Well! What does this mean?

Victor Oh! Forgive me.

Armandine You're not exactly shy, are you?

Victor Oh, I didn't know what I was doing. I haven't hurt you?

Armandine (*Reaching the right*) Not too much . . . Some sorts of impertinence don't hurt women.

Victor You won't tell the manager? I'd be thrown into the street.

Armandine (*Laughing*) As if I would! (*She sits on the sofa*)

Victor Oh, when I felt your hand on my cheek . . . It was so soft and warm . . . I trembled so much, I almost fainted . . . You see, I'm seventeen, and

since I've been seventeen, I don't know . . . Well,
I've got boils . . . Yes, look, there's one starting on
my neck. I showed the doctor this morning and
he said 'My boy, that's puberty.'

Armandine (*Seated on the sofa*) Puberty? What on earth's puberty?

Victor I don't know. Apparently I'm the age for love . . .
Oh, I've been feeling the sap rising!

Armandine Yes, yes, yes . . .

Victor So when you started to . . . Oh, you're not angry?

Armandine (*Rising*) Of course not . . . To prove it, here's
three francs.

Victor (*Taking it*) Three francs!

Armandine For you.

Victor Oh! No, no, no! (*He puts them on the table*)

Armandine What!

Victor Oh, no! Not from you! Not from you!

Armandine Now look . . .

Victor Oh, I'd give at least double that to . . .

Armandine To . . . ?

Victor (*Embarrassed, fighting back tears*) Nothing, nothing
at all! (*Changing his tone*) Here comes the manager.
(*He rushes upstage*)

Armandine Poor boy! (*She takes back the three francs*)
(*The Manager enters. Victor, who has reached the
door, stands aside to let him enter and then goes out*)

Manager You sent for me?

Armandine Yes, I did. About this room . . . (*She finishes packing
her trunk and travelling bag*)

Manager Yes, it's all arranged, we'll give you another at the
front.

Armandine Yes, I mean this one's dreadful. (*Looking at her
trunk*) Well, if I have to stay here ten days . . .
while I'm furnishing my new flat . . .

Manager I quite understand.

Armandine Of course you do. So, if you don't mind . . .

Manager	No, that's quite all right. Even if you'd wanted to keep this room, you couldn't have it now. I re-let it at once.
Armandine	Did you? Good. Who's the lucky man?
Manager	A Monsieur Vatelin. He telegraphed for a room, so I gave him this one.
Armandine	(*Closing her bag*) Vatelin? . . . Never heard of him. Anyway *I* don't care! Well . . . ? (*She sits, left of the table*)
Manager	So I'll give you No. 17, shall I? It's at the front.
Armandine	All right, if you say so . . . What I need is a comfortable room, on the large side, so if a friend or someone calls and happens to want to stay the night . . .
Manager	Ah, you're not alone, good, good, good . . . Yes, yes, yes, I understand, you want a room where you can . . . Oh, in that case I'll give you No. 23. It's got twin beds.
Armandine	Twin beds! What can I do with twin beds? Are you trying to make me look a fool?
Manager	Well, I . . .
Armandine	Really! Do you think I want an audience?
Manager	Oh . . . No, but I thought for your friend . . .
Armandine	(*Rising*) A second bed? . . . I'd like to see his face! . . . No, no, I'll take 17. (*She goes to the trunk and closes it*)
Manager	Very good.
Armandine	Please send someone for my trunk.
Manager	Yes, of course.
	(*The Manager goes through the door, but stops outside and speaks to someone who can't be seen*)
	Yes? (*Voices*) Yes, this is the room, I'll go and see. (*He comes back downstage*)
Armandine	What is it?
Manager	A gentleman for you . . .

Armandine	What gentleman?
Manager	I don't know. I'll go and ask . . .
Armandine	Oh, never mind, show him in. I'll have a look at him.
Manager	Come in, please.
	(*The Manager stands aside to let Rédillon enter and then goes out*)
Rédillon	(*In the doorway*) Good evening.
Armandine	You!
Rédillon	Me. (*He comes downstage and puts his hat on the mantelpiece*)
Armandine	Oh! Well . . . I mean . . . You know . . . I mean . . . well!
Rédillon	That's the way I am.
Armandine	How have you been since the other evening?
Rédillon	Fine. May I?
Armandine	What?
	(*Rédillon pouts his lips to show he wants to kiss her*) Yes. Yes.
	(*They kiss*)
Rédillon	Marvellous!
Armandine	So you love me?
Rédillon	I adore you.
Armandine	You're quick off the mark. What's your name?
Rédillon	Ernest.
Armandine	Ernest what? You do have another name? Or doesn't your father acknowledge you?
Rédillon	Yes, yes, yes. Rédillon.
Armandine	What a silly name!
Rédillon	It's been in the family a long time.
Armandine	Anyway the name doesn't make the man, does it? Look at me. You're really rather nice.
	(*Rédillon makes a face*) Do you know something?
Rédillon	No.

D

Armandine   You're a little like my lover.

Rédillon   Oh!

Armandine   Has no one ever told you?

Rédillon   No. Who the devil is your lover?

Armandine   (*Pushing him away*) Who the devil is my lover? He's very special, I'll have you know. Baron Finkelstein. (*She goes to the sofa and sits*)

Rédillon   He's Jewish? (*He sits*)

Armandine   Yes, but he hasn't been baptised . . . He's the amateur jockey, of course you know him. He made all that money on the Stock Exchange . . .You must know, the papers were full of it. But that means nothing nowadays.

Rédillon   There are so many of them.

Armandine   I know. Well, his sister married the Duke of . . .

Rédillon   Now look, I didn't come here to talk about your lover's family tree.

Armandine   Poor man! That Army's called him up for a month's training. That's why he's not here.

Rédillon   Well, it's an ill wind . . . (*Rising*) Armandine, darling

Armandine   What?

   (*Rédillon pouts his lips as before*)
Ah! (*She gives him a long kiss*) You know, I saw right away you were eyeing me the other evening in the theatre.

Rédillon   I certainly was.

Armandine   Was that Pluplu in the box with you?

Rédillon   Yes. You know her?

Armandine   Oh, I know her. The way she knows me. By sight. She's a wonderful girl. That's why I took a fancy to you. (*Going downstage left*) Otherwise I'd never have responded, because usually of course when I don't know people, I . . .

Rédillon   Aha?

Armandine   Well, of course. If a man's with a girl like that . . .

It's a challenge . . . That's why I got the attendant to give you my card in the interval.

Rédillon I see. So I owe this to Pluplu.

Armandine Don't tell her. If we ever . . .

Rédillon Silly girl!

Armandine Oh no. Or there's nothing doing. . . . Because I wouldn't want to play her a dirty trick. (*She goes upstage to the fireplace*)

Rédillon (*Following her*) Now stop worrying . . . You know, you've a marvellous figure . . . Is that all yours?

Armandine Of course. Whose do you want it to be?

Rédillon (*Taking her in his arms*) Mine. (*He kisses her*)

Armandine Greedy thing! . . . You'll let me have it back?

Rédillon Of course.

Armandine Good. Or Finkelstein would be miserable.

Rédillon (*Leaving her and coming downstage*) Damn it, will you stop talking about the man!

Armandine (*Coming downstage*) Oh! He loves me so much . . . He's so funny. He keeps on saying 'I love you because you're stupid'. I'm not stupid, am I?

Rédillon Of course you're not stupid. Ohhh! Darling Armandine!
   (*They kiss*)

Armandine Ohhh! Darling . . . What is your name?

Rédillon Ernest.

Armandine Darling Ernest!

Rédillon (*Sitting left and pulling her onto his knee*) Come and sit on my knee.

Armandine Oh! Already!

Rédillon Yes, already. Oh, Lucienne! Dearest Lucienne!

Armandine (*On his knee*) My name's not Lucienne. It's Armandine.

Rédillon (*Still enraptured*) No, Lucienne! Let me call you Lucienne. Why should you mind, I prefer it. Oh, Lucienne!

Armandine You are funny! . . . That reminds me of . . .

Rédillon (*As before*) No, it doesn't remind you of anything.
Shut up, don't talk, just kiss me. Lucienne!
Lucienne darling! . . . Is it you? Is it really you?

Armandine No, it isn't.

Rédillon Shut up. I don't need an answer. Oh, say it's
you . . .
      (*A knock at the door*)

Armandine Who's there?

Rédillon (*Drowning the offstage voice*) Oh, Lucienne! Lucienne
darling . . .

Armandine (*To Rédillon*) You shut up now. I can't hear a thing.
(*Towards the door*) Who's there?

Victor (*Off*) Victor. The page.

Armandine Oh, it's you. Come in.
      (*Victor enters*)

Victor (*As he enters*) Can we . . . (*Scandalised at seeing
Armandine on Rédillon's knee*) Oh! (*Despondently*) Oh!

Armandine (*Kindly*) What do you want?

Victor (*Tenderly*) I came to ask if we could take the trunk?

Armandine Yes, yes.

Rédillon (*To Victor*) What trunk?

Victor (*Sharply*) That trunk over there of course.
Whose trunk do you think?

Rédillon (*Rising and going towards him*) Don't you answer me
like that. I'll show you whose trunk. I've never
heard of such a thing.

Armandine Oh, don't hit him, he's very sweet.

Rédillon I don't care how sweet he is. I'll teach him how to
talk to me.

Armandine No, it's all right. Don't bother. Just give him
twenty francs.

Rédillon What! After the way he . . .

Armandine You're not going to refuse me twenty francs!
(*She sits left*)

Rédillon Of course it's not the twenty francs . . . But really
. . .(*Quietly*) You make do with five. (*Aloud*) All
right, (*Giving him the coin*) here's twenty francs this
time, but don't let it happen again. (*He passes to
the right*)

Victor (*Curtly*) Thanks. (*Between his teeth as he pockets the
coin*) Swine!

Rédillon (*Not having heard*) That's the way I am.

Victor (*Tenderly to Armandine*) I'll go and get the chambermaid to help me with the trunk.

Armandine (*Seated left*) Yes, good. Run along.
   (*Victor goes out*)

Rédillon (*Grumbling*) That will teach him to be rude to me.

Armandine Poor boy, you mustn't be angry with him. He's
upset at the moment. He's ill.

Rédillon I don't give a damn if he is ill.

Armandine You haven't got what he has.

Rédillon What has he got?

Armandine I don't know exactly. Apparently it's puberty.

Rédillon Puberty! What do you mean, puberty?

Armandine (*Leaning on the arm of the chair*) The doctor said so.
That's what he has.

Rédillon Has he? . . . I must say, I'm really sorry for him.

Armandine It's serious?

Rédillon Puberty? Oh, yes.

Armandine (*Rising immediately*) It's not catching?

Rédillon No, unfortunately. Or the germs would be worth a
fortune.
   (*Victor enters, followed by Clara*)

Victor (*To Clara*) Come on, give me a hand.

Clara This trunk here?

Victor Yes, it's to go down to No. 17 . . . (*Coming back
to take the bag from the table*) Ah, the bag!
   (*Victor and Clara go out with the trunk and bag*)

Rédillon (*Going towards her*) You're moving then?

Armandine Yes, I don't like this room. I asked for one at the front.

Rédillon I don't see why that should be nicer. Right, the new room! Off we go. (*He takes his hat from the mantelpiece*)

Armandine We? What for?

Rédillon (*Coming downstage*) What do you mean, what for? (*Teasing*) You are stupid!

Armandine Oh! Very sorry my dear. Not tonight.

Rédillon Oh, no!

Armandine Oh, no! Correct. (*Passing to the right*) I'm sorry, but it's quite impossible.

Rédillon Aha, it's serious. How can you dare to . . . ? Now, look . . . you don't imagine I'm going away like this . . . In the middle of the aperitif!

Armandine (*Leaning back on the table*) It can't be helped. I'm expecting a friend at eleven.

Rédillon (*Going to the bed and sitting*) A friend! That's no reason. Who the devil is this friend?

Armandine He's from Berlin. You don't know him. His name's Soldignac. Every time he's in Paris . . .

Rédillon That's disgusting!

Armandine (*Passing to the left*) I'm sorry, I'm expecting him here.

Rédillon (*Rising and coming downstage*) Well, don't be here. I know, come to my flat.

Armandine Your flat!

Rédillon (*Taking her arm. Business*) Yes, my flat. I have got one. Do you think I live in the street?

Armandine But what can I tell him?

Rédillon Leave a message your mother's ill and you've got to look after her. It's as old as the hills, but it always works.

Armandine Oh! It's not very nice.

Rédillon Yes, yes, it's terribly nice. Put your hat on and let's go.

Armandine (*Going towards the fireplace and taking her hat from the mantelpiece where she had put it before the beginning of the Act*) It's not very nice. But I'm tempted.
(*Knock at the door*)

Rédillon
Armandine } Come in.

(*Manager enters*)

Manager (*As he comes in*) I'm sorry to disturb you, but the people who've taken the room have arrived . . . so . . .

Armandine (*Putting on her hat*) You want to kick us out.

Manager Oh, I didn't say that.

Armandine I'll finish putting my hat on and they can have it all. Ask whatever his name is . . .

Manager Vatelin.

Rédillon Vatelin?

Armandine . . . to give me two minutes.

Rédillon Vatelin! Here! How on earth . . . Well, show him in, I'd love to see him.

Armandine You know him?

Rédillon He's my best friend.

Manager (*Off*) This way please.

Rédillon (*Going upstage*) My dear fellow!
(*Pinchard enters, wearing an Army doctor's uniform, followed by Mme Pinchard*)

Rédillon (*Seeing Pinchard*) Oh, I'm sorry. (*Aside*) It's a different one.

Pinchard (*As his wife bows to Armandine and Rédillon*) I'm so sorry to turn you out like this . . . (*Aside*) Dammit, a lovely girl!
(*He gives his bag to his wife, who goes and puts it on the table, then comes back to him*)
(*Aloud*) I booked this room for tonight by telegram and you can see from the telegram they sent me back . . . 'Reserved Room 39' . . . This is the one.

Armandine	(*Putting on her gloves*) I do apologise for still being here. We were getting ready to go.
Pinchard	Please, don't hurry. I'd hate to disturb you in the slightest. Two's company. But so is four.
Armandine	How very charming of you!
Pinchard	Not at all. (*To Rédillon*) Congratulations, you've a damned pretty wife.
	(*Rédillon bows, flattered*)
	I wish I could change her for mine.
Rédillon	⎱ (*Astonished, looking at Mme Pinchard, who is still
Armandine	⎰ smiling and bowing*) What!
Pinchard	It's a fact. And I'm not afraid to say so in front of my wife.
Rédillon	Doesn't she mind?
Pinchard	It's not a question of her minding. She's deaf as a post. (*He goes upstage a little*)
Rédillon	⎱ Ah! Ah! (*They stifle their laughter*)
Armandine	⎰
Mme P.	Please don't put yourself out for us.
Armandine	(*Thanking her*) That's what your husband was kind enough to say.
Mme P.	(*Not having understood*) Oh, not at all, not at all.
Pinchard	Do you understand?
Rédillon	No.
Pinchard	Nor do I. She does ramble a bit. That's because she hasn't heard a word.
Mme P.	(*Very affable*) And my husband too!
Pinchard	You see! You have to get used to it. I've had to for twenty-five years. In fact we were married twenty-five years ago today. We've come to Paris to celebrate. I'm taking her to the Opera.
Rédillon	(*To Armandine*) He's taking a deaf woman to the Opera! (*To Pinchard*) The Opera? This evening? (*He looks at his watch*)
Pinchard	Yes, it is rather late, but they're doing La Traviata,

followed by Coppélia. We'll get there for the ballet. You see I can't stand music and my wife only wants to see ballets. She likes to look at the dancing, she just says it would be better with music. (*Tapping her arm*) Don't you, sweetheart?

Mme P. What? (*He has both thumbs in his jacket pockets and, as he speaks, taps his stomach with the other fingers*)

Pinchard You miss the music in the ballets?

Mme P. (*Who has been looking at his hands*) Oh, much better. It's settled itself now. The train was the trouble. (*Rédillon and Armandine look at each other*)

Pinchard Ah, yes . . . No, that's something else. As soon as you set eyes on her, she starts talking about her stomach. She gets these slight liver attacks, but she's better now. Splendid! Splendid! She rambles a bit. Have to get used to it. Have to get used to it.

Armandine Well, I won't delay you any more. Are you ready, Ernest? (*To Pinchard*) Goodnight. (*She bows and goes upstage to the fireplace*)

Pinchard Delighted to have met you. (*To Rédillon*) Both of you.

Rédillon So am I. There's something I'd like to tell you . . .

Pinchard What is that?

Rédillon You'll never believe it, but my best friend's called Vatelin.

Pinchard (*Taken aback*) Oh!

Rédillon Yes.

Pinchard Yes . . . Well, one confidence deserves another. My best friend's called Piedlouche.

Rédillon (*Now he's taken aback*) Oh!

Pinchard Yes.

Rédillon Yes. (*Aside*) Why does he think I care? (*Armandine comes downstage*)

Pinchard (*To Rédillon*) Goodnight. I'm most grateful.

Rédillon Goodnight.

Rédillon }
Armandine } (*To Mme Pinchard*) Goodnight.
(*Pause*)

Pinchard (*Tapping his wife on the arm*) Sweetheart! (*She turns towards him*) They're saying goodnight.

Mme P. What?

Pinchard (*Shouting*) They're saying goodnight!

Mme P. I can't hear!

Pinchard Of course. Wait. (*Articulating with his lips, so that he is inaudible*) They're saying goodnight.

Mme P. Oh, I'm sorry. Goodnight.

Rédillon (*Aside*) Extraordinary! She can only hear when we can't!

Pinchard There!

Armandine You're coming, Ernest?

Rédillon Yes.
(*They go upstage a little. Knock at the door*)

All (*Except Mme Pinchard*) Come in.
(*Victor enters*)

Victor (*To Armandine*) You've nothing else to go?

Armandine No, that's all, thank you. Oh! Tell them at the desk that if a gentleman asks for me, they're to say I couldn't wait because my mother's ill and I've had to go to her. You understand?

Victor (*With a sigh*) Yes.

Armandine Run along then. And get well soon.

Victor Thank you.

Pinchard Is he ill?

Armandine Yes, he's got boils. Take care of yourself. (*To Rédillon*) Come along then. (*As she is going through the door, to Rédillon, who is following her*) Oh, my bag!
(*Armandine goes out*)

Rédillon Yes, yes. (*To Victor*) The bag over there!

Victor Here it is. (*He takes Pinchard's bag from the table and gives it to Rédillon*)

Rédillon (*Taking it. Aside*) Is this really hers? Ah well . . .
(*Rédillon goes out. The Pinchards are talking on the right and do not see what is happening. Victor's eyes follow Armandine and he sighs*)

Mme P. I'll get ready, if we have to go to the Opera.
(*Mme Pinchard goes out into the bathroom*)

Pinchard That's it. (*To Victor*) Well, my boy, don't just stand there like a flagpole. (*He goes and adjusts his uniform in front of the mirror above the mantelpiece*)

Victor Sir?

Pinchard So you have boils, have you?

Victor Yes, sir. Oh, but it's nothing.

Pinchard All right, I know 'em. MO in the cavalry, I've seen hundreds in my time. Let's have a look. (*He reaches the right*)

Victor (*Coming downstage*) Yes, sir. I have them all right!

Pinchard Don't chitter chatter, boy. Take your trousers down.
(*Mme Pinchard enters from the bathroom*)

Victor Sir?

Pinchard Are you deaf, boy? I said 'Take your trousers down'.

Victor (*Taken aback*) But, sir . . .

Pinchard Does my wife embarrass you? Take no notice of her, she's deaf.

Victor Oh! Good. (*He puts his hand on the belt of his trousers then hesitates*)

Pinchard Well! What are you waiting for?

Victor Well, sir, if it's out of curiosity, all right, but if it's for the boil, that's on my neck.

Pinchard Your neck! What are you blathering about? A boil on your neck! That doesn't keep you off horseback! Any more than pimples in your dimples! You want to be excused parade for a boil on your neck! (*Going to him and marching him upstage*) Boiling in oil's what you deserve! Malingerer! (*He puts his cap down on the mantelpiece*)

Victor But, sir . . .

Pinchard All right, on your way! Dismiss! Quicker than that!

Victor Yes, sir. (*Aside, as he runs out*) What a man!
(*Victor goes out*)

Pinchard (*To his wife*) Have you ever seen the like of that! For a boil on his neck!

Mme P. At ten thirty, so you've no time to spare.

Pinchard I'm not talking about that. I'm talking about his boil.

Mme P. Look at the programme. You'll see.

Pinchard (*Leaving her*) Yes, all right, I'll get ready. Where's the bag?

Mme P. What?

Pinchard (*Shouting*) Where's the bag? (*Articulating inaudibly*) Where's the bag?

Mme P. Where's the bag? You were carrying it.

Pinchard (*Shouting*) I was carrying it? (*Inaudibly*) I was carrying it?

Mme P. Definitely. Where have you put it?

Pinchard Oh! She's marvellous. Where can I have hidden it?
(*Knock at the door*)
(*Still searching*) Come in.
(*Pinchard goes and looks under the table; his wife under the armchair. Clara enters*)

Clara I've come to turn down the bed. Are you looking for something?

Pinchard (*Without looking at her*) Yes, a travelling bag. Damnation! Where did I put it?

Mme P. (*To her husband*) Why don't you go and see if the page has put it in the bathroom?

Pinchard You think so? Oh, I'd have seen him.
(*Pinchard goes into the bathroom*)

Clara (*To Mme Pinchard*) What pillows do you like,

feathers or horsehair?
>   (*Mme Pinchard says nothing*)

What pillows do you like, feathers or horsehair?
>   (*Mme Pinchard says nothing*)

Oh, what's the matter with her! (*Standing in front
>   of her*) What pillows . . .

Mme P.   Oh! Good evening. (*She reaches the left*)

Clara   (*Following her*) Eh? Good evening. I was asking . . .
>   (*Pinchard enters from the bathroom, still looking
>   about him for the bag*)

Pinchard   Were you? . . . Well, don't, you're wasting your
time. I must have left it downstairs. What were
you asking?

Clara   I wanted to know . . .

Pinchard   I say, I say! A pretty face!

Clara   . . . what pillows you want, feathers or horsehair?

Pinchard   I say, I say! You're marvellous!

Clara   What! I was asking . . .

Pinchard   I don't care if it's feathers or horsehair, half of
yours, that's what I want.

Clara   (*Scandalised*) Really, sir, I . . .

Pinchard   What's your name?

Clara   Well, dearie, what's yours?

Pinchard   (*Reaching the right*) Dearie! She called me dearie!

Clara   (*Going upstage to the bed*) You're being rather familiar.
(*She starts to turn down the bed*)

Pinchard   (*Going to her*) Never you mind about that, my girl!
(*Gripping her waist*) Ah! You called me dearie!

Clara   (*Releasing herself*) Will you leave me alone, sir!
(*Calling*) Help! Help!

Pinchard   Go on, go on. As loud as you like.

Clara   (*To Mme Pinchard*) Will you tell your husband to
stop!

Mme P.   We're only stopping till tomorrow.

Clara   She's deaf!

Pinchard As a post. But you're enchanting. (*He kisses her*)

Clara (*Slapping his face hard*) Take that! (*She goes upstage right*)

Pinchard Oh!

Mme P. (*Turning round*) Well? Have you got it?

Pinchard (*Holding his cheek*) I've got it all right.

Clara Is there anything else you'd like, sir?

Pinchard (*Reaching the right*) No. No, no, thank you. (*Aside*) Ohhh! She's tougher than she looks.

Mme P. Have you got toothache?

Pinchard No, no, it's nothing. (*After a new approach to Clara*) Ask the Reception to send up my bag, I must have left it downstairs. See it's here when I get back. (*He takes his cap from the mantelpiece*)

Clara Very good, sir. (*She goes to the bed*)

Pinchard (*To his wife*) Come along, sweetheart. (*Inaudibly*) Come along.

Mme P. (*Rising*) Let's go. I'm ready.

Pinchard That's right. (*Going upstage*) La Traviata must be over by now.

Mme P. What's La Traviata about?
    (*Pinchard speaks inaudibly*)
Oh, I don't approve of that sort of woman.

Pinchard They do fill a need, sweetheart.
    (*Pinchard and Mme Pinchard go out*)

Clara I think I've cooled him off all right. He's marvellous. Half of my pillow indeed! Does he really think that if I'd wanted a bad bargain, I'd have waited for him! No, really . . .
    (*Pontagnac half-opens the door and puts his head round. He then enters, carrying a small parcel*)

Pontagnac I thought I heard someone go out. Vatelin's taken this room for tonight, he'll be here any minute. Let's start getting things ready. (*He tiptoes towards the door on the left*)

Clara Who do you want, sir?

Pontagnac (*Aside*) Dammit, the maid!

Clara (*Repeating*) Who do you want, sir?

Pontagnac (*Aloud*) I . . . Eh? . . . Who . . . Who do I want?

Clara Yes.

Pontagnac The . . . The King of the Belgians.

Clara He's not here.

Pontagnac Ah! He's not here . . . What a pity! . . . Ah, well! . . . I thought as much.

Clara Well, in that case . . .

Pontagnac I knew it was room 39, but I wasn't sure it was the right hotel . . . I see it isn't.

Clara Oh! Well, I hope that's all that's wrong.

Pontagnac You see, when I saw the King today, he said 'My dear fellow, we're staying at the Ultimus, Room 39'. Now I'm sure about the room. But the Ultimus . . . I mean, with that accent! I heard Ultimus, but he might have said Continental.

Clara You're from the Court?

Pontagnac Yes, yes, slightly, quite an unimportant minister. So, to be near him, I've taken room 38 . . . (*Going towards the door on the left*) . . . The room through there.

Clara Yes, yes.

Pontagnac (*Trying to take the key out of the lock*) It's through there. Number 38.

Clara I know that. (*She goes towards the bed*)

Pontagnac (*Having taken the key. Aside*) There! I've got the key. (*Aloud*) Oh, well! He's not here. He's not here. We'll have so much to talk about . . . Or nothing . . . Won't we? . . . Goodnight, goodnight.
  (*Pontagnac goes out, humming. Clara looks at him amazed*)

Clara (*Laughing*) What an extraordinary man, our poor little, wandering minister! . . . I must get those pillows.

(*Clara goes out. A key is heard in the door, left and
Pontagnac, followed by Lucienne, enters warily*)

Pontagnac You can come in. She's gone.

Lucienne So it's here!

Pontagnac It's here.

Lucienne In this room!

Pontagnac Number 39. Exactly.

Lucienne (*Sitting in the armchair*) Oh, the depravity! . . . To
think that in this room . . . But it looks a decent
honest room. Liar! To think that in this room,
my husband and another woman . . .

Pontagnac (*Taking off his gloves*) Exactly.

Lucienne (*Rising*) Yes. And then the two of them . . . He as
I've always known him, with his sweet words and
caresses . . . And she . . . I don't know her . . .
with her . . . oh, I've no idea! . . . And then . . .
Oh, no! No, I can't, I won't! Ohhh! . . . You can
stand there, coolly and calmly?

Pontagnac Well . . . if the deed is beautiful!

Lucienne (*Passing to the right*) Oh, be quiet. I can see it all.
Terrible pictures appear before my eyes. Oh no, no,
I won't look at them, I won't. (*She puts her hand over
her eyes*) No, I'd rather keep my eyes open. When I
close them, I see much too much.

Pontagnac Please, don't get upset like this.

Lucienne Oh, I think I hate everything around me. (*She goes
upstage, passing behind the sofa*) These walls, for their
complicity, this mirror for what it's going to witness,
and that, that . . . Oh, no, no, I won't have it, I
won't. The bell, where's the bell?

Pontagnac (*Stopping her*) Bell! What for?

Lucienne They must take away the bed.

Pontagnac No, no, do think . . . Do you want to catch your
husband or don't you?

Lucienne I most certainly do.

Pontagnac Well, if you want physical proof, don't remove the means of getting it.

Lucienne You're putting me through a terrible ordeal.
(*They come downstage a little*)

Pontagnac I'll try not to make it last longer than necessary.

Lucienne Oh, yes.

Pontagnac We must arrive at the psychological moment.

Lucienne Before. Oh, before.

Pontagnac Well, yes, that's what I mean, not too soon while the orchestra's arriving, or too late . . .

Lucienne After the music's begun.

Pontagnac Precisely.

Lucienne Yes. But how will we know?

Pontagnac (*Going to the table*) I've thought of that. This is how. (*He points to two electric bells, wrapped in paper, which he has put on the table*)

Lucienne Whatever's that? Electric bells?

Pontagnac Correct. Do you know what fishing with a bell is?

Lucienne No.

Pontagnac Well, that's what it is, fishing with a bell. You tie a bell on the end of the line and the fish rings it to announce he's been caught. That's what I'm doing with Vatelin.

Lucienne You're going to fish for my husband with a bell?

Pontagnac Correct. Then he and his . . . companion will kindly ring for us at the right moment.

Lucienne That's ridiculous.

Pontagnac Ridiculous? I'll show you how easy it is. (*Going upstage towards the bed, followed by Lucienne*) Which side of the bed does your husband usually sleep?

Lucienne Away from the wall.

Pontagnac Right. Then the lady will be next to the wall. So, I take the two bells. The big one. (*He rings it: deep note*) That's your husband. And the other. (*He rings it: high note*) That's the lady. (*He rings them, one after the other*) Him. Her. Good. Now I put him here. (*He slides the first bell under the mattress in the place which Vatelin ought to occupy and then goes round to the other side*) And her there. (*He slides the other bell under the mattress on the other side*)

Lucienne Then what?

Pontagnac Then what? Then the line's baited. We're ready.

Lucienne Ready?

Pontagnac (*Between the bed and the wall*) Yes. We simply have to wait for a bite. One of them gets into bed, ting a ling, bell number one. We don't stir, we've only hooked one of them. When the second rings too, right, we've got them both. (*He comes out from behind the bed*)

Lucienne How ingenious!

Pontagnac No, I am a genius, that's all.
　　　(*Voices off*)
　　　(*Taking his hat and stick*) Someone's coming. Perhaps it's them. (*He goes upstage left*)

Lucienne Them! I'll tear their eyes out!

Pontagnac (*Stopping her*) Now look, they haven't arrived yet, and you want to tear their eyes out already! Come along quickly. There's not a moment to lose.
　　　(*He makes her cross in front of him*)

Lucienne (*As if speaking to her husband*) Oh! A few minutes more won't help you!
　　　(*Lucienne and Pontagnac go out left and can be heard turning the key in the lock. At the same time, Heidi enters through the other door, followed by Clara, carrying pillows*)

Heidi I asked you for Room 39. This is Herr Vatelin's room? (*She puts her bag down on the table*)

Clara I've told you, when visitors are not in their rooms, I can't let anyone else in without their permission.

Heidi (*Sitting near the table*) For heavens sake! I keep telling you he asked me to wait if he's not here.

He put it in a telegram. Here, read it . . . if you won't (*Searching for the word*) relieve me . . .

Clara (*Correcting her*) Believe me.

Heidi Yes, I believe you . . . (*Showing her the telegram*) Look, read it yourself . . .

Clara Ja.

Heidi Ah, you speak German?

Clara I can say Ja, that's all. (*Reading*) 'Your husband knows all, he found the letter in the wastepaper basket . . .' (*Stopping*) Oh!

Heidi (*Rising and taking back the telegram*) No, that's for me, not you. Nein, read the end . . . 'Come to the Hotel Ultimus'.

Clara (*Taking the telegram and reading*) 'Ask for my room, and if I'm not there, wait for me. Vatelin'.

Heidi (*Taking back the telegram and unpacking a nightdress, a box of tea, etc.*) Well, does that convince you?

Clara All right, yes, do wait.

Heidi Jawohl.

Clara Good.

Heidi (*Picking up a lighted candle*) Where's the bathroom?

Clara (*Opening the bathroom door*) In here.

Heidi (*Taking her nightdress and nightcap into the bathroom*) Now bring me a teapot, teacups and boiling water. I lived a long time in England and I can't do without my tea at night.

Clara Very good.

Heidi Danke schön.

(*Heidi goes into the bathroom*)

Clara She and her tea! No need to tell me she'd lived in England!

(*Victor enters, showing in Vatelin, who is carring a bag*)

Victor This is your room, sir.

Vatelin Ah, thank you.

Clara (*To Victor*) There's something wrong, this room's occupied. It's Monsieur Vatelin's.

Vatelin I am Monsieur Vatelin.

Clara But the two people who were here just now . . .

Vatelin (*Coming downstage and putting his bag down behind the sofa*) Yes, yes, never mind them. The manager's discovered what's happened. They should be in 59, but the telegram said 39 by mistake. The porter's going to tell them when they come back.

Clara Oh, good.

Vatelin Thank you, boy.

(*Victor goes upstage towards the door*)

Tell them downstairs, if anyone asks for me, I'm in Number 39, and show them up. (*He sits down next to the table*)

Victor Very good, sir.

(*Victor hurries out*)

Clara Are you looking for a lady?

Vatelin No thank you, I've all I need.

Clara Oh, I'm not offering you one. A lady was asking for you just now. She's in there.

Vatelin She's here! Already!

Clara Shall I tell her?

Vatelin No, she's all right where she is, leave her there.

Clara Very good, sir. I'll go and get the tea.

(*Clara goes out*)

Vatelin (*Rising*) Yes, leave her where she is. I'll see her soon enough. Oh, I'm furious. (*He sits left*)

(*Heidi is heard humming a German song, off*)

There she goes!

(*Heidi enters from the bathroom*)

Heidi Crépin! You're here!

Vatelin (*Rising*) For at least an hour!

Heidi Oh, no. I've been here ten minutes, so I . . .

Vatelin Oh!

Heidi   Ja. I was waiting in there. Oh, Crépin, I'm so happy.
But what are you doing standing there, gloomy as a
bitch?

Vatelin   A bitch?

Heidi   Yes, the gloomy one. Blood bitch, blood dog.

Vatelin   Blood bitch? Blood dog? Oh, you mean bloodhound. Not blood dog.

Heidi   Oh, hound, dog, dog, hound, what's the difference!
Oh, Crépin, darling!
    (*She falls on his neck. He turns his face away*)
What! You don't want me to kiss you?

Vatelin   No.

Heidi   Nein?

Vatelin   (*Passing to the right*) No. You wanted me to come
here, so I have. It was the only way to avoid a
scandal in my own house. But will you please get
it into your head that everything's finished between
us!

Heidi   Oh, Crépin, why do you say that? Oh, you're so
wicked . . . And I loved you because you were so
kind and my husband's such a brute.

Vatelin   (*Aside*) Oh, is that why you loved me! Right, just
you wait!

Heidi   You were so gentle to women.

Vatelin   Oh no, you're wrong there. Ha, you thought I was
gentle! Well, I'm not. I'll show you how gentle I
am! Bang! Crash! Take that. . . . and that. (*He
pretends to hit her, his left hand striking down behind
her neck, his right hand slapping the air in front of her
face*) That's how gentle I am! (*He goes and sits near
the table*)

Heidi   (*Passing to the right, laughing*) Oh, you're so funny.

Vatelin   Funny! Ha, you think I'm funny! Ha! You don't
know me. I'm not kind. Or gentle. (*Rising*) In
Germany, perhaps, because I wasn't at home. But

          here in France I'm a violent bad-tempered brute.

Heidi *You* are?

Vatelin I am. And I strike women. (*In a deep voice*) Ah! Ah! Ah!

Heidi (*Nearly collapsing with laughter*) Oh, Crépin . . .

Vatelin Don't move or I'll hit you.

Heidi (*Picking up the gauntlet*) What did you say?

Vatelin (*More timidly*) I said 'Don't move or I'll hit you'.

Heidi You'll hit me? *You* will?

Vatelin That's right.

Heidi (*Going towards him*) Just try.

Vatelin (*Pushing her away with his hand flat on her arm*) There!

Heidi Ha! You want a fight do you! All right. Ein, zwei. (*She takes up a boxing stance*) Fight away. (*She boxes him*) Take that. Eh? And that, eh? And that! And that! And that!

Vatelin (*Falling into a chair left*) Ohhh! What's the matter with her?

Heidi Ha! He wants a fight, does he?

Vatelin That's enough! All right! Ohhh!

Heidi Damned Frenchman! (*Seizing him round the neck from behind and kissing him*) Never mind. I adore you.

    (*Knock at the door*)

    Come in. (*She reaches the right*)

Vatelin (*Aside*) She packs a punch all right. Bloody German!

    (*Clara enters, with the tea things on a tray*)

Clara Here's the tea.

Heidi Ah, good. Put it down there. Thank you.

    (*Clara goes out*)

Heidi Well! (*Putting tea and hot water into the teapot*) I gave you a thrashing.

    (*Vatelin makes a face*)

    Do you still want to hit your little Heidi?

Vatelin Taking advantage of your strength like that!

Heidi (*Taking a few steps towards him*) So you're going to be nice to your little Heidi then?

Vatelin Oh, will nothing stop you? Look, you know your husband smells a rat.

Heidi Smells rats?

Vatelin It's an expression. He knows everything, if you'd rather. In my telegram I said . . .

Heidi Oh yes. And I thought he was a tame little laphound.

Vatelin Exactly. (*Changing his tone*) But you say dog, not hound. Lapdog.

Heidi You've just told me to say hound, not dog.

Vatelin No, that was a bloodhound. How could you take a hound in your lap! Well, never mind . . . (*Resuming*) The point is I can't go on like this, I can't. I can't. If you won't be reasonable, I will. Goodbye. (*He goes upstage*)

Heidi (*Seizing his sleeve*) Crépin! Crépin! Do stay. Do stay.

Vatelin No. Let me go. Let me go.

Heidi Nein.

Vatelin No?

Heidi All right. I'll kilt myself!

Vatelin (*Putting his hat on the bed*) Not again. This is blackmail. All right, kilt yourself and leave me in peace. (*He comes downstage*)

Heidi All right . . . I'll drink my tea. And die. (*She pours out a cup*)

Vatelin Go ahead and die then.

Heidi Would you like a cup of tea?

Vatelin Eh?

Heidi I asked if you'd like a cup of tea?

Vatelin I don't mind.

(*She pours a cup and hands it to him*)

Heidi (*Holding the sugarbowl*) One lump? Or two?

Vatelin (*Modestly*) Four. (*He sits at the table*)

Heidi (*Who has also taken four*) That's a lot.

Vatelin (*Stirring his tea*) Mm!

Heidi (*Taking a flask from her bag*) Take a drop of something in it.

Vatelin Not a drop! Fill it up.

Heidi That's a lot.

Vatelin I need it at the moment.

Heidi (*Pouring*) As you wish. That's enough to kill a regiment.

Vatelin (*Rising*) Eh? What on earth is it?

Heidi Strychnine. (*She raises the flask to her lips*)

Vatelin (*Rushing to her and seizing the flask*) Put that down.

Heidi No. I want to drink it all and die at your feet.

Vatelin Oh, my God! Heidi! I beg you!

Heidi (*Trying to raise the flask to her lips*) No. Goodbye Crépin. (*In the struggle they do a waltz turn*)

Vatelin (*Preventing her*) All right, I'll do anything you want. Anything you want.

Heidi Oh, you just say that.

Vatelin No, no. Anything. Anything. I swear it.

Heidi Ja?

Vatelin Yes . . . Ja . . . Ja . . . Yes.

Heidi (*Putting the flask away*) That's better.

Vatelin (*Aside*) Right . . . If it's got to be, let's get it over. (*Aloud, trying to work himself up*) Yes, yes, you're right. Come then, come. I want you, I desire you. Darling! Be mine. (*He takes her in his arms and tries to drag her towards the bed*)

Heidi (*Frightened*) No, Crépin. Not like that.

Vatelin Dammit, you know me. I'm always like this.

Heidi (*Going towards him*) All right. Yes, I will, I will.

Vatelin That's cooled my enthusiasm completely.

Heidi Never mind, it was just that I didn't like being dogged into bed . . .

Vatelin That wasn't dogging you, it was hounding you.
Dammit, you can't see a dog doing that.

Heidi (*Pushing him away*) Dammit yourself! You do it on
purpose. Whenever I say dog, it's hound and hound,
it's dog. I can never be right.

Vatelin No, it's not that. But go on, be angry with me.

Heidi (*Immediately becoming gentle and putting her arms round
his neck*) No, no, I'm not angry. It was a joke.
You love me, I love you.

Vatelin We love each other.

Heidi Wait. I'm just going into the bathroom. (*She goes
upstage right*)

Vatelin Bathroom?

Heidi Ja. You don't want me to stay dressed like this!

Vatelin Oh! Right. But why not here?

Heidi Here! In front of you! Naughty boy!
(*Heidi goes out*)

Vatelin (*Going upstage near the bed*) Oh, what a lesson! What
a lesson! There's no way out. (*He sits on the edge of
the bed and gets lost in thought. The deeper bell rings.
A long pause. He doesn't move*) Extraordinary noise
the bells make in this hotel!
(*The door of Room 38 opens noiselessly and Lucienne
puts her head round. Recognising her husband's back,
she raises her arms to heaven and opens her mouth
wide. Before she can scream, Pontagnac rushes to her,
shaking his head to indicate it's not yet time. His
right hand has seized her right hand and he passes her
quickly in front of him, as with his left hand he closes
the door sharply behind them. This must all be
absolutely silent and completed in a flash*)
(*Rising and turning round suddenly*) Eh? (*Seeing nothing*)
Nothing there. It's a miracle. The room's completely
empty. But I heard something. (*Going to the door,
left*) No, the door's shut. And locked. Strange

what illusions you can get. I thought I felt a
draught from the door. I must have had a nightmare.
Thanks to Heidi, damn her . . . and her strychnine
tea. (*He rings the bell*) I'll ring the bell to get them to
take away the tea. (*Reading the sign on the wall*)
'Chambermaid: ring twice.' Damn!
(*He rings twice, then comes downstage*)
Just in case she gets the same idea again . . .
    (*Knock on the door*)
That chambermaid's quick. (*Calling*) Come in.
    (*Soldignac enters*)

Soldignac Hullo.

Vatelin (*Aside*) Soldignac! Her husband! (*Aloud*) Oh, it's
you!

Soldignac Ja. It's me.

Vatelin Oh, yes . . . How did you get here?

Soldignac (*Going to the table*) Ah, that puzzles you, eh?

Vatelin Well . . . (*Aside*) Oh, God! His wife's in the
bathroom!

Soldignac (*Sitting*) I was downstairs at the Reception desk,
when the pageboy brought your message that if
anyone asked for you, he was to be shown up to
Room 39.

Vatelin (*Aside*) Oh, why did I ever think of that? (*He tries
to go upstage towards the bathroom door*)
    (*Soldignac rises and, still at 1, seizes his arm. Vatelin
    is very preoccupied and keeps on trying to get near
    the bathroom door. Soldignac, arm in arm with him,
    takes him for a walk round the stage*)

Soldignac Would you believe it, I've come here for a
rendezvous with a girl who wouldn't wait for me!

Vatelin (*His mind elsewhere*) Yes, yes, yes.

Soldignac She's had to go and look after her mother, who's
very ill. (*Stops and looks at him*) Aren't you interested
in what I'm saying? (*He's let go of his arm*)

Vatelin (*Apparently emerging from a dream*) Terribly interested. I'm with you. Ill, you said. Splendid . . . You're ill?

Soldignac Who?

Vatelin You!

Soldignac Nein, not me. Her.

Vatelin Oh! Her.

Soldignac Ja. Her mother.

Vatelin Ah, her mother . . . The old lady, yes of course, she's ill.

Soldignac So what can I do? . . . I know, you'll say you can go . . .

Vatelin (*Taking him upstage towards the door*) Go! Well, of course! That's it. Go on then. Never mind me.

Soldignac (*Coming downstage left*) No, no . . . It was just a thought. (*He puts his stick down near the mantelpiece*)

Vatelin Oh, just a thought. (*Aside*) Pity! (*Aloud*) No, I said that because I know you're always in such a rush.

Soldignac Ah yes, in the day. But at night I've lots of time. (*He stretches out in the armchair*)

Vatelin (*Aside*) This is going to be amusing.

Soldignac Nein, I can't go. I knew I'd be at this hotel, so I've arranged to meet the police here.

Vatelin (*Falling into the chair next to the table*) Police!

Soldignac Of course . . . I'm going to catch my wife tonight.

Vatelin (*Aside*) Oh! Does he suspect? (*Aloud*) She's not here. She's not here.

Soldignac Who? My wife? I know. She's at Rue Roquépein.

Vatelin (*Rising*) Ah yes, yes. (*Aside*) He doesn't know.

Soldignac At this moment the police inspector should be catching them in the act.

Vatelin (*Going upstage towards the bathroom door*) Yes, yes, yes, yes.

Soldignac (*Rising*) To be on the safe side, he's had her followed. Chased all day. Aren't you interested in what I'm saying?

Vatelin (*Going towards him*) Yes, yes, yes . . . You were
     saying 'Ill . . . She's ill'.

Soldignac No, not any more.

Vatelin Oh, she's dead . . . That's always the next step.

Soldignac No, no . . . I was saying 'My wife . . .'

Vatelin Ah yes, your wife . . . She's there.

Soldignac What?

Vatelin She's there . . . in the Rue Roquépein.

Soldignac Ja . . . She's been chased . . .

Vatelin Chaste . . . Little does he know! (*He goes upstage*)

Soldignac As soon as it's over, the Inspector will send me
     word here.

Vatelin (*Upstage right*) Splendid. Splendid.

Soldignac What on earth are you so worried about?

Vatelin (*Going towards him*) Me worried? Nonsense! I look
     worried?

Soldignac Yes. Are you ill?

Vatelin (*Thumbs in his waistcoat pockets*) No, yes, oh, slightly,
     very slightly.

Soldignac Stomach?

Vatelin (*Absent-minded*) Ah?

Soldignac The man doesn't understand a word. (*Rubbing his
     stomach*) Stomach?

Vatelin Eh? No, yes. You know, betwixt and between.

Soldignac Betwixt and between! Are you often like this?

Vatelin Yes, there, you've got it. I'm often like this.
     It's nothing. (*Going upstage as Soldignac goes and
       sits on the sofa*) Oh, what am I going
       to do?
       (*Through the half-open bathroom door, Heidi's arm
       appears and puts her bodice on a chair near the door*)

Soldignac (*Having seen the arm*) Ah! Pretty! Very pretty!

Vatelin (*Having turned round at the sound of Soldignac's voice.
     Aside*) Dammit! Heidi! (*Aloud*) You saw? That . . .
     That's an arm!

Soldignac (*Still on the sofa*) Haha! I saw! Very pretty! You old
        devil! Whose arm? (*He puts his hat down on the table*)

  Vatelin I don't know. It doesn't belong here. It's an arm
        that's there . . . so it's there . . . It arrived. . . .
        It's the woman in the next room.

Soldignac Nonsense! It's your wife.

  Vatelin You're right. It's your wife . . . My wife. The
        woman in the next room, she's my wife.
        (*He picks up Heidi's bodice, but, as he is about to go
        upstage, Heidi's arm reappears, holding her skirt.
        Vatelin rushes forward and snatches it, then stuffs it and
        the bodice under the bed*)

Soldignac Well, my dear fellow . . . Where have you got to?

  Vatelin (*Coming downstage*) Here I am. Here I am.

Soldignac Come and sit down here, near me.

  Vatelin (*Sitting on the back of the sofa. Aside*) Here we go.
        He's settled in now.

Soldignac I congratulate you. She has a beautiful arm.
        (*Heidi, not suspecting her husband is there, walks
        straight in. She is in her dressing gown. Seeing her
        husband, she stifles a scream and rushes back into the
        bathroom. Hearing the scream, Soldignac turns his
        head, but Vatelin has realised what he's going to do
        and, seizing his head in both hands, turns him round
        so they are face to face*)
        Ohhh! What is it?

  Vatelin I'm sorry . . . it was my wife, she's not in a state
        to . . .

Soldignac Oh! Yes, yes, I'm sorry. Ohhh! You were quite
        right.

  Vatelin Exactly. Now, come and have a game of billiards.
        (*He takes him by the arm and drags him away*)

Soldignac Oh! Yes, all right. I will . . . (*He takes his hat*)

  Vatelin (*Aside*) It's the only way to get rid of him.

Soldignac Besides, we must be embarrassing the lady.

Vatelin   You're too modest. Speak for yourself.

Soldignac   Oh!

Vatelin   (*Aside*) I'll play for five minutes and leave him. (*Aloud*) Let's go.

Soldignac   Let's go.
> (*Knock on the door*)

Vatelin   What is it now!

Soldignac   Come in.

Vatelin   (*Aside*) Come in! What impertinence! (*He comes a little downstage right*)
> (*Rédillon enters, with the bag he had taken away with him*)

Rédillon   I'm sorry to bother you.

Vatelin   Rédillon! Here!

Rédillon   I must have taken the wrong bag just now. (*Recognising Vatelin*) Vatelin! You're here? (*He puts the bag down on the chair near the table*)

Vatelin   Hm! Yes. It's me. I missed the train . . . I'll explain later. Look, go and have a game of billiards. With him. (*He pushes him towards Soldignac*)

Rédillon   Him? . . . I don't know him.

Vatelin   Monsieur Soldignac, Monsieur Rédillon. Now go and play billiards.

Rédillon   (*Defensively*) I can't play.

Vatelin   Never mind. He can, he'll teach you.

Rédillon   (*Passing to 3*) No, he won't. Anyway I'm in a hurry. Someone's waiting for me. (*He sits on the sofa*)

Vatelin   (*Making him get up*) Are they? Then don't sit down . . . It's not worth it, we're going. (*He drags him upstage*)

Rédillon   Oh . . . All right . . . Would you believe it, I . . .

Vatelin   No, no, there's no time, you can tell us tomorrow. Where's my hat? (*He goes to the bed*)

Rédillon   Whatever's the matter with him? He's making me

worried. (*He goes to the table and is about to drink the cup of tea*)

Vatelin (*Wearing his hat*) Got it! Come along. (*Snatching the cup away*) No, don't drink that, we haven't got time.

(*Knock at the door*)

Soldignac (*Lighting a cigarette at the fireplace*) Come in.

Vatelin Not again! I'm fed up with him and his come in's.

(*Clara enters*)

Clara You rang, sir?

Vatelin Yes, I did. Half an hour ago. Take away the tea things. (*He takes the cup from Rédillon, who was putting it to his lips, and gives the tray to Clara*)

Clara Very good, sir.

(*Clara goes out with the tray*)

Vatelin (*Pushing Rédillon towards the door*) Now, let's hurry.

Rédillon My bag! I came for a bag!

Vatelin (*Giving Rédillon the bag he's just brought back*) All right, take your bag and come along.

Rédillon No, not that one. I've just brought it back.

Vatelin (*Giving him Heidi's*) Then it's this one?

Rédillon (*Taking it*) I don't know. It isn't yours?

Vatelin No. (*He puts Pinchard's bag on the table in place of Heidi's*)

Rédillon Then it must be this one. Let's go. (*He returns upstage*)

Soldignac (*Also going upstage*) Let's go.

Vatelin Right. Now you go on ahead. I shan't be a moment, I'll catch you up.

(*Soldignac and Rédillon go out*)

(*At the bathroom door*) Heidi! Quick!

(*Heidi enters*)

Heidi I can come out now? They've gone?

Vatelin Gone! They're waiting for me outside. I've got to

go and play billiards with your husband. Now
please, don't stir from this room, while I'm away.
To be doubly sure, I'll lock you in and take the key.
If anyone comes, hide in the bathroom and don't
move till I get back. Do you understand?

Heidi   Oh! Yes.

Soldignac   (*Off*) Vatelin!

Vatelin   (*Quickly*) Your husband! Hide in there.
> (*Heidi only has time to flatten herself against the bed.
> Soldignac enters*)

Soldignac   (*In the doorway*) Vatelin! Do come along.

Vatelin   All right. I'm just coming.
> (*Soldignac and Vatelin go out. Vatelin takes the key
> and double locks the door behind him*)

Heidi   (*Coming downstage*) Oh! I'm so frightened. Oh!
When I saw my husband, all my courage vanished.
Oh, no. No. I don't want to now. I want to go.
(*Looking for her dress on the chair where she thought she
had put it*) My dress! . . . Where's he put my dress?
> (*Voices in the corridor*)

Oh, no! What is it now?
> (*Heidi rushes into the bathroom*)

Pinchard   (*Off*) Damnation! The key's not in the door and
I forgot to ask for it downstairs. (*Calling*) Waiter!
Will you open this door for me please?

Waiter   (*Off*) Very good, sir.
> (*The key turns in the lock, the door opens and Pinchard
> and Mme Pinchard enter. The waiter stands back to
> let them pass*)

Pinchard   Thank you.

Waiter   Not at all, sir.
> (*Waiter goes out, closing the door*)

Pinchard   (*Supporting his wife as she walks*) There, there now,
stop whimpering. It will soon be over. Sit down.
(*He makes her sit*) Damn these liver attacks! They

would have to start again in the theatre. We had to leave before the end. (*Noticing the bag*) Ah, they've brought my bag up. I knew I left it downstairs. (*To his wife who is looking at him and is clearly ill; articulating*) Well, you don't feel any better?

(*She shakes her head*)

Still hurting?

(*She nods*)

Put your tongue out.

(*She does so*)

It's not bad.

(*She makes a face, meaning it can't be very good*)

You know, you ought to go to bed.

(*She gestures, meaning: You think so? Perhaps you're right*)

Yes, that's it.

(*She smiles sadly: Goodnight*)

Goodnight.

(*She goes upstage a little, then returns and kisses him*) (*Aloud*) Ah yes! The anniversary! (*He kisses her on the forehead*) Twenty-five years!

(*She goes listlessly to the far side of the bed and starts undressing*)

I'll make up a sedative for her. (*He goes to the fireplace, picks up the lighted candle and takes it to the table. He then searches in his bag*) Where's my medicine chest? (*Taking out his slippers*) My slippers! (*He throws them on the floor in front of him, then takes out another pair*) Ah hers! Look, Sweetheart! . . . Slippers! . . . Hey! (*He takes them over to her*)

Mme P. (*Behind the bed*) Thank you.

Pinchard (*At the bag*) Ah! A dressing jacket. (*To his wife*) Sweetheart! Dressing jacket! (*He hands it to her*)

Mme P. Thank you. (*She puts it on*)

Pinchard (*Delving into the bag*) Ah! Here's my medicine chest.

           (*Opening it*) Laudanum. Laudanum. Here's the laudanum.

Mme P. (*The other side of the bed*) My comb! Give me my comb.

Pinchard (*Taking it out of the bag*) Comb. Here it is. (*He hands it to her across the bed. Then he takes a glass, water jug and spoon from the table at the foot of the bed*) Now let's prepare the sedative.

        (*He comes back downstage to the table and prepares the sedative. Mme Pinchard, in her skirt but without her bodice, sits on the bed to comb her hair. The bell under the mattress starts ringing. Pinchard pays no attention*)

        (*Counting the drops*) One, two, three . . . Who on earth's ringing bells like that at this hour of the night! . . . Four, five, six, that's six drops. (*He puts the glass on the table and rises*) Oh, that ringing's getting on my nerves. (*He runs to the door, opens it and shouts*) Stop ringing that damned bell.

A Man (*Off*) Who's ringing that bell?

Pinchard (*Answering*) I don't know. It's unbearable. (*Shouting*) Stop it. People are trying to get some sleep.

Mme P. (*Rising, so that the bell stops*) What's the matter?

Pinchard Ah, it's stopped. High time too.

A Man (*Off*) Yes, high time. Goodnight.

Pinchard Sleep well. (*He shuts the door*)

Mme P. What was the matter?

Pinchard Nothing, nothing. (*Pushing her towards the bed*) Go on, go to bed, it's late. I will too. I've made that fellow shut up.

        (*He takes off his jacket. Mme Pinchard has got into bed, so the bell starts again*)

        Dammit, he's starting off again. It's driving me mad. (*Leaning on the bed to take off his shoes and put on*

his slippers, he starts his bell ringing)
Now another one's started. It's unbelievable.
Are they having a competition? I've never heard
such a row.

*(He starts to take off his boots, turning his back on
the door to Room 38. Lucienne bursts in, followed by
Pontagnac)*

Lucienne Ha, you beast, I've caught you!

*(She seizes him by the shoulders. Pinchard loses his
balance and falls, sitting, onto the floor. He still has
his back turned to them and has only taken off one
boot)*

Lucienne
Pontagnac } It's not him!

*(Lucienne and Pontagnac rush back into Room 38.
Pinchard rises, his boot in his hand and, seeing
nobody, limps round the room, looking everywhere)*

Pinchard Where are they? Where have they gone?
(Victor enters quickly)

Victor What is it, sir? What is it?

Pinchard *(Putting on a slipper)* Eh?
(Clara enters quickly)

Clara Are you responsible for all this ringing, sir?

Pinchard Me?
(Manager enters quickly)

Manager Really, sir, really! You mustn't ring like that.
You'll wake the whole hotel.

Pinchard What! You don't think *I'm* ringing!
(A guest enters in nightgown and nightcap)

Guest Do stop ringing. My wife can't sleep a wink.
(Second guest enters)

2nd Guest Why are you ringing like this?
(A succession of guests enter. Babble of protests)

Guests What's the matter? Why is he ringing? Why
won't he stop? *(Etc.)*

Pinchard Who the devil are all these people? Will you all
go away?

Manager Yes, when you've stopped ringing.

All Yes, yes.

Pinchard Me ringing? Where am I ringing? Can't you see
I'm not ringing? Nobody's ringing here.

Manager But really, sir!

Pinchard How dare you come into people's rooms like this!
Get to hell out of here.

Guests (*Booing him*) Oh!

Pinchard (*Furious, near the bed*) Will you get to hell out of here!
    (*He emphasises the last few syllables by striking the
    mattress with his hand. Each time the deeper bell
    replies briefly. Pinchard stops, amazed, looks at the
    mattress and deliberately punches it three times; each
    time the bell responds accordingly*)
Good God! It's ringing in the bed.

All In the bed!

Pinchard In the bed. (*He pulls out the bell*) I'd like to know
who thought this was funny.

All (*Amazed*) Oh!

Pinchard It's still going on. There must be another one under
my wife.
    (*Everyone goes upstage. The Manager and the guests
    get between the bed and the wall, looking for the other
    bell*)

Mme P. (*Not understanding anything*) What is it? What do you
want? Husband, husband! Men are after me!

Pinchard They're not after *you*.

Manager (*To Mme Pinchard*) There's nothing to be afraid of.
(*Finding the bell*) You're right. Here is another.

Pinchard (*Taking the bell and coming downstage*) There! What
did I tell you! Well! I'd like to know what all this
means.

Manager I simply don't understand it.

Pinchard If this is the way you amuse yourself with your visitors, I'll make a complaint, I promise you.

Manager Oh, I assure you . . .

Pinchard (*Giving him the bells*) All right, all right! Go away the lot of you and leave us in peace.
   (*They all go out. He slams the door behind them*) Well! There's a howdyedo! (*He reaches the right*)

Mme P. (*On her knees, holding a pillow in front of her*) What on earth is going on?

Pinchard (*Sitting near the table*) She hasn't heard a thing. Well, Sweetheart, you don't know how lucky you are.

Mme P. What did all those people want?

Pinchard (*Shaking his head*) Nothing. Nothing. (*He takes off his second boot*)

Mme P. Oh, they frightened me. My pains were beginning to go away. Now they've started again worse than ever. (*She lies down again*)

Pinchard (*Rising*) Oh, the brutes! You'd better have a poultice. (*He puts on his second slipper*)

Mme P. What?

Pinchard (*Articulating*) You need a poultice.

Mme P. How do you expect me to understand? You're speaking in front of the light. I can't see a word you're saying.

Pinchard (*Taking the candle and illuminating his face. Articulating*) You ought to have a poultice.

Mme P. Oh yes, you're right. With a little laudanum, that will help. But where can you get one?

Pinchard (*Pointing to his bag. Articulating*) I've everything I need in the bag. I just have to make it up. (*He rings the bell, then takes a packet of linseed from the bag*) (*Aside*) Thank heavens I brought everything, just in case! When she saw there was room in the bag, she wanted to fill it with food. I preferred a poultice. How right I was!

(*Victor enters*)

Victor You rang sir?

Pinchard (*Throwing the bag behind the bedside table*) Yes, this time I did. I want a hot poultice made up for Sweetheart . . . for my wife. She's ill.

Victor But, sir, there's no one in the kitchen now.

Pinchard Naturally! A moment ago this room was full of people and now there's no one in the kitchen! There is at least a gas stove?

Victor Oh yes, sir, there's a stove.

Pinchard (*Putting on his jacket. Victor helps him*) Good. Take me down there and I'll make the poultice myself.

Victor Very good, sir. Will you allow me, sir?

Pinchard (*Giving him the jacket*) No, I won't allow you, I order you. (*Business*) If ever I find you in hospital, I'll give you poultices! (*Candle in hand, to his wife. Articulating*) I'm going downstairs to make the poultice, I'll be back in five minutes. Try to go to sleep.

Mme P. Try to go to sleep! Don't worry . . . If only I can! . . . Don't be long.

Pinchard No.

(*Mme Pinchard turns over to face the wall. Pinchard and Victor go out. The stage is empty for a moment. Heidi enters*)

Heidi The noise has stopped. What is going on? Why doesn't Vatelin come back? I'll get dressed and go home . . . Where has he put my clothes? (*She begins to search for them and finally goes to the bed, where she sees Mme Pinchard facing the wall*) Mein Gott! Someone's in the bed!

(*Heidi rushes out into the bathroom. The stage is once again empty for a moment, then the key is heard in the lock and someone pushes against the door. It remains shut*)

Vatelin (*Off*) Damn! What's the matter with this lock?
    (*The key is heard again and Vatelin pushes hard
    against the door. It opens. Vatelin enters*)
How stupid, I was turning the wrong way. I double
locked it, instead of opening. (*He shuts the door*)
What a leech that man is! . . . I thought I'd never
get rid of him . . . Now, let's liberate Heidi.
    (*Snore from the bed*)
Is that someone snoring? (*He pulls back the curtain*)
She's in bed! She is amazing. Nothing bothers her.
(*Taking his bag from behind the sofa, he puts it on the table
and takes out a pair of slippers which he throws down by
the bed. Then he puts a chair next to the bedside table ready
for his clothes*). Germans are marvellous! Thank
heaven she's asleep, don't let's wake her. That's
something gained. I'll get into bed as quietly as I
can . . . to make sure I don't disturb her rest . . .
(*Starting to get undressed*) So I can get some rest myself.
(*Coming downstage, he stumbles over Pinchard's shoes and
picks them up*) God, German women have big feet!
(*He has taken off his own shoes and puts them outside the
door with Pinchard's*) Whew! I'm thirsty. (*Seeing the
glass which Pinchard has left on the table*) Just what I
wanted. Madame Soldignac, I'll know your thoughts!
(*He drinks*) Ah! That's good. (*He finishes undressing*)
I feel sleepy. It won't take me long to drop off . . .
Well, into bed . . . as quietly as we can, to avoid
waking my mistress. (*He slips into bed*) Whew, she
takes up a lot of room! . . . I daren't push her over,
I might wake her up. Oh, I forgot my hat. (*He
throws it to the foot of the bed*) It'll keep my feet warm
. . . as a stovepipe hat should . . . Oh, I'm sleepy . . .
I don't know, a lot more since I drank that glass.
What can she have put in it? . . . Strychnine again.
Strychnine . . . (*He goes to sleep*)

> (*Victor enters, showing in Pinchard with his poultice.*
> *He puts the candle on the mantelpiece*)

Pinchard Thank you.

> (*Victor goes out. Pinchard blows on the poultice and*
> *pours laudanum on it*)
>
> (*Going towards the bed*) Are you awake, Sweetheart?
> Be careful, it's hot. (*He uncovers Vatelin with his right*
> *hand and with his left applies the poultice to his stomach*)

Vatelin (*Screaming*) Oh!

Pinchard What the devil's this?

Vatelin Who's there? Burglars!

Pinchard A man in my wife's bed!

Mme P. (*Waking up*) Who's there? . . . Oh! A man in
my bed!

Vatelin Who the devil's this woman?

Pinchard (*Seizing him by the throat*) Villain! What are you doing
here?

Vatelin (*Getting out of bed*) Let go of me.

All Three Help! Help!

Pinchard (*Shouting*) There's a man in my wife's bed!

Vatelin Let me go.

> (*Lucienne bursts into the room, followed by Pontagnac*)

Lucienne Oh, you brute!

Vatelin Oh, no! My wife!

> (*Vatelin pushes Pinchard away, picks up his clothes*
> *in full flight and rushes out, carrying the chair with*
> *him*)

Pinchard (*To Lucienne*) You're a witness. He was in
Sweetheart's bed.

Lucienne I saw it all.

Pinchard Catch him. He was in Sweetheart's bed. My wife's
bed.

> (*Pinchard rushes out in pursuit, during the last line.*
> *Mme Pinchard gets out of bed and picks up her skirt*
> *and slippers*)

Mme P.	Husband! Pinchard! Where are you going? (*She rushes out after them*)
Pontagnac	There! Are you convinced?
Lucienne	Yes, yes. The traitor!
Pontagnac	Was I right to make you stay when you wanted to go?
Lucienne	Oh yes, you were right. Thank heavens! That settles it.
Pontagnac	I hope you know how to get your revenge?
Lucienne	Ah yes, indeed I do.
Pontagnac	You know what you promised: 'If ever I have proof my husband's unfaithful, I'll pay him back in the same way'.
Lucienne	I won't go back on my word. Oh, I'll show you.
Pontagnac	Bravo!
Lucienne	I said I'd take a lover. Well, I will.
Pontagnac	Ah, I'm the happiest man alive.
Lucienne	If my husband ever asks you who my lover is, you can tell him.
Pontagnac	Oh, it's not worth the trouble.
Lucienne	It's his best friend. Ernest Rédillon.
Pontagnac	(*Choking*) What! Réd . . . !
Lucienne	Goodbye. I'm going to get my revenge. (*Lucienne goes out quickly into Room 38*)
Pontagnac	(*Running after her*) Lucienne! For heaven's sake! Lucienne! (*He rushes at the door, but finds it locked*) It's locked! (*He rushes to the other door and bumps into the first Police Inspector who enters, followed by two policemen and Soldignac*)
Inspector	Stop . . . In the name of the law.
Pontagnac	A Police Inspector!
Soldignac	(*Holding a billiard cue*) Ah, so this is her Herz. (*He puts his cue down near the fireplace, takes off his coat and practises boxing against the wall*)

Inspector (*To Pontagnac*) We know everything. You were here with this gentleman's wife.

Pontagnac Me?

Inspector Where is your accomplice?

Pontagnac Accomplice?

Inspector Policeman! Search the room.

Pontagnac (*Aside*) What's he saying?

    (*The policeman, who had gone into the bathroom, returns, dragging Heidi with him*)

Policeman Here she is!

Pontagnac Who on earth's that?

Heidi (*Seeing Soldignac*) My husband!

Soldignac (*Turning round*) My wife!

    (*They argue in German. Second Inspector enters from Room 38, followed by Mme de Pontagnac*)

2nd Insp. In the name of the law . . . !

Pontagnac Another one! . . . (*Recognising his wife*) My wife!

Mme Pont. Inspector! Do your duty.

    (*Mme de Pontagnac goes out quickly into Room 38*)

Pontagnac (*Running after her*) Clotilde!

Soldignac (*Barring his way*) Put your hands up.

    (*He boxes with him, while at the same time Heidi boxes with the policeman, who won't let her go. Rédillon enters, carrying Heidi's bag*)

Rédillon What is going on?

    (*Seeing the two Inspectors, who are looking at him*)

I'm sorry, I took the wrong bag.

    (*Rédillon hurriedly changes his bag for Vatelin's, which is on the table, and goes out. The boxing continues.*

CURTAIN

Act III

(Rédillon's study.
In the back wall a door into the hall. Midstage right
a door into Rédillon's bedroom. Another door downstage
right and another midstage left.
Gerome enters upstage, carrying Rédillon's suit and
Armandine's skirt, folded on his arm, together with
their boots which he has just cleaned)

Gerome Another skirt to iron! Skirts all the time! He's
incorrigible. I wonder what he can do with them
all. There's young men for you today . . . burning the
candle at both ends. Running hither and thither . . .
They all do . . . except me. On the go all the time.
(He goes to the door midstage right and knocks)

Rédillon *(Off)* What is it?

Gerome It's me, Gerome.

Rédillon *(Putting his head round the door)* Well, what's the
matter?

Gerome It's eleven o'clock.

Rédillon All right, it's eleven o'clock.
(He slams the door in his face)

Gerome Yes. *(Aside)* Look at that. Slams the door in my
face. A child I've known from birth. No respect
at all . . . And his father, my foster brother, made
me promise on his deathbed to keep an eye on him
. . . How can I keep an eye on him? What influence
have I got? He won't even listen to me. You might
as well ask the Prince of Monaco to keep an eye
on Africa. If I lecture him, he thinks I'm an old
fool. And to cap it all, I have to valet his
girlfriends.

(Voices can be heard in Rédillon's room and the door
opens)

Ah, they've made up their minds at last.
> (*Gerome goes out downstage right, still carrying the
> clothes and boots. Armandine enters, followed listlessly
> by Rédillon. Her hair is loosely knotted on her neck
> and she is wearing a man's dressing-gown. As she enters,
> she catches her feet in it and stumbles*)

Armandine Your dressing-gown's so long. (*She goes to the
fireplace*)

Rédillon (*Having collapsed on the sofa*) Long for you. Not for
me.

Armandine (*Arranging her hair*) Possibly, but I'm wearing it . . .
How did you manage to collect every single bag
in the hotel except mine?

Rédillon I don't know yours.

Armandine Well, you collected so many, you might have had
the luck to pick on mine. (*She leaves the fireplace*)

Rédillon (*Yawning*) Oh, well . . .

Armandine (*Looking at him*) Well, what?

Rédillon Eh?

Armandine Do you feel ill?

Rédillon No . . . I'm tired, that's all.

Armandine (*Sitting near the table*) After eleven hours in bed!
> (*Gerome enters, a feather duster in his hand. He stops
> and looks pityingly at Rédillon*)

Rédillon Less than six hours sleep. (*He yawns*)

Gerome (*Going towards the door midstage*) How does anyone
dare get in a state like this?

Rédillon What do you want, Gerome?

Gerome (*Sulking*) Nothing.

Rédillon Then what are you staring for?

Gerome Oh, Ernest! You're wearing yourself out.

Armandine Eh?

Rédillon What?

Gerome You break my heart.

Rédillon Go to hell. Nobody asked your opinion.

Gerome I don't have to be asked. I'm telling you. You break my heart.

    (*Gerome returns upstage and goes out*)

Rédillon (*On the sofa*) Glad to hear it. I've never heard of such a thing. I'm sorry, he's an old servant of the family.

Armandine (*In the armchair*) He certainly is familiar.

Rédillon He's a sort of relation. My foster uncle.

Armandine Foster uncle?

Rédillon His mother was my father's foster mother. He's not a blood relation, a milk one.

Armandine He seems so much more familiar to you than you are to him.

Rédillon Naturally. He was present at my birth. I wasn't at his. (*Yawning*) Oh! I'm so tired. (*He stretches out on the sofa, head towards the audience*)

Armandine (*Rising*) Poor Ernest! You definitely don't hold the record. (*She goes to him*)

Rédillon I never claimed to be the champion of France.

Armandine (*One knee on the sofa between his legs*) You do all right. (*She kisses him*) My kisses seem to bore you.

Rédillon (*Without conviction*) No.

Armandine (*Seated*) There. Already.

Rédillon No. But look . . . after all . . . (*Imploringly*) Rest!

Armandine Oh! That's typical. Men! They're only nice the day before. (*She rises*)

Rédillon Oh! . . . Or the day after.

Armandine (*Standing in front of him, looking at a water-colour above the sofa*) What a nice picture! Is it your family's house?

Rédillon That's the Capitol in Rome.

Armandine The Capitol? Ah, so that's the Capitol! How funny!

Rédillon (*Still stretched out on the sofa*) What's so funny about it?

Armandine	(*Sitting*) Oh, nothing. Because of my lover. You know, he's . . .
Rédillon	Yes, yes.
Armandine	He's so boring about it. I don't know why, but he keeps on insisting I saved the Capitol.
Rédillon	*You* did?
Armandine	It's not true, you know, I didn't. I've never even heard of it . . . so . . .
Rédillon	Well then . . . ?
Armandine	He will keep on about it. He says I deserve a medal. Do you think he's mad?
Rédillon	Do you?
Armandine	Never mind him. Darling! (*She kisses him*) (*Gerome enters with a glass of wine on a tray*)
Gerome	Not again! (*To Armandine, placing himself between them*) Please! For his sake!
Armandine	(*Reaching the left*) Well, what's the matter with him?
Gerome	(*Looking at Rédillon*) Just look at him.
Rédillon	I'll throw you out of the house.
Gerome	I don't care, I won't go. Here, drink this.
Rédillon	No.
Gerome	Drink it up.
Rédillon	(*Crossly*) Ohhh! You need the patience of a saint. (*He takes the glass*)
Armandine	What's that?
Gerome	(*Going towards her*) Something special. (*Aside to her*) Be kind, remember he's still a child. Only thirty-two. He's not like me.
Rédillon	(*Seated on the sofa, drinking*) What are you whispering about over there?
Gerome	Nothing, nothing, nothing.
Armandine	(*Teasing*) We have our own little secrets.
Gerome	There! It's no business of yours.
Rédillon	Oh! I apologise. (*He gives the glass back to Gerome*) Has no one called this morning?

Gerome (*Contemptuously*) Yes. To begin with, your so-called Pluplu.

Armandine (*Rising quickly*) Pluplu's been here? (*She sits in the armchair to hear better*)

Gerome Yes. She insisted on seeing you.

Rédillon What did you tell her?

Gerome You're with your mother. Then she wanted to wait, so I told her when you're with your mother, it usually lasts three or four days.

Armandine (*Rising*) Well done! Thank you, if we'd met face to face. . .

Gerome Then Monsieur Emmenthaler arrived. . .

Armandine (*Back to the audience, leaning against the table*) Emmenthaler! Wait now . . . Emmenthaler . . . Emmenthaler . . .

Rédillon No, you don't know him, he's too old for it.

Armandine Oh! (*She turns round*)

Rédillon He's an antique dealer. His shop's in a flat across the landing. So sometimes when he has a bargain, he . . .

Armandine Yes, yes, you're right, I was thinking of a Monsieur Liptauer . . . I knew it was some sort of cheese. (*She passes between the table and the fireplace*)

Rédillon It's slightly different. (*To Gerome*) Well, what did Liptauer want . . . I mean Emmenthaler. (*To Armandine*) You're muddling me up.

Gerome He's got a new acquisition to show you. Very rare. A chastity belt. Fourteenth he said.

Rédillon Oh?

Armandine (*Leaning against the table*) Fourteenth what?

Gerome I don't know. Someone's fourteenth lover, I expect.

Rédillon No, fourteenth century. Is that all?

Gerome That's all.
   (*Bell rings*)
  All right, I'll see who it is.

Rédillon   I wasn't going to . . . If it's a lady, I'm out.

Gerome   No need to tell me that!
>   (*Gerome goes out*)

Armandine   (*Coming downstage*) Yes, we're out. It's probably Pluplu again and there'd be a scene. Not for me! I don't want a fight. (*She goes back upstage*)

Rédillon   Ah, well! Where are you going?

Armandine   (*At the door, right*) To get dressed of course. If it is a woman . . . Gooodbye. I'll slip away.

Gerome   (*Off*) No, he's out. I'm sure.
>   (*Gerome puts his head round the door*)
>   (*Whispering but so that Rédillon can hear him*) Another woman! Hide.

Rédillon   Come on.
>   (*Armandine and Rédillon go out midstage right.*
>   *Gerome enters*)

Gerome   (*Opening the door upstage*) There, look for yourself, if you don't believe me.
>   (*Lucienne enters*)

Lucienne   Nobody here!

Gerome   I said there wasn't.

Lucienne   Very well. Tell him Madame Vatelin wants to speak to him.

Gerome   Madame Vatelin! Is your husband, Monsieur Vatelin, the friend he's always going to see?

Lucienne   Precisely.

Gerome   Oh! That's different. I beg your pardon, I thought you were a tart.

Lucienne   What!

Gerome   (*Calling through the door, right*) Ernest! It's Madame Vatelin!

Rédillon   (*Off*) What's that?

Gerome   (*Calling*) It's Madame Vatelin! (*To Lucienne*) Here he comes.
>   (*Rédillon enters quickly*)

Rédillon It can't be true! You! You! In my flat! . . .
How . . . ? (*He indicates a chair*)

Lucienne (*Sitting near the table*) You're surprised? Oh, I am
too.

Rédillon (*Aside to Gerome*) Tell the lady next door, I'm very
sorry, but important business . . . anything you
like. Then as soon as she's dressed, show her out.

Gerome I've got it.
(*He knocks at the door right*)

Armandine (*Off*) Don't come in.

Gerome Right you are.
(*Gerome goes out right*)

Rédillon You here! You!

Lucienne Me. You know why, don't you?

Rédillon No.

Lucienne What! I'm here, so you should have guessed.

Rédillon What?

Lucienne (*Rising and passing to 2*) Last night I caught my
husband redhanded. Committing adultery.

Rédillon No! . . . So you've come here to love me!

Lucienne I always keep my word.

Rédillon (*Taking her hands and making her sit on the sofa*) Oh,
Lucienne! I'm so happy. Command me. Take me.
I'm yours. (*He sits next to her*)

Lucienne No, I'm here to tell you that.

Rédillon That's what I meant.
(*Gerome enters upstage*)

Gerome Psst!

Rédillon What?
(*Gerome signals to him to move away so that Armandine
can come out. Then he shuts the door*)
Right.

Lucienne What is it?

Rédillon (*Rising*) Someone's going to go across the room.
Hide behind me, so you won't be seen.

> (*Lucienne has risen. She hides behind Rédillon, who is standing. He looks upstage. Gerome enters, accompanying Armandine, now fully dressed. With her head she signals goodbye to Rédillon, who answers in the same way. Then she and Gerome go out*)

Lucienne Well?

Rédillon Sh! Wait a moment.
> (*Gerome enters and signals that she has gone by tapping with his left hand on the back of his right*)
>
> Yes?
> (*Gerome nods and winks maliciously. Then he goes out*)
> (*To Lucienne*) All right, they've gone.

Lucienne Ah! (*They abandon their stance*)

Rédillon Do sit down. (*He goes and shuts the door upstage*)

Lucienne (*Sitting*) Ohhh! Really! What a beast!

Rédillon Who?

Lucienne What do you mean, 'Who'? My husband, of course.

Rédillon (*Coming to sit next to her*) Oh, yes, yes. How silly of me! My thoughts were miles away.

Lucienne I've been such a faithful wife. I've always rejected the advances of my poor Rédillon.

Rédillon Yes, poor Rédillon.

Lucienne Well! I won't any more . . . You love me . . . Very well. I'm yours. That's my revenge.

Rédillon Yes. Oh, Lucienne! Lucienne!
> (*Gerome puts his head round the door*)

Gerome I say! I'm going to get some cutlets.

Rédillon (*Rudely*) All right. All right.
> (*Gerome goes out*)
>
> Coming in here to discuss cutlets! . . . Oh, Lucienne! (*Running quickly upstage*) I say! Get some beans too. All right? . . . Beans!

Gerome (*Off*) Yes.

Rédillon (*Coming downstage*) He will give me cauliflower every day. I'm fed up with it . . . (*Sitting*) I'm sorry,

he's an old family servant, terribly down to earth.
He's not like us, floating in heaven.

Lucienne (*Rising and reaching the left*) I'm certainly not floating
in heaven. (*She goes upstage between the table and
fireplace*)

Rédillon What was I saying?

Lucienne You're fed up with cauliflower.

Rédillon (*Rising*) No, before that.

Lucienne You were saying 'Oh, Lucienne, Lucienne'.

Rédillon (*Ecstatically, as he tries to remember what he was going
to say*) Oh, Lucienne! Lucienne! . . .Ah, yes . . .
(*Continuing*) Oh, Lucienne! Lucienne! . . . (*Taking
her back to the sofa*) Tell me it's not a dream. You're
really mine? All mine?

Lucienne (*Seated*) Yes, really yours. All yours.

Rédillon Oh! I'm so happy!

Lucienne Good. It's some compensation that one person's
misery can be another person's happiness.

Rédillon Oh yes, yes. Look, rest your head on my chest.

Lucienne Just a moment, my hat's in the way. (*She takes
it off*)

Rédillon (*Taking it*) Give it to me. (*He holds it on his right
fist, while he puts his left arm round her waist*) Ah,
I'm intoxicated with the scent of your hair . . .
Ah, to feel you here in my arms . . . mine, all
mine . . . (*He closes his eyes with delight*)

Lucienne Are you going to keep holding my hat all the time?

Rédillon (*Rising*) No, just a moment! (*He goes and puts it on
the table, then comes back to Lucienne who has moved*)
(*Kissing her*) Ah! That's the first time my lips have
been allowed to touch your skin.

Lucienne It is. Now, let's take our revenge. My revenge.

Rédillon Oh, yes!

Lucienne From now on, I'm not his wife. I'm your wife . . .
You're going to marry me!

G*

Rédillon Oh yes! Yes!

Lucienne (*Speaking towards upstage*) I gave him everything . . .
I was faithful to him . . . I loved him.

Rédillon Stop. Stop. Look, don't talk about your husband
. . . Not at this moment. Don't let him stand
between us. Oh, Lucienne, my dearest . . . (*He
kneels in front of her*)

    (*Gerome puts his head round the door*)

Gerome I'm back.

Rédillon Don't come in.

Gerome Well! What are you doing there?

Rédillon Mind your own business. Go away.

Gerome Yes.

Rédillon And shut the door.

Gerome Why? Are you cold?

Rédillon Because I tell you to! . . . And don't come in
unless I call.

Gerome (*Sighing and going upstage. In the doorway*) I couldn't
find any beans.

Rédillon I don't care.

Gerome So I got cauliflower.

    (*Gerome goes out, closing the door*)

Rédillon I'm sorry. He's an old family servant, he takes
everything for granted. Now . . . (*Still on his knees*)
Oh, Lucienne! Let me hold you in my arms.

Lucienne Do you really love me?

Rédillon Do I love you! . . . No, just a moment, this isn't
very comfortable . . . I'm not close enough to you.
Make room for me at your side. (*He sits on her
right*) That's better . . . Now I can hold you against
my heart.

Lucienne So the fortune-teller was right.

Rédillon (*Eyes half-closed*) What fortune-teller?

Lucienne A fortune-teller said I'd have two romantic
adventures in my life. One at twenty-five . . . the

other at fifty-eight. Well, the first has come true.
I was twenty-five last week.

Rédillon   Yes, and it's happened with me! . . . (*Changing his tone*)
Just a moment . . . no, like this. (*He stretches out full
length behind Lucienne, his head towards the audience*)

Lucienne   What are you doing?

Rédillon   There! That's better. I can see you better . . .
Hold you better. (*He kisses her*) Oh, Lucienne!
Lucienne!

Lucienne   (*Sitting upright again, sighing*) Oh!
> (*Rédillon's face expresses great anxiety. He caresses
> her hand mechanically, but his thoughts are clearly
> elsewhere. Lucienne turns to look at him. He immediately
> smiles*)

Well?

Rédillon   What?

Lucienne   Is that all?

Rédillon   Is that all? Oh, Lucienne! Lucienne! (*Aside*) Why
on earth did I bring Armandine back here last
night!
> (*Lucienne looks at him again*)

Oh, Lucienne! Lucienne!

Lucienne   (*Rising*) Oh, Lucienne! Lucienne! Can't you say
anything else?

Rédillon   (*Sitting upright*) Lucienne, I don't know if it's the
worry . . . or the excitement . . . but I swear it's
never happened to me before.

Lucienne   Oh! There speaks the man who says he loves me!

Rédillon   (*Rising*) I do love you. But try to understand . . .
I never expected . . . So the happiness . . . the joy!
. . . I'm *over*joyed . . . That's why. Besides I do have
scruples. They won't last long, but they exist.
I can't help thinking of your husband; he's my
friend! So playing a dirty trick like this . . . Give
me time to get used to the idea.

Lucienne (*Going upstage to the fireplace*) It's a little late to start having scruples now.

Rédillon They won't last long . . . But give me time to think. Come back tomorrow . . . Or tonight.

Lucienne (*Upstage of the table*) Tomorrow! Tonight! . . . I can't. My husband's coming here now.

Rédillon What!

Lucienne (*Coming downstage*) By the time he arrives, my revenge must be consummated.

Rédillon Your husband? . . . Your husband . . . here?

Lucienne Yes. I left a message for him: 'You've been unfaithful. Now it's my turn. If you don't believe me, come to Rédillon's flat at twelve. (*A slight movement of her head, as she looks at him*) You'll find me in the arms of my lover.'

Rédillon You're out of your mind! . . . We're making a terrible mistake! It's funny, I had an intuition . . . Thank God! Heaven has given me the strength to be sensible.

Gerome (*Off. Stopping someone coming in*) No, you can't, no!

Mme Pont. (*Off*) Yes, I tell you, yes!

Rédillon Oh! What is it now?

Mme Pont. (*Off*) Get out of my way.

(*Mme de Pontagnac enters*)

Rédillon
Lucienne } Madame de Pontagnac!

Mme Pont. Yes, it's me . . . You didn't expect to see me so soon, did you? . . . Yesterday, Monsieur Rédillon, I told you if ever I had proof my husband was unfaithful, I'd come to you and say: 'Avenge me. I'm yours.'

Lucienne What!

Mme Pont. (*Taking off her jacket and throwing it on the sofa*) Well, Monsieur Rédillon, here I am. Avenge me. I'm yours.

Rédillon   Her too!

Lucienne   What did you say?

Rédillon   (*Aside*) Oh! I'm fed up. Fed up! No, no, no!
(*He goes upstage*)

Lucienne   I'm sorry but 'Avenge me, I'm yours' . . . You're
behaving rather freely.

Mme Pont.   I beg your pardon! It's all been settled with
Monsieur Rédillon.

Lucienne   I'm sorry, I was here first.

Mme Pont.   That may be, but I booked him yesterday.

Lucienne   Booked him! I don't give a damn.

Mme Pont.   Really!

Lucienne   Really!

Rédillon   (*Coming between them*) For heaven's sake! Don't I
have any say?

Lucienne   All right. Say something.

Mme Pont.   Correct. Say something.

Rédillon   I'll say something all right! I am amazed. You both
want to get your revenge on your husbands . . .
so I have to . . . Do you think I'm a professional
co-respondent?

Lucienne   Well, which of us is it to be?

Mme Pont.   Yes?

Rédillon   Right! Neither of you! There!

Both Women   What!

Rédillon   Goodbye! (*He goes upstage*)

Both Women   Ohhh!
(*Gerome enters*)

Gerome   I say . . . Pluplu . . .

Rédillon   What about Pluplu?

Gerome   She's come back. She wants to see you.

Rédillon   What! Pluplu too! No, no, no! I've had enough.
I'm not at home. Tell her I'm dead.

Gerome   All right.
(*Gerome goes upstage and goes out*)

Lucienne	⎱ *(Together)* ⎰	Rédillon!
Mme Pont.		Monsieur Rédillon!

Rédillon No!

      (*Rédillon goes out right and shuts the door*)

Both Women (*Who have rushed with the same instinctive movement towards the door*) Locked!

Mme Pont. (*Coming downstage left*) See what you've done.

Lucienne I'm sorry, what *you've* done!

Mme Pont. (*With a bitter laugh*) Ha, so it's my fault! I'd like you to know I hate all this.

Lucienne You don't think I've come here for pleasure!

Mme Pont. Thank you. Oh, I wish I didn't have to get my revenge.

Lucienne Me too.

Mme Pont. Me too! Can't you say anything else!

Lucienne What do you expect me to say? We're both in the same situation.

Mme Pont. Created by our husbands.

Lucienne Oh! Life is hard for faithful wives.

      (*Gerome enters*)

Gerome A young man's asking for Madame Vatelin.

Lucienne Asking for me? . . . A young man? . . . Who is it?

Gerome Monsieur de Pontagnac.

Mme Pont. (*Who has gone upstage to the fireplace*) My husband!

Lucienne You call him a young man?

Gerome He's young to me . . . Remember I was grown up when he was still at his mother's breast.

Mme Pont. What does my husband want?

Lucienne I don't know. He's asking for me . . . Good! . . . He's come at the right moment. I need a man for my revenge.

Mme Pont. What! You don't mean . . .

Lucienne Don't worry. It's just to play a trick on my husband.

Mme Pont. Oh! Well!

Lucienne Will you give me your husband?

Mme Pont. Agreed. Besides it will give me another cause for complaint.

Lucienne Thank you. (*Taking Mme de Pontagnac's jacket from the sofa and giving it to her*) Go in there.
    (*Lucienne makes Mme de Pontagnac go out midstage left*)
    (*To Gerome*) You can show him in.

Gerome Very good. (*Aside*) I don't know what's going on.
    (*Gerome shows in Pontagnac and goes out*)

Pontagnac (*Very excited*) Alone!

Lucienne You asked for me?

Pontagnac Yes. Have you been here long?

Lucienne I've just arrived.

Pontagnac And . . . Rédillon?

Lucienne I'm waiting for him.

Pontagnac Thank heaven, I'm here in time. (*He puts his hat on the table*)

Lucienne What do you mean by pursuing me here? What do you want?

Pontagnac Want? . . . I want to stop you doing something silly. I want to place myself between Rédillon and you, fight for you, tear you away from him.

Lucienne How dare you!

Pontagnac How dare I? I'd dare anything after all I've gone through. For love of you, I'm in the most appalling mess. Two cases of adultery . . . which I didn't commit. Caught by a husband I don't know . . . with a wife I don't know. Caught by my own wife . . . with the same woman I don't know. My own divorce pending . . . Another divorce of the woman I don't know and the man I don't know, with me as co-respondent . . . A quarrel with my wife. The woman I don't know arrives this morning and tells me in a German accent I owe her reparation, complicated by the man I don't know taking the law into his own hands. Worries, lawsuits, scandals, the lot. All to throw you into the arms of another man! Sauce for the goose you said. But not with some other gander! No, no, no! You wouldn't do it!

Lucienne (*Aside*) Oh, wouldn't I? (*Aloud*) Yes, things do happen. . . . Isn't it strange, when you arrived just now, I was thinking about my revenge and I wondered why it should be Rédillon. After all, *you* told me about my husband.

Pontagnac Exactly.

Lucienne If anyone's to give me my revenge, you should.

Pontagnac No! It can't be true!

Lucienne So if I asked you . . .

Pontagnac Asked me! . . . You know I'd be the happiest man alive!

Lucienne Would you? Very well, be the happiest man alive. You shall be my avenger.

Pontagnac No!

Lucienne Yes.

Pontagnac It can't be true. And here at Dodillon's – I mean, Rédillon's! That makes it even more exquisite.
      (*He closes the door and lowers the blinds*)

Lucienne (*Going to the table*) I'm ready. (*She takes off the top half of her costume and reveals a black velvet bodice, sleeveless and completely décolleté, only attached across the shoulder by a strap of diamonds. At the same time she loosens her hair with a shake of her head*) This is how my husband thinks I'm most beautiful. Am I really beautiful like this?

Pontagnac (*Taking off his gloves*) Oh, yes. Beautiful. Very beautiful.

Lucienne You do love me?

Pontagnac (*Taking her in his arms*) With all my heart.

Lucienne You'll love me for ever?

Pontagnac For ever.

Lucienne (*Leaving him and moving to 2*) Good. Now, go and sit down.

Pontagnac (*Astonished*) Sit down?

Lucienne Yes.

Pontagnac But I thought . . .

Lucienne Yes, I know. But suppose I happen not to want to, like that, right away. Suppose it suits me to choose my moment. The man who loves me must be the slave of my every whim. I said 'Sit down'. Sit down.

Pontagnac Yes. (*He sits near the table*)

Lucienne (*Going upstage a little*) Thank you.

Pontagnac I've obeyed you.

Lucienne (*Approaching him*) Good. Take your coat off.

Pontagnac What?

Lucienne (*Reaching the right*) Take your coat off. I can't bear to see you wearing it. You remind me of my husband.

Pontagnac Oh! All right. But then I'll be in my shirtsleeves.

Lucienne (*Sitting on the sofa*) I don't mind.

Pontagnac Good. (*He takes his coat off*) And now . . . ?

Lucienne Sit down here, next to me.

Pontagnac (*Sitting*) There.

Lucienne Good.
(*Pause*)

Pontagnac What are we waiting for?

Lucienne My good will.

Pontagnac Oh!

Lucienne Take off your waistcoat, you look as though you've come to remove the furniture.

Pontagnac What! You want . . .

Lucienne Please. And sit down.

Pontagnac (*After taking off his waistcoat and putting it down upstage*) All right, if you insist. (*Sitting*) Don't I look ridiculous like this?

Lucienne	Never mind about that. (*Unbuttoning one of his braces*) Braces are so ugly . . . Like your hair . . . Why do you have your hair cut like that? . . . You look like a waiter.
Pontagnac	(*Having unbuttoned the second of his braces*) Oh!
Lucienne	Turn round. (*Ruffling his hair at the back*) There. At least that makes you look like an artist.
Pontagnac	Does it? (*Forgetting his promises at the touch of her hand*) Oh, Lucienne! Lucienne, darling!
Lucienne	Well, what is it?
Pontagnac	Oh! I'm sorry.
Lucienne	Do please behave yourself when no one's here.
Pontagnac	Oh! What do you expect? I'm not made of wood.
Lucienne	All right. That's enough.
Pontagnac	Yes.
	(*Lucienne has risen and gone to the table. She picks up a newspaper, goes back, sits down and starts to read it. Pause*)
	(*Having watched her*) What an extraordinary attitude to love! (*Reading the name of the paper*) The Figaro. (*Pause*)
Lucienne	Ah-ha! There's a first night tonight at the Champs Elysées.
Pontagnac	Is there?
Lucienne	Are you going?
Pontagnac	No.
Lucienne	Oh!
	(*She continues reading the paper. Pontagnac, not knowing what to do, starts to whistle under his breath, as he looks round the room. Then he rises and, with his hands behind his back, inspects the ornaments*)
	(*Without raising her head*) Do sit down.
Pontagnac	Oh! Yes. (*He sits obediently*)
	(*Pause*)
	Well, what are we waiting for? . . . Do I have to

beg to get the sugar?
> (*Voices off*)

Lucienne Sh!

Pontagnac (*Having risen when he heard the voices*) What is it?
> (*Lucienne has risen at the same time. She screws her newspaper into a ball and throws it across the room*)

Lucienne (*Aside*) At last! (*Aloud*) Why should we care? People. . . . Possibly my husband.

Pontagnac Your husband!

Lucienne I hope so. It will make my vengeance the more complete.
> (*The blinds upstage are parted and heads appear at the window*)

Inspector (*Off*) Open in the name of the law!

Pontagnac It's them! Hide.

Lucienne Hide me then. Do you love me enough to fight my husband for me?

Pontagnac Of course, but . . .

Inspector (*Off*) Will you open this window!

Lucienne This is how I want it to be, in front of them all. Take me, Pontagnac, I'm yours.

Pontagnac Eh? You mean now?

Lucienne Now or never.

Pontagnac (*Moving away*) Oh, no! No, no, no!

Inspector (*Off*) Open or I'll break the glass.

Lucienne Go on, open, or he'll break the glass.

Pontagnac (*Panic-stricken*) Eh? Yes.
> (*Pontagnac goes to the window and opens it. Lucienne sits down on the sofa and, with her legs stretched out one across the other and her body thrown back supported on her arms, stares defiantly at her husband. Vatelin enters with the Inspector, followed by two policemen*)

Vatelin (*To Lucienne*) Oh! How dare you!

Inspector Don't move, anybody.

Vatelin	So it's true!
Pontagnac	(*To the Inspector*) Now look here . . .
Inspector	(*Looking at him*) You again! You seem to make a habit of this.
Pontagnac	I don't understand, I was just paying a social call.
Inspector	Dressed like this? Put your clothes on.
	(*Pontagnac gets dressed, forgetting his braces. Rédillon enters downstage right*)
Rédillon	Well! What on earth's going on?
Inspector	(*To Lucienne*) I'm the police inspector in charge of this district. I'm here at the request of your husband, Monsieur Crépin Vatelin . . .
Rédillon	Forgive me interrupting you, but you mean there's been adultery in my flat! (*Aside*) Pontagnac!
Lucienne	(*Still in the pose she adopted when they entered*) All right, Inspector, I know what you have to say. (*Aside*) I looked it up this morning. (*Aloud*) I'll make your task easier. Monsieur de Pontagnac may tell you all sorts of things to try to save me. That's his duty as a gentleman. But I want you all to know the truth.
	(*She looks defiantly at Vatelin, who is standing between the table and the fireplace, with his back almost turned on her*)
	I came here of my own free will and for my own pleasure. To meet Monsieur de Pontagnac, my lover.
Vatelin	She admits it!
Lucienne	Inspector! I authorise you to include my statement in your report.
Vatelin	(*Collapsing into a chair near the fireplace*) Ohhh!
	(*Madame de Pontagnac enters left*)
Mme Pont.	It's my turn now.
Pontagnac	My wife!
Mme Pont.	Inspector, will you please make another report and include a statement that I, Clotilde de Pontagnac,

	this gentleman's wife, was found in this flat, where I'd come to meet my lover.
Pontagnac	What's she saying!
Mme Pont.	Goodbye!
	(*Mme de Pontagnac goes out left*)
Pontagnac	(*Running after her, his braces flapping against the back of his legs*) Clotilde!
Inspector	(*Stopping him*) Please stay here, sir, we need you.
Pontagnac	But, Inspector, you heard what she said! She has a lover!
	(*The Inspector shrugs his shoulders and comes downstage*)
	Where is this man? I'll strangle him. I'll kill him.
	(*Gerome enters*)
Gerome	(*Aside*) He's going to hurt my Ernest.
Pontagnac	(*Walking up and down furiously*) If this lover doesn't show his face, he's a coward.
Gerome	(*Coming forward*) It's me.
Pontagnac	You!
Rédillon	(*To Gerome*) What are you saying?
Gerome	(*Quietly to Rédillon*) Shut up, I'm saving you.
Pontagnac	Very well, we shall meet again. Your card!
Gerome	I don't have one . . . I'm Gerome, valet to Ernest here . . . poor Ernest! (*He gives him a friendly tap on the cheek and goes upstage*)
Pontagnac	The valet!
Inspector	(*Coming downstage; to Pontagnac*) Look, can't you see they're all making a fool of you – including your wife. Don't you understand she's behaving like this because she's outraged, not because she's guilty!
Pontagnac	(*Going upstage between the table and the fireplace and taking his hat*) Oh, I knew it!
Inspector	(*Going upstage*) In the meantime we still need you you here. Where can I write my report?
Rédillon	In there. (*He points to the door upstage*)

Inspector   Thank you. (*To Pontagnac*) Will you come with me please . . . And Madame Vatelin.

Lucienne   Very good. (*She rises and goes slowly upstage, still staring at her husband. Midstage, suppressing her emotion with difficulty, she nods towards him and silently mouths*) A man I loved!

> (*At this moment, Vatelin, to show a bold front, rises and looks scornfully towards her. She immediately resumes her air of bravado and tosses her head back*) Let's go.

> (*Lucienne goes into the room upstage, where the others, except Rédillon and Vatelin, have already gone. Through the doorway can be seen one of the policemen, seated at a table, with the Inspector standing next to him, dictating, and Lucienne and Pontagnac on each side of the table. Gerome has disappeared. Vatelin puts his hat on the table and collapses into an armchair completely exhausted. He puts his head in his hands.*)

Rédillon   Well! This is a dreadful mess. (*Noticing Vatelin*) Come Vatelin, take a grip of yourself.

Vatelin   My dear fellow, you've no idea how upset I am.

Rédillon   (*Tapping him on the shoulder*) You'll be all right in a moment.

Vatelin   All right in a moment! You may be, I won't. Of course if it were someone else's wife, I wouldn't give a damn. But try to imagine you've a wife and she's been unfaithful . . . lt's hard.

Rédillon   May I talk to you as a friend?

Vatelin   My dear fellow, of course!

Rédillon   Well . . . you're a fool.

Vatelin   Am I?

Rédillon   Of course.

Vatelin   Deceived husbands always are.

Rédillon   You're not a deceived husband. It's because you think so, you're a fool. Don't you see! Isn't it

obvious from the fact that she told you to
come and find her here in her lover's arms? An
unfaithful wife doesn't usually send her husband
that sort of invitation.

Vatelin You're right! . . . But then . . .

Rédillon Then she must have a reason. To make her husband
jealous! I'll say to you what the Inspector just said
to Pontagnac: Can't you see she's an outraged wife
taking her revenge! Everything shows it . . . This
eagerness to accuse herself . . .

Vatelin Yes . . .

Rédillon The whole scene . . .

Vatelin Yes . . .

Rédillon This extraordinary costume . . .

Vatelin Yes.

Rédillon Choosing a man she only met yesterday.

Vatelin Yes.

Rédillon I happen to know something about it, because she
came here to ask me to play the part . . . and I
refused. (*Aside*) With good reason!

Vatelin (*Stretching out his hands*) Oh, my dear friend!

Rédillon (*Taking his hands*) And you fell right into the trap.
It wasn't very clever of you.

Vatelin I admit it.

Rédillon There!

Vatelin Oh, I'm so happy. (*He puts his head on his hands*)
(*Lucienne enters and comes downstage with the same
arrogant air. She stops, surprised, and looks
questioningly at Rédillon, who puts his finger on his
lips and signals her to be silent and listen*)
I'm so happy!

Rédillon Splendid!

Vatelin Be a good fellow, see my wife and tell her she's the
only woman I've ever loved. Make her understand
I'm the most faithful husband in Paris. Which is true.

Rédillon In spite of your little escapade last night?

Vatelin My little escapade last night! Do you think I got any pleasure out of that? I wish you'd been there.

Rédillon I'd have thought I was being indiscreet.

Vatelin Oh, you could have been there. That damned German woman . . . And her feet! I wish you'd seen her boots. It's silly to say so, but apart from that single foreign affaire, I've never been unfaithful to my wife. It happened that once in Berlin, a month away from home, alone . . . I'm not made of wood. I thought it was all over. But she came to my flat yesterday to start all over again. Blackmail! From a female! She threatened to create a scandal, I was afraid of upsetting my wife, and I yielded.

Rédillon What a pity your wife can't hear you! (*He looks at Lucienne who is softened*)

Vatelin I wish she could hear me. I know she'd believe me. She'd see I love her. I'd put out my hand towards her, she'd put her little hand in mind and I'd hear her say 'Crépin, I forgive you'.

  (*Rédillon has taken Lucienne's hand and puts it in his*)

Lucienne Crépin, I forgive you.

Vatelin (*Rising*) Lucienne! Oh, my dear, you've hurt me so much.

Lucienne So have you.

Vatelin I adore you.

Lucienne Darling!

Rédillon And I love you both.

Vatelin (*Shaking his hand, as does Lucienne*) My dear fellow!

  (*All three embrace*)

  (*To Lucienne*) He has been very kind.

   (*Rédillon and Lucienne reach the right. The Inspector enters and comes downstage*)

Inspector I've finished my report.

Vatelin We don't need a report now . . . Let's tear it up.

Inspector What!

Vatelin Come along, Inspector. Let's tear it up together.
(*He takes him upstage*)

Inspector What sort of a joke is this?
(*Vatelin and the Inspector go out*)

Rédillon Well?

Lucienne Well?

Rédillon All's forgiven?

Lucienne All's forgiven.

Rédillon And for me . . . it's all over?

Lucienne All over. Remember what the fortune-teller said. I'd
have two adventures in my life. The first has
happened, the second will be when I'm fifty-eight.
If that tempts you?

Rédillon Hm! At fifty-eight!

Lucienne Oh! Really!

Rédillon Oh, not because of you, you'll always be enchanting.
But by then I'll be exhausted.

Lucienne (*Gently mocking*) As always!
(*Vatelin enters and comes downstage, followed by
Pontagnac*)

Vatelin There, it's all settled. As for you, Pontagnac, I ought
to be angry with you, but I can't be. To prove it . . .
I give a dinner-party every Monday, will you be
one of my regulars?

Pontagnac Me? . . . Oh, thank you.

Vatelin It's men only. On Mondays my wife dines with
her mother.

Pontagnac (*Understanding*) Oh, with pleasure. (*Aside*) Then
that's the end of that.

Rédillon (*Aside*) Lucienne, if ever you get the same idea
again, please give me a day's warning.
(*Gerome enters*)

     Gerome (*Upstage*) Is nobody going to have lunch?
    Rédillon Yes.
          (*Vatelin, Lucienne and Rédillon go upstage*)
  Pontagnac (*Coming downstage. Aside*) I knew it. Sauce for the
          goose, she said. My goose has been cooked all right!
          (*He joins them*)

CURTAIN